CHEERS!

CHEERS!

AN INTEMPERATE HISTORY OF
BEER IN CANADA

NICHOLAS PASHLEY

Collins

First edition

Published by Collins, an imprint of HarperCollins Publishers Ltd

HarperCollins Publishers Ltd
2 Bloor Street East, 20th Floor
Toronto, Ontario, Canada
M4W 1A8

www.harpercollins.ca

Library and Archives Canada Cataloguing in Publication
Pashley, Nicholas, 1946–
Cheers! : an intemperate history of beer in Canada / Nicholas Pashley.

ISBN 978-1-55468-257-7

1. Beer—Canada—History.
2. Beer—Canada—Humor.
I. Title.

TP573.C3P37 2009   663'.420971   C2008-908010-6

Printed and bound in the United States
RRD 9 8 7 6 5 4 3 2 1

Text design by Sharon Kish

For Anne,
Thanks for encouraging me to quit my day job.
And, of course, for everything else.

I tell you, if there is a heaven for fools, the man who believes in the saloon will be on the front seat, for, if the saloon is not the dirtiest thing on the face of God's earth, the devil ought to be canonized.

—Billy Sunday,
Victoria, BC, August 1916

In the first place there are a certain number of deeply religious, patriotic, and estimable people who actually believe that in passing a law to make it a crime for a man to sell a glass of beer they are doing the work of Christ on earth. Let them be entitled—along with Torquemada and Philip of Spain—to the credit of their good intentions. Along with these are a vast number of people who are animated by the evil spirit that for ages has vexed the fortunes of humanity: the desire to tyrannize and compel—to force the souls of other men to compliance with the narrow rigor of their own.

—Stephen Leacock,
The Tyranny of Prohibition, 1919

Who are you going to believe: Billy Sunday or Stephen Leacock?

—Nicholas Pashley

Contents

Canadians and Beer: Something of an Introduction   1

**Monks and Bootleggers, Ladies and Escorts:
  Beer in Canadian History**

Frère Ambroise, Who Started It All (Unless He Didn't)   9

And What Happened Next   14

There Was a Tavern in Our Town   20

Prohibition: Who Thought *That* Was a Good Idea?   25

So Nobody Had a Drink for, Like, How Long?   35

Prohibition Ends: So Everything Was Fine Once Again, Right?   50

**Heroes and Villains, Stubbies and Killer Beers:
  Beer in Canadian Life**

Us Against Them: Canadians and Our Neighbours to the South   65

When Canadians Knew Squat: The Stubby in Our Lives   73

Domestic or Imported?   78

Home or Away: Where We Drink   83

Yes, but Isn't It Bad for You and Bad for the Planet?   89

Ale or Lager? East Is East and the West Isn't   97

Tycoon Taylor Tinkered: Canada's Beer Villain   102

Oland the Family   108

You Can't Do That: Beer and the Law   111

Wouldn't a Dow Go Good Now? When Beer Kills   121

Hey Mabel! Marketing Beer   126

Barkeep! Gimme Another Light Dry Low-Carb Ice Beer with
    No Aftertaste!   135

Geeks and Angels, Spitters and Burpers:
    Becoming a Connoisseur

Are You a Beer Geek? (There's No Right Answer)   147

The Future of Beer: Can I Afford to Drink It? (Can You Afford
    Not to Drink It)?   155

Get Real: The Day I Met a Beer Angel   160

Beer Festivals: Why You Should Care   165

Name That Beer: What's This Stuff Called Again?   182

Beer vs. Wine   189

Patty O'People: Drinking Outdoors   197

The Author Goes Back to School   203

The Biggest Damn Beer Company in the History of the Universe   214

Sparge That Malt, Pitch That Yeast!   218

Trains and Boats and Planes (Plus a Couple of Greyhound
    Buses, Not to Mention Plenty of Urban Mass Transit):
    Looking for Canada's Beer

The Author Gets Out of the House   227

Party Towns: Drinking in Halifax and St. John's   230

Offrez-Vous Une Autre: Drinking Beer in Montreal   246

"This Might Be the Greatest Beer I've Ever Had!":
    Winnipeg, Regina, Calgary, Edmonton   255

West by Northwest: Vancouver, Whitehorse, Victoria   281

Bibliography   299

Acknowledgements   305

Index   309

Canadians and Beer: Something of an Introduction

We like beer in this country. We really, really like it. And it's not just a fly-by-night, sordid little affair. We're in it for the long haul. We've made our vows and we mean to keep them.

We spend something like nine billion dollars a year on beer, of which the federal and provincial governments take more than the lion's share. From barley growers to label designers, more than 170,000 Canadians owe their full-time jobs directly or indirectly to beer. The rest of us just do what we can to help. Beer accounts for 80 percent of alcoholic beverages consumed in Canada. A MasterCard survey in 2006 revealed that 56 percent of Canadians regard beer as "the most priceless Canadian drink." Rye was in second place, at a mere 8 percent.

This is not a book about numbers, but in 2005, according to the Brewers Association of Canada, we bought nearly four billion pints of beer. Or, if you prefer bottled beer, nearly six and a half billion standard bottles. And that's not even counting homebrew.

Who's drinking all this beer? Yukon drinkers, that's who. Sure, they account for only 0.2 percent of the beer consumed in Canada, but man for man and woman for woman, they're drinking us under the table. If you've ever been up there, you'll remember that there are a lot of wide-open spaces with not many people. You can go miles without seeing another member of our species. When you actually see a human being, there's a very good chance that he or she has consumed a skinful of beer. In 2005, Yukoners of legal drinking age threw back an average of 163.46 litres of beer. Newfoundlanders were a distant second, with 108.15. (And don't accuse Yukoners of being beer specialists; they're number one in wine consumption and spirits consumption as well. If there's a branch of the Woman's Christian Temperance Union up there, she's probably pretty lonely.)

There is a suggestion, made most frequently by disgruntled Newfoundlanders, that the Yukon figures are skewed by the small population and the fact that so much of the drinking is performed by tourists and seasonal workers who don't count as actual Yukoners. There's also the indisputable argument that many of Newfoundland's finest drinkers are most often to be found in other provinces, jacking up other people's figures at the expense of their native province's. It is no coincidence that the first person I met in Whitehorse in the summer of 2008 was a Newfoundlander.

We Canadians have a reputation for drinking beer; there was even an episode of *That '70s Show* that featured a trip to Canada for beer. We pride ourselves on our beer drinking, but how well do we stack up against the world? Surely the land of Bob and Doug McKenzie takes a back seat to no one. Not so fast, hosers. At last count, we occupied twentieth place on the planet, just behind Poland and ahead of Iceland. Even the Americans are ahead of us, in fourteenth place, though as roughly half their intake is either Bud or Bud Light, it hardly counts. (In our defence, mind you, we are the second most highly taxed beer drinkers in the world, trailing only the Norwegians.

According to the aforementioned Brewers Association of Canada, you and I donated an estimated $4.3 billion to our assorted layers of government in 2005. And did we get a thank-you card?)

As a nation, we down 68.3 litres a year each, every man, woman, and child, which is roughly the equivalent of 120 pints. (If you count only Canadians of legal drinking age, the number rises to 88.2 litres per capita.) This may sound like a fair bit, given that we have numerous infants among us, but even if we doubled our intake we'd still only be in second place, sneaking in ahead of the Irish and the Germans, but well short of the Czechs. The Czechs manage a whopping 156.9 litres apiece. Are they drinking the stuff at breakfast? Yes, I'm afraid they are. If you donate blood in the Czech Republic, they offer you two half-litre glasses of beer. Now, *there's* an incentive. Mind you, the average Czech's donated blood is approximately half beer, which needs replacing.

A hundred and twenty pints a year is a mere ten pints—or slightly less than seventeen standard bottles—a month, which really isn't all that much. Most readers of this book can manage that without breaking a sweat. Many of us will have consumed our annual national average before the snow melts in a normal year. (Readers in Victoria will have to make up their own imagery; this is a book about beer, not weather.)

Someone's letting the side down, friends. I'm not suggesting we start drinking beer with our breakfast—or drinking even more with our breakfast (you know who you are)—and I'm not proposing feeding beer to our infants to improve our international standing. But something needs to be done. People in Luxembourg are drinking sixteen litres a year more than we are, and they're only in eleventh place. We are being outdone by New Zealanders and Hungarians. We would each have to drink another seventeen litres a year just to edge ahead of Finland and make the top ten.

Take Austria, if you like. We don't think of Austrians as a great beer-drinking people. Quick: think of a great Austrian beer. But Austrians are in fifth place, just behind the Australians. Evidence of the importance of beer in Austrian life is an announcement made by the Ottakringer Brauerei of Vienna at the beginning of the Euro 2008 soccer championships. Austria was not a highly regarded team in this tournament, having been included only because it (along with Switzerland, an appallingly low twenty-seventh in the beer rankings) was co-hosting the event.

In an effort to kick-start the national team after a loss in their first match, the Ottakringer people promised free beer for life to the first Austrian player to score a goal. The chief executive even promised to deliver the first year's supply himself. An official of the Austrian Football Association rejected the offer, citing the danger of beer bellies, though in fact it probably had more to do with a sponsorship deal with another brewery. In any case, spare a thought for Ivaca Vastic, the Austrian who did actually score for his homeland but will forever have to pay for his own beer.

Where are the Canadian brewers? Who's ponying up for beer for our athletes? The 2010 Olympics in Whistler would make a good starting point for such an offer. What am I saying? This is Canada: free beer is illegal. And I'm reluctant to point out that our three biggest breweries—the companies best equipped to make a generous gesture to Canadian athletes—are actually owned by foreign companies, so might be more likely to support Belgian, American, and Japanese athletes instead.

But back to our national pride. Have we no ambition in Canada? Are we content with twentieth place? Are we proud merely to be ahead of Cyprus and Gabon? Is that the spirit that beat the Soviets in 1972? Do you think for a moment that Phil Esposito is happy to be eight spots behind Slovakia? These questions are rhetorical; you know the answers.

There are people among us who pull their weight, who drink beer like the Czechs (twenty-three pints a month). Sadly, there are others who drink beer like the French (not even five pints a month). And worse: there are people who drink no beer at all. It is highly unlikely these people will read this book, so it is up to the rest of us to show them the light, to let them know that Austrians and Australians and even the Spanish laugh at us and our paltry habits. If someone says to you, "But I'm only four years old," cut that person a bit of slack. If an adult says, "But I don't like the taste of beer," take him or her to a bar that offers a range of tastes. There is no single "taste of beer" any more than there's a single taste of cheese. Nowadays, we have beers that range from virtually tasteless to beers that make grown men exclaim, "Holy Cow!" (or, as you will learn later in this book, make a grown woman announce, "This might be the greatest beer I've ever had!").

Right now, we are the Toronto Maple Leafs of international beer drinking. Perhaps we need to draft some Czechs (I hate to think where we'd be on the scale if more than twenty thousand Czechs and Slovaks hadn't fled to Canada in 1968).

But the point here is that Canadians who like beer like it a lot. There's an advertising slogan in there somewhere. There are Canadians who would rather drink beer than do just about anything else. Even in Toronto, where people are proud to spend sixty or seventy hours a week in their offices, there are people who would rather drink beer than work.

This book is for people who would rather drink beer than work. It's for the people who believe that we should be higher than twentieth in the world in terms of beer consumption. It's for the people who grew up believing that we were better than Americans because we played better hockey and drank better beer. If you're that sort of Canadian (cue the stirring patriotic music), this book's for you.

Monks and Bootleggers, Ladies and Escorts: Beer in Canadian History

Frère Ambroise, Who Started It All (Unless He Didn't)

Let's be totally honest, right at the beginning: we don't know who brewed the first batch of beer in Canada.

When we talk about when things first happened in Canada, of course, we usually mean things done by people with pale skins, people of European origins. And in this case, oddly enough, we're right. People with a lot of book learning are adamant that aboriginal North Americans were alcohol-free before the rest of us got here. It was the last time North America was devoid of alcohol until Prohibition, and I'm only kidding about Prohibition. Many early European arrivals were given a kind of spruce beer when they arrived, but, while this potion was good for fending off scurvy, it lacked the alcoholic kick Europeans were accustomed to. Many native tribes had other substances that bucked them up when they were low, but fermentation was foreign to them—if these particular historians are correct.

It is said that the Inuit were the only society on the planet that lacked any sort of mind-altering substances, the result of not having any significant plant life. You can't overestimate the importance of plants: some you smoke, some you eat or inhale, and some you make into beer. And people have been doing all those things for a very long time.

Okay, you say, then who's the first European to brew beer in Canada? It is unlikely we'll ever know, given that we can't even identify the first European to get here. When I was in school, we were told that John Cabot was the first white dude to get here, back in 1497; mind you, John Cabot was possibly still alive when I was in school, so he might have been a sentimental choice. That, and the possibility that he was English, unless he was actually Italian.

Since then, of course, we know that Basque fisherpersons working the Grand Banks routinely landed on our east coast long before Cabot learned to sail. People in boats have historically needed alcohol, as plain water goes brackish and becomes unhealthy. The Basques would certainly have sailed with lots of wine, but if they ran out on their long journey across the Atlantic, they may have needed to brew up some beer to get them home.

But what about the Vikings? They got here a thousand years ago, while the Basques were in knee pants. They called the place where they arrived Vinland because of the grapes they found (we call it Newfoundland), but it seems unlikely they would suddenly have become makers of wine. Is it possible they made beer while they were here? Well, duh, as people say. They were Vikings, for Pete's sake. The Vikings are believed to have brewed with a grain called *bere* (pronounced "bear," and etymologically unrelated to beer), which contends admirably with a cold, short growing season. A Shetland brewery called Valhalla, Britain's northernmost brewery, now brews a bere beer, possibly the first-ever commercial brew of its sort. (I'd write at greater length about it, but I'm reluctant to become a bere beer bore.)

And then there's St. Brendan the Navigator, an Irish medieval monk who may have sailed to Newfoundland in the sixth century in a very small boat with a crew of other clerical gents. If you've read your *Navigatio Sancti Brendani Abbatis,* the ninth-century (or so) account of Brendan's voyage that should be on all our bedside tables, you'll know that it took Brendan and his shipmates rather a long time, travelling via the Hebrides, the Faroe Islands, Iceland, and Greenland, to get to what became called St. Brendan's Isle—or Newfoundland, as we call it today, if in fact that is where Brendan stopped, if in fact he actually made this voyage, and if this isn't all the product of some overexcited ninth-century imagination. (Or some mad Irish attempt to claim sovereignty over Canada.) But if Brendan did get to Newfoundland, what are the odds that a team of Irish monks who had been out at sea for some considerable period wouldn't brew up a kettle or two of ale?

So it's certainly possible that St. Brendan or one of his crew was the first European to brew beer in Canada. Just in case, it's worth opening a bottle of something bracing to acknowledge the courage and outright foolishness of the monk who sailed out into the unknown in a leather boat.

The Europeans who really started settling Canada in a serious way (and I'm trying to think of a frivolous way of settling a very cold, rocky country with fierce animals and even fiercer bugs) were French. But they weren't effete, southern, wine-swilling, beret-wearing French people. They were, for the most part, northern French folk, from Normandy and Brittany. They had been beer and cider drinkers back home, and they didn't see much reason to change their ways when they got here. It is safe to assume that they crossed the Atlantic on a diet of ale, and that they endeavoured to continue that diet once they landed. And who can blame them?

We can be sure they had brought grain with them so as to be able to make beer and bread as soon as they settled, and they would have been quick to grow more as soon as they could. Beer would have been made in the home at first, for family consumption.

In 1617, a man named Louis Hébert was the first settler given land for agriculture, and he began growing wheat (primarily for bread) and barley (primarily for beer). So he might well be the first European in Canada to make beer for people beyond his own domestic sphere. (Hébert has a descendant living in Toronto today, and if I don't mention this early brewer I'll hear about it.)

According to Allen Winn Sneath's fine book, *Brewed in Canada,* this country's first institutional brewery was built in 1646 in Silléry, just outside Quebec City, for the exclusive use of the Jesuit fathers. The brewer was a monk named Frère Ambroise, by anyone's measure a great Canadian. Thirty popes from that day have outrageously failed to canonize the good brother, but the McAuslan brewery in Montreal finally did the decent thing in 1989 and declared this Canadian brewing pioneer a saint, naming two of their best beers after "St." Ambroise.

The reader's religious leanings and affiliations are no business of the author's, but I would ask you to raise your next glass of beer to the memory of Frère Ambroise. And make it soon. [*Editor's note*: The author of this book sometimes gets carried away when he writes about beer. Please practise moderation when taking his advice. Do not read this book while driving.]

Another Quebec brewery of the era sold beer to people who weren't Jesuit clerics, at least until it was destroyed by fire. Draw your own conclusions; I'm not about to sully this work with idle speculation or conspiracy theories. There were an awful lot of fires in the seventeenth century.

History, as you may have learned in high school, is very confusing. I will note that Stephen Beaumont, in *The Great Canadian Beer Guide,* makes a case for one Louis Prud'homme as Canada's first institutional brewer. He was granted a royal decree in 1650 to operate a brewery in Montreal, but was never sainted.

Soon afterwards, Jean Talon, Intendant of Justice, Public Order and Finances for New France, declared the need for a commercial brewery in the colony. If a colony is ever to become self-sufficient, he reasoned, it needs its own brewery. Talk about truths being self-evident. Talon imported two large vats from the motherland and encouraged the growing of barley and hops. The resulting Brasserie du Roy (opened in 1670 and named for Louis XVI) lasted only as long as Talon's term of office, whereupon the building was turned into a military prison.

(This was not the last interesting use of a former brewery. In 2004, police raided the former Formosa Springs brewery in Barrie, Ontario, and found old beer vats turned into seedling incubators, as well as thirty thousand flourishing marijuana plants. For what it's worth, hops and marijuana, along with deadly nightshade, are botanically related.)

It should be noted that the French government had limited enthusiasm for supporting brewing in New France. In the great tradition of colonialism, it was in France's financial interest to ship great quantities of brandy and wine to its new colony, in ships that would return home heavy with furs. It was only after James Wolfe won his set-to with Louis-Joseph Montcalm (6–4, 3–6, 7–6, 4–6, 6–4) and the British became a force in Quebec, that beer once again became a big deal in these parts. A hundred and eighty-five years after Jean Talon's display of initiative, an Irishman named John Boswell discovered that the site of La Brasserie du Roy still had its underground storage vats and built a new brewery above, one that proved greatly successful. The province of Quebec has been an important factor in Canadian brewing ever since, and today produces some of our best and most interesting beers.

Now, have you raised that glass to Frère Ambroise yet?

And What Happened Next

Anyone who has ever hauled a two-four of beer any distance knows that beer is heavy. Even light beer, paradoxically, is heavy. And the low percentage of alcohol means that beer doesn't last very long, which was especially the case back in the days before refrigeration and pasteurization. All this guaranteed that, for most of human history—or at least human history since beer arrived, which is the human history that you and I are interested in—beer was, by definition, local. You could transport your beer as far as a team of horses could haul it along usually unreliable roads. If you were near water, you could, possibly, ship it slightly farther by boat.

Transporting beer still has its hazards, especially if the beer is made by Moosehead. It is presumably a compliment to the brewmaster that Moosehead shipments get so frequently hijacked: 60,000 cans in 2004 on a run from Saint John to Mexico, 77,000 cans and 44,000 bottles in 2007 on a run to Mississauga. Back in, say, the eighteenth century, no one would have even considered shipping beer from Saint John to Mississauga, even if Mississauga had existed.

This being Canada, of course, we have distances. We have distances the way some countries have quaint old thatched cottages. Everywhere, almost by definition, is a long way from everywhere else. Consider Saskatchewan. Which means that the distance problem was more pronounced here. If you lived in, say, Medicine Hat, you drank beer made in Medicine Hat. If you wanted a Moosehead, you packed your bags. The Moosehead wasn't going to come to you. Often, it still doesn't, but that's because it keeps getting stolen.

This state of affairs made it difficult to establish a national brand back in the eighteenth century. (Nowadays, it's wacky interprovincial regulations that make it difficult. As Dave Broadfoot says, "Americans are plagued with organized crime. We have provincial liquor boards.") But it didn't stop people from expanding and forming dynasties. As Allen Sneath observes, by the time Gerard Adriaan Heineken bought his brewery in Amsterdam in 1863, the third generation of Molsons was on the job in Canada. Molson is predated slightly by Guinness and Bass, but it beat the upstarts of Anheuser-Busch by a century.

John Molson arrived in Canada from his native Lincolnshire in 1782, though it was touch and go on the way over. It was a bad year for travel, given that Britain was, as usual, at war with France, and the Americans were being characteristically stroppy as well. Military ships from those two nations were prowling the seas with an appetite for British blood, as were freelance pirates. But it was a gale that nearly ended John Molson's prospects two weeks into his trip, a journey undertaken only because he had contracted some mysterious ailment, which, it was hoped, would be cured by means of a long sea voyage. As he tossed about on his ship, he must have wondered if the cure was worse than the disease.

All right; there's no point trying to build up the suspense. You can go into any beer store in Canada and find Molson products, which would not have been the case had John Molson perished at sea in 1782. Eight weeks after leaving Portsmouth, he arrived at Quebec City. From there, he travelled to Montreal and began working for a brewer named Loyd. The next year he became a partner, and three years later he bought Loyd out and returned to England to buy brewing equipment, barley and hops and seeds, some barrels, and a how-to guide (the first English-language guide to brewing was published in 1762). In 1786, he opened what we eventually came to know as Molson Canada, the second-oldest business in Canada. It's older than CCM, Canadian Tire, Laura Secord, you name it (unless you name the Hudson's Bay Company). Business seems to have been good from the start. In that first year, he testified, "My beer has been universally well-liked beyond my most sanguine expectations."

In the 1990s, the Molson corporation took a lot of heat for diversifying into other, non-beer-related businesses—Diversey Corporation, Réno-Dépôt, Beaver Lumber, and much more—but John Molson would have been supportive. He himself went into banking and invested in the first Canadian commercial railway, as well as building Montreal's first luxury hotel and the first Canadian-built steamship. He liked steamships a lot, and built the first steamship used in war and one of the first two ever to collide. He was an ambitious man, but even he could not have imagined brewing from coast to coast.

The story of the Molson family is one of generations of worthy businessmen who tried to stay out of the news. A twentieth-century Molson told Shirley E. Woods, Jr. (author of *The Molson Saga, 1763–1983*) that the only times a Molson gets his name in the papers are when he is born, gets married, or dies. Occasionally, a Molson performed one of these feats in a dramatic way—most notably Harry Molson, who went down with the *Titanic*.

The Labatts were a similar family. Like the Molsons, they became pillars of their community—London, Ontario, in their case—and did good deeds while trying not to draw attention to themselves. But

1934—on the surface a good year, because Ontario allowed public sale of beer by the glass for the first time since Prohibition—was an uncharacteristically high-profile year for the Labatts. In January, Henry Labatt disappeared at sea while sailing to the West Indies. In August, a gang of desperados kidnapped company president John Sackville Labatt and demanded a ransom of $150,000, serious money during the worst of the Depression. A ransom note, signed by someone purporting to be "Three-Fingered Abe," was found in Labatt's car. It was initially assumed that Labatt's abductors were American gangsters, possibly the famous Purple Gang of Detroit, just because they were so good at that sort of thing, but nobody really knew anything. The *Toronto Star* asked, "What has 'Three-Fingered Abe' done with John S. Labatt?"

The next day, the *Star* reported that suspicion had fallen on a dodgy character named Joe Massei, known in Detroit as Joe "The Bum" Massei (he had been named Public Enemy #1 in Detroit in 1930). He strongly denied any involvement: "'Me a snatcher?' Massei commented at his home. 'Of all the bum raps this is the worst and I have had plenty. I'm no snatcher and I'm just as much against kidnapping as the chief of police. It's a dirty racket and if I can help find out who pulled this I'm willing to help.'" There is no record that Mr. Massei (often known as Massey) played any further role in the case, but his indignation at being associated with a foul crime like kidnapping is evidence of his worthy moral character. One can only wonder how such a good man earned a nickname like The Bum.

Attempts to negotiate a drop of the money near a bridge spanning the Humber River in Toronto failed as the kidnappers feared getting caught, and, sixty hours after the initial abduction, they left Labatt at the corner of St. Clair Avenue and Vaughan Road with a dollar for cab fare. (When the dishevelled Labatt arrived at the Royal York Hotel, where his brother had set up camp, no one at first believed his claim to be the kidnapped millionaire.) As *The Globe* put it breathlessly, "When word was flashed in Toronto yesterday morning that John Labatt, wealthy London brewer, had been released by his kidnappers and was with his family in London, Ont., there was climaxed a series of events of drama, tragedy and mystery unequalled in Toronto newspaper history." Nothing so exciting has happened in Canadian brewing ever since, unless you count the development of ice beer. I don't.

John Molson's success led to a growing number of Canadian breweries, operated by men (and at least one woman) with names like Alexander Keith (1820), John Sleeman (1836), Thomas Carling (1843), John Kinder Labatt (1846), Eugene O'Keefe (1861), and Susannah and John Oland (1867). (Susannah was the brewing brains behind the Oland operation, as is right and proper; for millennia, brewing was a female occupation, until men figured they could make more profit and took it over.) One could add to this list names like Dow and Brading, now largely forgotten figures in early eastern Canadian brewing.

As Canada spread westward, so did beer. It was getting closer to the best places to grow barley, after all. The latter quarter of the nineteenth century saw huge settlement in Manitoba and places west, and breweries quickly opened to cater to the thirsts that were moving in. Edward Drewry and Patrick Shea dominated in Winnipeg, Alfred Cross in Calgary, Fritz Sick in Lethbridge. Breweries came and went. Some went bust, others burned down. A lot of proud brewing pedigrees disappeared with the arrival of Prohibition. Others died out at the hands of E.P. Taylor. But those are different stories.

The realities of shipping a very heavy product over long distances kept brewing in Canada a local industry well into the twentieth century, when the big guys started swallowing up smaller companies and setting up their own operations in far-flung parts of the country. It would be a long time before the companies started by the great Canadian Johns, Molson and Labatt, became national forces.

In fact, much of what we think of as national institutions are surprisingly modern. Labatt introduced Pilsner Lager, which eventually became Labatt Blue (apparently in honour of the Winnipeg Blue Bombers), in 1951. It was the first attempt by a Canadian brewer to create a national brand. It took Molson another eight years to launch Molson Canadian, its first national brand. I know, it feels as if they've been around forever.

There was, for a long time, federal legislation that insisted that beer could be sold only in the province in which it was made, legislation designed to promote employment, particularly in smaller provinces. In order, then, to become a truly national brewer, companies needed at least ten breweries across the country. They achieved this goal either by opening new breweries or by buying out existing companies. Later on, we'll talk about E.P. Taylor, the Canadian who made practically an art form out of brewery takeovers.

John Molson could not have foreseen, back in 1786, the rise of massive national brewing corporations, one of which still bears his name.

There Was a Tavern in Our Town

The drinking history of North America can be broadly divided into two eras: pre- and post-Prohibition. We will see in a later chapter how the hangover from Prohibition affected Canadians' drinking habits for decades (and still does), but what was it like before the fun-haters turned drinkers into criminals?

There was a lively drinking scene in most of Canada before we started to go dry, mostly centred on either beer or spirits. (Our American friends, before the arrival of German brewers in the 1840s and later, were for the most part spirits drinkers, but Canadians from the start had a keen taste for beer. Which, I'm happy to say, we have retained.) Many Canadians drank at home—often potables they had made for themselves, especially in rural Canada.

But humans have always taken an interest in drinking outside the home, whether to go to a place that was heated or to avoid one's family at home or merely to be out in society. Canadians were no exception to this rule of human nature.

In Canada's earlier days, there were two distinct forms of licensed premises: the tavern and the inn. Taverns were generally in towns. They might have had rooms for travellers, but they existed by and large to cater to their townspeople. Inns, on the other hand, were in the business of caring for travellers, offering lodging as well as food and drink.

As Gordon Lightfoot's many fans will know, there was a time in Canada before the railways. Travellers in those years moved about on stagecoaches, and they moved slowly and uncomfortably. After a day of bouncing about on unpaved roads, sometimes having to get out and push, the traveller looked forward to a night's lodging at an inn along the way. For the most part, this entailed sleeping in a large room, possibly on a mattress on the floor, with your fellow travellers, sharing everything down to—and including—the fleas and bedbugs.

In their excellent book, *Tavern in the Town: Early Inns and Taverns of Ontario,* Margaret McBurney and Mary Byers note that the stage-coach line between York (now Toronto) and Kingston opened in 1817. They also point out that some travellers found it less danger-ous and uncomfortable to walk the 160 or so miles—you could also complete the trek a day faster on foot.

Given the sluggish pace of the stagecoach, many inns were required along the coaching routes. Innkeepers had to be able to provide food, drink, and lodging for humans and horses. It could be a lucrative business for the men and women who owned these inns, and many of them became prominent citizens. Three major thor-oughfares in the northern throes of Toronto were named for the inn-keepers who maintained their businesses on the busy coaching route up Yonge Street: Thomas Sheppard, John Finch, and Thomas Steele. (It has to be conceded that there is some spirited debate as to whether Sheppard Avenue is named for Thomas Sheppard, proprietor of the Golden Lion at what is now Sheppard and Yonge, or for Joseph Shepard, who lived across the street and was deficient to the tune of one "p." There are no points for guessing which claim I support.)

The coaching routes would have been untenable without inns. At the same time, many of the inns were untenable without the stage-coach, and the arrival of the railways doomed most roadside inns. A few had become anchors of growing, prosperous communities and had a chance of surviving as a result, but most did not. Even some of the prosperous communities did not survive the steam revolution, turning into ghost towns. As most of western Canada was settled only after the appearance of the railways, most of that part of the country never had quite the same tradition of the inn. Communities formed instead around the railway routes.

The more urbane tavern was a better bet over the long haul. Even in a modest-sized town, the tavern was often the biggest space available, so was often used as a courthouse, meeting hall, even a Sunday school. As McBurney and Byers tell us, Jordan's Hotel in York even hosted Upper Canada's legislature in 1814 after the blasted Americans burned down the building actually designed for that purpose. Still, if the Americans are going to burn down a building, better it should not be a tavern, though there were a number to choose from. The figure I never tire of repeating from the McBurney/Byers book is that, in 1837, the tiny bit of Toronto bordered by King, Front, Yonge, and Church streets held no fewer than fifty licensed premises. Toronto had a tavern for every 127 men, women, and children. I don't use the expression "golden age" lightly, but I'll mention it in this context.

So, the legislators of Upper Canada repaired to Jordan's Hotel, a spot McBurney and Byers suggest was familiar to many of them. Politics and taverns were a natural mix. As we know, the Upper Canadian rebels of 1837 began their fateful march down Yonge Street at Montgomery's Tavern, their customary meeting place. After William Lyon Mackenzie's massively unsuccessful rebellion, however, Governor Sir Francis Bond Head ordered the tavern destroyed (he watched on horseback as the place went up in flames), and its owner, John Montgomery, was sentenced to hang. Because I know you like a happy ending, I can inform you that Montgomery was pardoned in 1845 and went on to open and operate more taverns in Toronto. Francis Bond Head had won the battle but lost the war, and he returned to England and never held public office again. And did you know that a member of the militia that did battle with Mackenzie's rebels was a young lawyer named John A. Macdonald, later to become the first prime minister of Canada and one of this country's premier drinkers?

It is safe to assume that Canadian taverns of the early nineteenth century saw their share of raucous occasions and sporadic drunkenness; their customers were human beings, after all. There was, however, a growing cadre of people who didn't hold with alcohol, and there were travellers who appreciated quiet lodgings that were unspoiled by the din and hubbub of abusers of drink. For these people, there were temperance inns and taverns. In Port Credit, Ontario, a man named Wilcox opened a temperance inn specifically for teetotal sailors, which sounds counterintuitive.

One advantage the temperance houses had over taverns was that they didn't have to pay tax. A reading of *The Globe* (not yet *The Globe and Mail*) of February 11, 1845, is rewarded by an account of a debate before the Parliament of Upper Canada over a piece of legislation proposed by one Mr. Cummings: the Dog and Temperance Bill, which aimed to tax dogs and temperance houses. A Colonel Prince supported the bill because the country was overrun with dogs and because "he had no great opinion of Temperance people, he had always found them the greatest gluttons in the world," and, "in spite of all their protestations, there was generally a sly bottle to be found in the cupboard." *The Globe* noted: "The hon. gentleman was greeted with shouts of laughter throughout."

Next to rise was one Dr. Dunlop, who objected to the pairing of these two items in the proposed bill, as "he was a friend to dogs, but he was no friend to temperance houses," which occasioned more laughter.

Mr. McDonald, member for Glengarry, thought it impolitic to tax temperance houses, and he was disinclined to tax dogs: "He could not say how it might be in other parts, but the dogs of Glengary [*sic*] were a most intelligent race of animals." This was greeted not just by laughter but by cries of "You are a specimen."

The Globe then reported: "Mr. Roblin replied at some length to Messrs. Prince and Dunlop, but as his speech was only a temperance lecture, we refer our readers to the *Temperance Advocate,* or any similar publication." *The Globe* would take the voices of temperance more seriously in years to come.

Prohibition: Who Thought That Was a Good Idea?

You don't know what's going to get people excited, do you? Back in 1975, an American advertising guy got together with some friends over drinks and invented the Pet Rock, which made him rich. A million people paid US$3.95 for, yes, a rock, packaged in a box like a cardboard pet carrier. You can google it if you don't believe me. But that's what the 1970s were like. You had to be there. Baby Duck and disco. The hair. The clothes. The Captain and Tennille. What were they thinking?

This sort of group madness happens more often than you might think. Why, as recently as 2000, an unruly mob of five US Supreme Court Justices went bonkers and elected George W. Bush president, which makes Pet Rocks seem pretty harmless. What were they thinking?

In the nineteenth century, a new and irrational craze took off. Without the benefit of modern media, it took longer to take off than the Pet Rock, but take off it did. A whole bunch of people decided that not only were *they* not going to drink any more, but that nobody else would, either. It took them about a hundred years to carry it off, but they succeeded. What was *anybody* thinking?

The crusaders who initiated the temperance movement had a bit of a point. There was, by all accounts, a fair bit of drunkenness going on—committed mostly by men, it must be said. And the temperance movement, it must also be said, was largely instigated by women.

There are lively accounts of alcohol abuse in the period during which the temperance movement got going. A lot of fellows were doing their best to drink everything the brewers and distillers of this country were able to produce. In 1880, the city of New Westminster, British Columbia, had a licensed establishment for every thirteen people, and that doesn't count the unlicensed ones. Fifteen years later, Governor General Lord Aberdeen passed through town and was put up in a hotel—unfortunately, in a room above the hotel's bar. Lady Aberdeen reported in her journal: "At 1:15 H.E. [His Excellency, and I wish my wife referred to me in such respectful terms] rang to ask the night porter when the hotel was shut up. 'Not at all,' was the answer. 'When does the bar close?' 'Not at all, Sir.'" Lady Aberdeen went on: "[B]ut happily the singing and shouting were so continuous that I was finally sung to sleep and woke only to hear the carousal being closed by God Save the Queen shortly after 8 a.m. But as we are guests of the city on this occasion, we must say nothing."

Now, the word "temperance" does not mean—or did not always mean—total abstinence and the enforced abstinence of others. A temperate climate is a moderate one, seldom too hot or too cold. "Temperance" is another word for "moderation," and in its early days the movement favoured just that. Indeed, beer was held up by many as the ideal temperance beverage because of its healthy ingredients and low alcohol content. It was hard liquor that was doing the damage. Thomas Jefferson, a home brewer himself, had once said of beer, "I wish to see this beverage become common instead of the whisky which kills one-third of our citizens, and ruins their families."

In fairness to the ladies of the Woman's Christian Temperance Union, I should observe that, according to their website (and who among us is not a bit surprised to discover that the WCTU still exists *and* has a website?), their definition of "temperance" differs from mine. They cite no less an authority than that great ancient Greek pubgoer Xenophon: "Temperance may be defined as moderation in all things healthful; total abstinence from all things harmful." (We will address the "harmfulness" of beer in a later chapter.)

Be that as it may, the original goal of the temperance movement was to encourage drinkers to consume less alcohol (one group in Quebec resolved to take no more than six strong drinks a day), but inevitably some hothead is bound to come along, start quoting Xenophon, and then take an axe to the nearest saloon. Which is pretty much what happened.

The anti-booze people had two advantages over the drinkers. Drinking folk, bless us, have lots of good intentions, but we are apt to forget about them later. The chronically sober not only remember, but they also have more free time to attend meetings, take minutes, and organize. The sober people also had some very good songs. Drinkers have lots of good songs, too, often better ones, but they can't remember the lyrics or agree on a key.

The prohibitionists had a variety of songs, but their mainstay was the Drunken Dad song, of which there were many variations. These songs were usually presented as sung by an undernourished child. This poor waif occasionally attempts to discourage Dad from going to the tavern in the first place, but is more often standing at the tavern door, pleading with Dad to come home before somebody dies. There is inevitably someone dying at home—another child or its mother, dying from hunger, cold, neglect, abuse, or just plain nineteenth-century melancholy. I'm not aware of any instances in these songs of Dad actually coming home and doing the right thing by his family. No, he is destined to keep drinking while little Benny expires. In "Come Home, Father" (1864), little Benny survives until the third verse before he is taken by the angels of light. Sad enough, you might think, but no: "And these were the very last words that he spoke, 'I want to kiss Papa good night.'" (If you find that a bit mawkish, you'll want to avoid "Father's a Drunkard and Mother Is Dead.") With any luck, the enormity of these fathers' crimes will overtake them later on and they will see the error of their ways and join the Band of Hope. If they haven't drunk themselves to death first. (Though, interestingly, the drinkers seem to live in good health; it's their presumably non-drinking dependents who flutter their eyes and succumb at the first sign of starvation or cold.)

The sheer quantity of songs of this sort suggests they were, in fact, mirroring some very real social problem, though it strikes me that, if so, it must have been difficult to get into a nineteenth-century tavern, having to push past all those singing, shivering children. "Outta the way, kid, outta the way, kid, how you doing, Jimmy, outta the way, kid . . ."

The movement toward Prohibition happened over a long period. Nova Scotia was praised, by those who think this sort of thing praise-worthy, for having the first temperance unions in Canada. The first temperance union in what was then Upper Canada was established in 1828, in the wonderfully named Bastard Township in Leeds County. (No one seems sure if it was already called Bastard Township or if that's how it got its name.)

At first, the anti-drink people relied on their gifts of persuasion, demonstrating to tavern-goers their moral weakness and showing them a better way. Ruth Spence, in *Prohibition in Canada,* her in-depth and enthusiastic study of the rise of Prohibition, records the triumphs of some of these campaigners. One man launched into an impromptu debate with a brewer he met in a public place, denouncing the evils of beer so convincingly that the brewer declared that he would immediately turn his brewery into a tannery.

This campaign of persuasion met with some success but was followed by a lot of backsliding. An awful lot of backsliding. It became apparent that the only long-term remedy for the drinking problem was to remove temptation from boozehounds and get the demon alcohol out of their lives altogether.

For a much fuller history of the buildup to Prohibition, I recommend *Booze: a Distilled History* by Craig Heron. I will tell you, however, that it was a sneaky, insidious process, as you'd expect. The movement was a mix of religious folk and social reformers, reflecting a rising, sober, middle class of respectable people who were not reluctant to deliver bracing speeches to those less fortunate than themselves.

There was, you'll be surprised to learn, the occasional outbreak of hypocrisy in the movement. One of the leading anti-drink proponents in Quebec was a Catholic priest named Father Charles Chiniquy, a speaker who could charm the whisky out of a glass. He is said to have converted two hundred thousand Quebecers to the cause between 1848 and 1851. In 1849 alone, the Molson company in Quebec lost fifteen thousand pounds sterling. Chiniquy appealed effectively to Quebec nationalism, arguing that only temperance could prevent the extinction of French Canada. There is no saying how much damage Father Chiniquy might have done had he not displayed the sort of human weakness that has brought down many a pious man. A year after publishing his treatise *Manuel de la Société de Tempérance,* he was apprehended trying to have it off with a female parishioner of a church in which he had spoken. It was not, it turned out, an unusual example of Father Chiniquy's behaviour.

As the evidence against him piled up, the priest was quietly removed from Montreal, and he washed up in Detroit, where similar offences followed. He then, according to Allen Sneath, wound up in Illinois, where he was accused of corrupting women and setting fire to his chapel, not necessarily at the same time. His lawyer was Abraham Lincoln. He eventually returned to Montreal as a married

Presbyterian and spent the rest of his long life loudly lambasting the Catholic church. Now, *that's* an interesting Canadian character. I bet you didn't learn about Father Chiniquy in school, did you? You have to read books about beer to get proper history.

The keen prohibitionist Ruth Spence praises Father Chiniquy for his role in encouraging his flock to see the light, but she neglects to mention his human flaws, noting only that he "broke" with the Catholic church.

The self-destruction of Father Chiniquy did not deter the forces of abstinence, any more than the repeated moral failures of American preachers have silenced that nation's Bible Belt. On they marched, winning some battles, losing others. (Incidentally, the first act of liquor-related legislation in Upper Canada had taken effect back in 1792, banning the sale of alcohol in prisons. For more than two centuries, Ontario prisoners have been forced to make their own.)

For a long time, large-scale efforts to pass legislation failed, but smaller measures sometimes worked. The Dunkin Act of 1864 (surprisingly, nothing to do with doughnuts) and the Scott Act of 1878 allowed for local option, whereby counties or municipalities could vote to go dry. The first city to exercise this option was Fredericton, in 1879. The Maritime provinces were enthusiastic adopters of abstinence, which seems surprising if you go there today. By 1901, Charlottetown was the only remaining wet part of Prince Edward Island, but in that year all was lost. PEI remained dry until 1948, an unconscionably long time, and didn't permit tavern drinking until 1964. Luckily, the province was blessed with rather a lot of potatoes, which can be readily transformed into alcohol by those to whom the law is more a guideline than a binding ordinance.

Local option was an effective tool for dry campaigners; by the time Prohibition arrived across Canada, there was already a sizeable proportion of the population who lived in dry areas. In Ontario, for instance, there were 4,794 licensed taverns and 1,307 shops selling alcohol in 1875. By 1916, before the arrival of Prohibition, there were only 1,224 taverns and 211 shops. The prohibitionists had achieved much of their goal even before they succeeded in shutting everything down. Had they stuck with the gradual, insidious approach, they might have enjoyed more long-term success.

The enthusiasm for unadulterated cold water grew. In 1898, a national plebiscite actually approved cross-country Prohibition by a tiny margin, although Quebec, hardly surprisingly, voted overwhelmingly against. Prime Minister Wilfrid Laurier decided that the turnout was too low to be representative and that Quebec's vociferous position against Prohibition made the plebiscite invalid. It is small wonder that an Ontario university is today named for him.

It was World War I that finally turned Canada dry. Wartime is an occasion for urging sacrifice (historians will recall that President G.W. Bush gave up golf during his misadventure in Iraq), and it's even more fun to encourage people to sacrifice what you've already given up—or, even better, what you never indulged in in the first place. In 1914, the federal War Measures Act—which many of us think calls for sending tanks into Montreal—banned the use of grain for distillation, though it remained permissible to use grain to make beer.

In 1916, the other provinces began voting to follow PEI and go dry. Quebec banned spirits in 1919, but not for long, which will not astonish visitors to that province. And it never did ban beer and wine, thanks in great part to the Honourable Napoléon Séguin, a Quebec cabinet minister who argued, just before a provincial referendum on the subject, that Prohibition was a "Methodist plot" to undermine Catholicism by depriving it of the Sacrament. Quebec was always going to be a problem for the anti-drink forces. Ruth Spence notes Montreal's reputation for accommodating "ten times as many licensed places as any other city in Canada," and that the city, with a population of less than half a million, had more licences than Toronto, Winnipeg, Hamilton, Edmonton, Vancouver, Calgary, London, Ottawa, Quebec

City, Halifax, and Saint John put together, "although those cities had a combined population of more than a million people." Nevertheless, the dark veil of Prohibition spread across this land.

What had the brewers of Canada been doing to avoid this plague? Prohibition, after all, would be extremely bad for business. Surprisingly, the purveyors of alcohol failed to mount as active a campaign as you might expect. Both here and in the United States, brewers and distillers were in something of a state of denial. Governments, they reasoned, gained (I almost said "earned") so much tax from booze that no politician would dare outlaw the golden egg.

Maureen Ogle, author of *Ambitious Brew: The Story of American Beer,* demonstrates that American brewers were blindsided by the arrival of income tax in 1913, which made the American government suddenly less dependent on alcohol revenues. Canada followed suit in 1917, as a temporary means of paying for the First World War, by which time several provinces had already gone dry. The American drive for Prohibition was aided by virulent anti-German feeling: with such names as Busch, Pabst, Blatz, Schlitz, and so on, American brewers were intensely vulnerable as war approached. In 1916, a delegation of prohibitionists descended upon Quebec premier Sir Lomer Gouin to enlist his aid in their cause. According to Ruth Spence's book, one Judge Lafontaine, president of the Montreal Anti-Alcoholic League, "denounced beer as an unsanitary and mischievous beverage, pointing to the brutality of the German nation as an evidence of its evil effects." And he didn't even mention that beer also appears to make Germans want to wear leather shorts and play tubas.

In both countries, the well-organized campaigns against drink relied on fear-mongering, spurious statistics (remember: 64 percent of statistics are made up on the spot), and sometimes not very subtle racism. Many American brewers were using rice in their beer, which provoked the *Milwaukee Daily News* to observe in 1878 that the rice-eating "oriental races" wound up "dwarfed in features, body, morals and intellect." Maureen Ogle found another newspaper that blamed corn and rice in beer for causing "temporary insanity." (I discourage the use of corn and rice in beer, but I blame temporary insanity for causing people to drink such beer in the first place.) Canadian prohibitionists were no less ready to blame the evils of drink on any immigrant who didn't look like them. *We* were capable of self-control; *they* weren't. Southern Europeans, especially if they could be described as swarthy, were obvious choices, but anyone would do in a pinch.

There was much huffing and puffing in Canada about the evils of drink. In 1916, *The Globe,* allied with the Liberal Party, editorialized: "True Liberalism can have no alliance with the liquor traffic, either in Southwest Toronto or anywhere else. The traffic is a menace to the moral and material welfare of every citizen of Ontario." And a year later: "Intoxicants are a curse. Traffic in intoxicants during war time ought to be made a crime forbidden by Parliament." For most of us, that would constitute both huffing *and* puffing. *The Globe* had significantly altered its position since 1845.

(War, of course, brings on a lot of that sort of thing. A letter to *The Globe* from someone identified only as H.C. of Brantford, Ontario, lays into cats for their consumption of valuable milk and their destruction of birds, those reducers of the insect population: "The only thing a cat can do to help win the war is to die as quickly and quietly as possible. As a patriotic duty we ought to assist every milk- and bird-consuming cat to do this." Even in 1917 the world was divided into cat people and non-cat people.)

Prohibitionists were highly organized and well funded. On the west coast, the anti-drink people brought in the American Bible-thumper Billy Sunday to address crowds in Victoria and Vancouver. He told the assembled masses, "The saloon is an infidel. It has no belief in God and would close down all the churches and hang its filthy rags on the sacred altars. It is a moral clearing house for all the filth of the universe, and is a liar in every way for it holds out false hopes to its victims. It is God's worst enemy and hell's best friend." God's Worst Enemy and Hell's Best Friend would be a good name for a saloon, come to think of it.

Some have drawn a connection between the arrival of Prohibition and the vote being granted to women, along with the fact that hundreds of thousands of Canadian men were battling in the trenches of France and Belgium at the time. Which might make it appear to be women's fault. This, of course, is wrong. Like everything else, it's men's fault. If men hadn't, by and large, kept women out of their saloons, the women might not have built up this resentment. And if women had been allowed to vote much earlier, they might have felt included in the system and have been less likely to go off holding meetings and suchlike while their husbands were in the tavern.

That said, I hate to think of these men returning home from the unfathomable hell of World War I, if they were lucky enough to come home at all, looking forward to a nice, quiet glass of beer without anyone trying to shoot their heads off. For centuries, men have been going off to war, wondering all the while what their womenfolk were getting up to in their absence, but who could have imagined this? You leave the women in charge while you're off at the front, being shot at and gassed, and you come home to a total ban on alcohol. (The *Toronto Star*, in a 1916 editorial, actually opposed letting the soldiers at the front vote on an Ontario measure to outlaw drinking. They would, after all, be able to repeal the law once they got back.)

My theory is that the death toll from the Spanish influenza that swept the world after the First World War was as high as it was because Canadian men had lost the will to live. It's just a theory, that's all. I also have a theory that, nearly a century later, Canadian men harbour a suspicion that women are planning something behind their backs. It makes men nervous. If a man in your life drinks too much, it may be because he's afraid it's going to be taken away from him. It's happened before.

So Nobody Had
a Drink for,
Like, How Long?

In the United States, Prohibition was imposed by the federal government, through the Eighteenth Amendment and the Volstead Act, both passed in 1919, but here in Canada, after a bit of federal busy-bodying early on, it was primarily a provincial affair. The provinces went dry one by one, and then they went wet again one by one.

As noted earlier, Prince Edward Island went first and stayed dry the longest, handily winning the Prohibition championships. Nova Scotia is in second place, staying dry from 1916 to 1930. Quebec's dalliance was shortest, followed by Yukon Territory and British Columbia. For the record, here are the dates of Prohibition across Canada:

PEI: 1901–1948
Manitoba: 1916–1923
Nova Scotia: 1916–1930
Alberta: 1916–1924
Ontario: 1916–1927

Saskatchewan: 1917–1925
New Brunswick: 1917–1927
British Columbia: 1917–1921
Newfoundland (not part of Canada at the time): 1917–1925
Yukon: 1918–1921
Quebec: 1919–1921 (beer and wine never banned)

Under local option, there were areas within these jurisdictions that went dry before the above dates and remained dry afterwards. The last little bit of Toronto to go wet did not do so until 2000. Yes, 2000; it's not a typo.

It is difficult now to imagine the smugness of the Prohibition-minded as they shut down the saloons. *The Globe* had plenty to say on the subject. Two days before Prohibition arrived in Ontario, *Globe* readers read, "When 'Big Ben' sounds seven o'clock on Saturday evening he will toll the knell of Old John Barleycorn in Ontario. The hour rings out the existing license system, and rings in the new Ontario temperance act." The paper had already noted that liquor stores had been enormously busy in the weeks leading up to this point.

On the sad day itself, *The Globe*'s lead editorial went on at great length: "The sale of strong drink in the hotels, clubs, and liquor stores of Ontario ends to-night, and in all probability never will be resumed." And even greater length: "It is reasonably certain that in Toronto during the coming year thirty persons daily, who because of the open saloon have heretofore found themselves in the hands of the police, will go about their business free, unashamed, and contented. There will be thousands of happy wives and mothers in the homes of Toronto who now listen with horror and dread for the shuffling step that proclaims the return of the breadwinner—drunk." *The Globe* then went on to predict that prosperity would reign in a dry Ontario, that millions of dollars' worth of extra productivity would result from the "clear eye, the unfuddled brain, and the firm hand." Remarkably, the friends of

Prohibition seemed unable to imagine that anyone might attempt to circumvent this obviously flawless legislation.

During the years of Prohibition, of course, no one touched a drop. Remember the joke about how to get Canadians out of the swimming pool? (The punchline: Ask them to get out of the pool.) We may be a law-abiding nation, but we make an exception when we're told not to drink.

Canada's provinces made it illegal to sell or purchase alcohol, but not to manufacture it. In fact, it was not within the provincial bailiwick to ban the production of alcohol; that was a federal responsibility, and the feds saw no good reason to do so. You couldn't upset business and lose jobs, after all. So distilleries could distill, brewers could brew, and winemakers could make wine, but it was primarily for export. Given that, from 1920 to 1933, our major trading partner was dry as well, it's not clear where our businesses were going to export their product, but that was none of Ottawa's business. According to the official documentation, a lot of hooch was destined for Cuba or Mexico, but, generally, it was being hauled away on small boats across whatever body of water led most directly to the United States. These boats often returned for more the next day; the Cubans were a thirsty people. In the absence of water, bootleggers used the roads. Is there a more popular tourist destination in Moose Jaw today than the network of tunnels used by Al Capone and his staff as a major hub of illegal booze distribution? (Open every day but Christmas.)

Prohibition was a godsend for the criminal element, both large and small—except for the individuals, and sometimes groups, that got bumped off, to use a business term of the day. And it was all tax-free, unless you see protection money as a form of taxation.

Life was risky, too, for the consumer in those dark days. Wood alcohol was cheaper and easier to obtain for those who wished to make illegal hooch. It was also fatal in anything but very small doses. The newspapers of the day described it as "canned heat," which was not a reference to the sixties rock band. An untold number of Canadians breathed their last as a result of drinking wood alcohol.

There was a nasty outbreak of bootleg alcohol–related deaths in Ontario in July 1926; seventeen people died between Toronto and Brantford within a few days. More died, presumably from the same batch, in Buffalo and other nearby locations. These deaths were reported as far away as Vancouver, where Prohibition had long since ended. *The Vancouver Sun*—which generally took an anti-drink stance—editorialized: "Which is the greater evil to be assaulted, the controlled sale of liquor in government stores and beer parlors, or the uncontrolled sale of liquid death in bootleg joints and blind pigs . . . Let the prohibitionists get rid of the gin merchants first, tackle absolute prohibition afterwards."

Speakeasies and blind pigs sprang up across the country, providing employment for those willing to take that entrepreneurial risk. Prohibition created an almost perfect environment for pure capitalism. It really should be taught in economics classes.

And pure capitalists turned up in the oddest places. The British Columbia Prohibition Commissioner in 1919 was a man of good character named W.C. Findlay. He was a popular choice among prohibitionists, well known as a teetotalling, no-nonsense kind of guy. And he maintained that reputation right up to the day he was arrested for smuggling large quantities of hard liquor. He quietly paid his thousand-dollar fine and hightailed it to Washington State. It was widely felt that he had got off a bit lightly and that the public should know more about what went on behind the closed doors of the Prohibition Commission. Findlay returned to Canada but refused to testify before the inquiry, whereupon he was sentenced to two years in the slammer. The embarrassment to the righteous cause of abstinence was wonderfully incalculable.

There was a decent living to be made selling alcohol to Canadians, but there were outright fortunes to be made after 1920, when the

United States went dry. Under the Volstead Act, even the manufacture of alcohol was banned across the entire United States. So, for thirteen years, enterprising Canadians became very rich. Staggering amounts of alcohol crossed the border into the United States, keeping thirsty Americans supplied. As one bootlegger said, "They want it, we got it." And as Will Rogers said, "Prohibition is better than no liquor at all."

The Prohibition years were exciting ones down east. The Atlantic provinces are surrounded by a lot of open water, and a good many of the local people own boats, many of which are regularly moored in obscure coves. As the era was yet another bad one for the fishing industry, the prospect of facilitating the delivery of alcohol from Canadian sources to the heavily populated northeastern American states was an opportunity not to be missed. The French islands of Saint-Pierre and Miquelon—just off the Newfoundland coast— where Prohibition was merely something one read about, became a major hub for bootlegging. Al Capone, who seemed to get just about everywhere in the 1920s, himself visited the islands and apparently approved of the efficient operation. One of his colleagues—a Canadian named Bill McCoy—invented a quieter way (it involved straw and burlap) of passing large numbers of bottles of alcohol from one boat to another at sea, so as not to draw the attention of the authorities. Thousands of wooden whisky crates were broken up on Saint-Pierre, and many houses were built with wood from these crates. Flags there were flown at half-mast in 1933, when the Volstead Act was repealed, ending the lucrative times of illicit liquor.

A good many Maritime fishermen did very well out of Prohibition, and as bootlegging became more lucrative, the east coast shipbuilding industry boomed, as bigger and faster boats were needed. A ship named the *I'm Alone,* built in Lunenburg in 1923, was one of the most successful rumrunners of the era. It was finally fired upon and sunk by a US Coast Guard cutter off Louisiana in 1929, and one of its crew members drowned. The Canadian ambassador, future governor general Vincent Massey, protested this act of violence, and Canada sued the United States for $268,386.68. After years of legal backing-and-forthing (by which time Prohibition, which had triggered the entire incident, was a thing of the past, except in PEI), the Americans grumpily apologized and gave $25,000 to Canada and another $25,666.50 to Captain John Randell and crew.

Similar activities were reported on Canada's west coast. Roy Olmstead, an American known as the King of the Northwest Bootleggers, hired a Canadian, Captain Stuart Stone, and his five-masted schooner the *Malahat,* to run booze into Washington State and California. As the *Malahat* could hold sixty thousand cases of alcohol, there were vast sums of money involved.

Where there wasn't water, there were roads. We know of Al Capone's operation out of Moose Jaw, Saskatchewan, but there was a Mr. Big on the BC–Alberta border. Emilio Picariello, known as Emperor Pic or the Robin Hood of Blairmore (he was good to the poor), ran a major bootlegging operation across the US border, using powerful cars that could outrace the authorities. His downfall came when his son was shot and wounded by a Mountie. Emilio went to punish the uniformed wrongdoer and shots were fired. The Mountie, Stephen Lawson, died. Emilio persuaded his right-hand woman, Florence Lassandra, to take the rap, on the assumption that they wouldn't hang a woman, but they were both hanged in Fort Saskatchewan Jail in 1923. Florence was the only woman hanged in Alberta, but she got her reward eighty years later when Calgary Opera and the Banff Centre for the Arts produced an opera about her colourful life.

Most of the very successful entrepreneurs kept a low public profile, but not all of them. In 1924, the *Toronto Star* ran a remarkable front-page interview with Rocco Perri, a man the paper described as the "King of Ontario Bootleggers." Accompanying the interview was a very respectable photograph of the man in question, as well as a photograph of his "unpretentious looking" home at 166 Bay Street South in Hamilton. This issue of the *Star* was one of the paper's most successful ever, and it was said that copies that retailed at two cents were changing hands for as much as two dollars.

Perri comes across in this interview as a reasonable and honest businessman. Although Prohibition has brought him prosperity, he claims to favour government-regulated liquor sales. The law, he says, is unjust. "Am I a criminal because I violate a law which the people do not want?" Prohibition, he argues, encourages crime: "Now what have you? Many hundreds of cheap bootleggers selling poison liquor. That is bad." His men, he observes, do not carry guns: "Guns make trouble." He goes on, "There is no business, I don't care what you name, in which honesty is a more important factor than in the bootlegging business." The *Star* reporter, David B. Rogers, imagined himself "listening to a college lecture on business administration."

Perri was not finished: "Pure liquor, fair prices and square dealing. Those are the requisites of the trade." He was joined by his petite wife, Bessie, as he saw the reporter out. "'Good evening. Come again when I can help you.' Those were the parting words of Rocco Perri. Debonaire, polished and confident, he remained, bowing in the doorway, as The Star passed out into the night." In 1944, Perri disappeared, widely believed to have ended up in a cement grave at the bottom of Burlington Bay.

A safer way of making money during Prohibition was simply by making alcohol legally. The business successes of Sam Bronfman and his brother Harry are well recorded. Selling whisky was perfectly legal, as long as a B-13 customs form was filled in and signed, recording the ultimate destination for the liquor. Customs inspectors were routinely "tipped" by the alleged "exporters" of the alcohol, and some became wealthy enough to enter the bootlegging game themselves. Because spirits were so much more portable and long-lasting than beer, it was the distillers who made the big profits. Many distilleries actually expanded their operations during Prohibition, such was the appeal of Canadian rye whisky in the United States.

The Gooderham family, owners of the Gooderham and Worts company in Toronto (now the site of the trendy Historic Distillery District), was too respectable to traffic in illicit liquor and shut down its operation with the arrival of Prohibition. A pair of brothers, Harry and Herb Hatch, bought the company from the Gooderhams and made vast sums selling booze south of the border. As a Canadian magistrate observed in such a case, "There is no burden cast upon us to enforce the laws of the United States."

There was, in most provinces, additional scope for producers of alcohol to sell their products perfectly legally to Canadians. I am indebted to University of Toronto researcher Bridget Ker for her work on the subject of the medicinal role of alcohol in this era.

The process of distillation (probably discovered in China in about 3000 BC, but perfected by medieval Muslim scientists; "alcohol" is derived from an Arabic word) had originally been intended for medicinal purposes. It was only after some time that people—and you know what people are like—discovered that the end product of distillation could go down very well and make people feel happy. By the nineteenth century, alcohol had long been a part of conventional medicine. Indeed, it is safe to assume that many of the women of the temperance unions of the nineteenth and early twentieth centuries had cured their own ills with the generous application of the very popular tonics available. An enthusiastic British Columbia prohibitionist named W.H. Malkin was the creator of a potion called Malkin's Best, described by one observer as provoking a "jazzy jag" in its users. An anti-prohibition pamphlet on the west coast pointed to such popular tonics as Rexall's Rheumatic Remedy (a mere 9 percent alcohol) and Hamlin's Wizard Oil (a spectacular 32½ percent). That's a pick-me-up, all right.

Ms. Ker found a remarkable, book published in Toronto in 1888 and written by C. Gordon Richardson, entitled *Alcohol: A Defence of Its Temperate Use.* Mr. Richardson, a member of the National Liberal Temperance Union, wrote, "[F]or the literary man, delicate women or anaemic children with weak digestive power and capricious appetites there is nothing so exceedingly well adapted for general use as the ordinary light, dry wines of Bordeaux." Even then, literary men were linked with the use of alcohol, for what that's worth. (Richardson's book makes for fascinating reading. The National Liberal Temperance Union, whose president was the interesting and eccentric Goldwin Smith, was opposed to Prohibition, and this book is a serious rebuttal to the pseudo-scientific claims and "the vapid utterances of teetotal writers and lecturers." Richardson approvingly cites one Albert J. Bernays: "At the present day it is a common thing to meet a friend in very bad health, and you ask him the cause: often it is owing to some experiment in teetotalism." Richardson takes special offence at a textbook "recently foisted" upon Ontario's public schools, purporting to reflect intelligent scientific opinion. Richardson was a lecturer in chemistry at the Ontario Veterinary College.)

So it was possible, even in the dry years, to find a sympathetic doctor—or at least a doctor who was happy to take two dollars, the standard prescription charge of the era—who could write a prescription for a bottle of something that would end your pains, relieve your suffering, and get you back on your feet again. In 1919 alone, there were more than 180,000 prescriptions for alcohol issued in Vancouver. By all accounts, the drugstores of Canada were kept particularly busy at Christmas, filling great numbers of these prescriptions. One BC observer reported lineups a quarter of a mile long, which included "Hindus, Chinese, and Japanese." Provincial governments were regularly pressured by the temperance people to restrict the number of prescriptions a doctor was permitted to write. They may have suspected that not all of them were going to genuinely ill Canadians.

Canada's brewers fared poorly from Prohibition. It's a lot easier to transport large quantities of contraband hard liquor; beer takes up a lot more space. (That said, there was significant traffic in beer across the Detroit River. It was estimated at the time that 80 percent of the Canadian beer and 60 percent of the Canadian whisky that made its way into the US did so across the Detroit River.) There was a fair amount of home brewing during these bleak years, which was not much comfort for commercial breweries (especially the farther they were from Detroit), some of which survived by selling near beer, soft drinks, and baker's yeast, and operating as bottling plants. Home brewing was legal in many parts of Canada; in 1925, there were more than ten thousand such licences in operation in Ontario alone. (The *Toronto Star* wittily noted, "Ottawa has record of only 10,049 home brewers in Ontario. These are brewing beer; the others, who are unregistered, are mostly brewing trouble.")

Even without the homebrew, there was beer in many jurisdictions: near beer. Someone had decreed that any alcoholic beverage of 1.25 percent or less was not an intoxicating drink, so low-alcohol beer was widely available. Now, the best way to make weak beer is to brew strong beer and water it down, and brewers were already permitted to make strong beer for export purposes. Human beings are fallible, as we know, and if strong beer accidentally made its way someplace it shouldn't, who are we to stand in judgement? Well, you and I might not, but government agents kept busy raiding premises in which strong beer was believed to lurk.

There were invariably ways around Prohibition, and human ingenuity was, as always, up to the job. Which didn't prevent a good many people from winding up in trouble with the authorities. The newspapers of the era were filled with booze-related stories: deaths, arrests, raids, and rhetoric from either side of the social and political battle. By 1925, the tide was turning against total prohibition. British Columbia had already gone wet in 1921, and in 1925 it authorized licensed hotels for the sale of beer by the glass. In the early 1920s, Quebec was making five million dollars a year selling alcohol, while British Columbia took in three million, which must have drawn the attention of other provinces. Saskatchewan went into the liquor business in 1925, opening government liquor stores across the province. (They didn't go hog-wild, of course. A month after booze had become legal, *The Morning Leader* in Regina reported the case of one Rudolf Zulach of Melville, convicted of "giving information or direction to a party to obtain liquor." He was convicted and given the choice of a $200 fine, plus costs, or three months in the Regina jail. For giving someone directions to the liquor store?)

Also in 1925, Ontario premier Howard Ferguson passed a bill to permit the sale of beer of a whopping 2.2 percent, dubbed Ferguson Beer (or Fergie's Foam), to be sold in grocery stores and bars. The government defended this measure as being good for temperance, as it would discourage Ontarians from abusing hard liquor. Ferguson tried to mollify his critics in the Legislature, saying, "It will not be sold to boys under eighteen years of age, and it will not be sold in candy booths or dressmaking establishments, as certain people try to tell you." Tell that to *The Globe,* which opined: "The new beer means a headache for some of the consumers and a heartache for their dependents." The paper also found it odd that Ferguson Beer could be served to seated drinkers at tables but not to standing drinkers at bars: "The 4.4 beer [it appears to have been 4.4 proof, which is 2.2 percent alcohol by volume] seems to be intoxicating when drunk at a bar, but non-intoxicating when drunk at a table. It is surely a magic brew."

(The stand-up bar, by the way, was an object of fear for many people at the time, synonymous with the infamous saloons of the pre-Prohibition era. Most provinces, when they once again permitted beer by the glass, were adamant that beer parlours should not have a bar. There was a serving area, where waiters came to fill their trays, which members of the public were not to approach. Even in 1949, a British journalist named Noel Monks, clearly unaware of the way we do things in Canada, was twice refused service at the counter of a beverage room in London, Ontario. When he reached Vancouver, Monks was interviewed by the *Province* newspaper and expressed his admiration of Canada as "a tremendous, virile country and I know from personal experience that your fighting men can match the finest in the world. Yet you've apparently let yourselves be legislated into a state of adolescence when it comes to the use of alcohol." By contrast, Al Capone professed to know nothing at all about Canada. When asked if he dealt with Canadian criminals, he replied, "Do I do business with Canadian racketeers? Why, I don't even know what street Canada is on.")

There was a common disconnect within the newspapers of the day between the editorial board and the anonymous hacks who wrote the paper. A *Toronto Star* editorial of 1925, as Premier Ferguson was planning a return to beer, predicted that "[T]he province will experience again conditions which existed fifty years ago, and which the people hoped had gone forever." The previous day's front page, over a piece about the number of places expected to be able to sell the new beer, ran one of the funniest headlines of that newspaper's long history: BEER CAFES OF TORONTO MAY BECOME AS FAMOUS AS THOSE OF CONTINENT. Perhaps I'm thinking of a different continent, though to this day it's hard to think of a continent whose cafés are not more famous than those of Toronto. Antarctica, perhaps.

American defenders of Prohibition referred to it as the Noble Experiment, but it succeeded in getting a lot of people killed, one way or another, and it just plain didn't work. You could easily draw parallels with America's wildly successful war on drugs. From a government perspective, Prohibition was a disaster. Governments at all levels lost massive amounts of revenue, while at the same time having to spend millions of dollars trying to enforce a seriously unpopular law. The mayor of Vancouver complained that enforcing Prohibition cost his city $100,000 a year (nearly a million dollars in today's money). There were still, however, lots of sober voters who clung to their principles and promised to unseat any candidate who upheld the rights of drinking folk.

Throughout the 1920s, though, province after province looked for ways to placate the drys and please the wets and get their mitts back on alcohol taxes. It was a delicate balancing act in most provinces, but the pendulum was swinging in the direction of drink.

Ontario was dry for eleven years, but went wet again on June 1, 1927, though not without a struggle. An election was held late in 1926, with temperance as its central issue. *The Globe,* in late November of that year, reprinted the following piece of moral suasion from the *Bowmanville Statesman:*

Both Sides
Which Will You Choose?
Dry or Wet?

Profit or Loss?

Youth or Crime?

Thrift or Waste?

Asset or Liability?

Business or Booze?

Principle or Party?

Home or Grog-shop?

Control or Uncontrol?

Sinclair or Ferguson?

Happiness or Misery?

Progress or Reaction?

Kindness or Brutality?

Confidence or Distrust?

Optimism or Pessimism?

Education or Ignorance?

The Boy or the Bottle?

Stability or Uncertainty?

Democracy or Autocracy?

Industry or Lawlessness?

Sobriety or Drunkenness?

Performance or Promise?

Safety First or Accidents?

Certainty or Uncertainty?

Dry Goods or Wet Goods?

Respect Law or Bootleggers?

Temperance or Intemperance?

Water Wagon or Black Maria?

Retail Stores or Liquor Stores?

Less Alcohol or More Whiskey?

Bank Accounts or Bankruptcy?

Plebiscite or Liquor in Politics?

Party Leader or Party Betrayer?

Protect Youth or Booze Profits?

Will of the People or Dictatorship?

Home Comforts or Liquor Shops?

Consideration for Others or Selfishness?

Thriving Industries or Busy Breweries?

People's Choice or Brewers' Choice?

Better Conditions or Worse Conditions?

Full Pay Envelope or Liquor Store Tills?

Nickle's Word or Ferguson's Promise?

True Conservatives or Ferguson Followers?

Exclude Importation or Liquor Importation?

Liquor Restrictions or Increase Liquor Sales?

Public Opinion or Liquor Interests' Demands?

When you put it like that, when you spell out the alternatives that clearly, there can be only one result. You guessed it: Premier Howard Ferguson—publicly linked with misery, crime, drunkenness, ignorance, lawlessness, dictatorship, brutality, bootlegging, and grog-shops—was re-elected shortly thereafter, and Prohibition ended.

A nation, or at least a province, or at least much of a province, cheered.

Prohibition Ends: So Everything Was Fine Once Again, Right?

Not so fast. You may have seen photographs from the past, taken on the day Prohibition ended. You've seen crowded barrooms filled with grinning, enthusiastic drinkers and an army of barkeeps primed to satisfy hundreds of thirsts. With few exceptions, those photographs were not taken in Canada.

Alberta, in 1924, went straight from Prohibition to licensed taverns, as did Newfoundland the following year, but they were the exceptions. Elsewhere, the end of Prohibition usually meant the arrival of government-operated stores, bleak places that reminded the drinker that the consumption of alcohol was a privilege (and a sin), not a right. We were not going back to the good old days—or bad old days, depending on your perspective.

The balance of wet and dry voters in most of the country was such that provincial governments had to tread carefully. In much of Canada, treading carefully was what provincial governments did anyway, but in this case they were determined to appease the temperance side by exercising draconian control over the drinking community.

In Ontario, for instance, the end of Prohibition meant the creation of two universally admired institutions: the Liquor Control Board of Ontario stores, run by the government, and Brewers Retail (now the much cosier "Beer Store"), originally set up as a distribution co-operative operated by the breweries of the province but now owned by the big three foreign-owned breweries.

Alcohol purchased in these stores was intended for consumption at home only. Many provincial laws stipulated that customers were required to travel straight home with their purchases. (Though in 1927, a sensible Whitby, Ontario, magistrate named Willis ruled that "a man who buys a bottle at the vendor's under a permit need not take the shortest way to his home.") Purchasing alcohol for a friend was bootlegging, plain and simple. Technically, in some jurisdictions, it might still be.

The government liquor store was not somewhere you went to browse. There was not a bottle to be seen. The stock was kept behind the scenes, where it would not tempt the drinking person. Drinkers wrote their choices on a form, handed it to a cashier, and paid their money (cash only, thank you very much), whereupon another staff member went back into another room and brought out the custom-er's order, already bagged. At no point did the patron see any actual booze. If the drinker felt shamed and demeaned, that was the point.

It is difficult to exaggerate the role of shame built into post-Prohibition drinking legislation in most of Canada. For instance, in all provinces except Quebec and New Brunswick, liquor purchasers were required to possess an individual liquor permit, issued by pro-vincial authorities. In most cases, the amount of liquor purchased on each occasion—and some provinces limited the amount you could buy in one visit—was recorded in this permit, which was in fact a small book, so that the customer's purchasing history could be reviewed at a glance. This was meant to deter problem drinking and bootlegging, as well as adding to the sense of shame experienced by the drinker. Although much of this punitive legislation has disappeared, every now and then Canadian drinkers still get a sulphuric whiff of the shame that was etched into every alcohol-related law passed all those decades ago.

The end of Prohibition in Ontario, July 1, 1927, coincided neatly with the diamond jubilee of Confederation, and it is difficult to tell from this distance how much of the celebration of that Friday had to do with national pride and how much was the effect of legal hooch. Ontarians who hadn't touched a drop for sixteen years—apart from what their doctors had prescribed or friends had located for them—joined long lineups for the privilege of purchasing alcohol from their government.

The Liquor Control Board had managed to open all of thirty-eight stores across the province by opening day, with another twenty-two on the way. Come July 1, only one of the three stores in Ottawa was ready. On the fourth of July, twenty thousand American cars crossed the brand-new Peace Bridge into Canada, presumably not looking for maple syrup. Sadly, there was no liquor store in Fort Erie, so most of those cars headed for Niagara Falls, whose single store was overrun. In Windsor, the rush for liquor was such that women fainted and had to be carried outside. *The Globe* reported that Sault Ste. Marie was as dry as it had ever been: there was, as yet, no liquor store, and the local bootleggers had unloaded their stock before the Temperance Act expired.

The *Toronto Telegram* ran an upbeat story from Peterborough headed; ALL BEER CLEANED OUT YET NO ILL EFFECTS SEEN. Like Niagara Falls and Windsor, Peterborough seems to have attracted many American tourists, wittily described as "tourists from the domains of Uncle Volstead," a clever reference to the hated Volstead Act. Still, there were no arrests, "and as far as the *Telegram* can learn, not one person was seen the worse of liquor."

Toronto was less well behaved, though the *Telegram* was send-ing mixed messages. Its front page boasted two pieces immediately next to each other, headed BIG ARRAY OF DRUNKS and SAFE AND SANE HOLIDAY RECORD. The more positive article observed that, between Thursday and 6 a.m. on Monday, "there were but 57 'drunks' arrested in the entire city." A full twenty of those "drunks" were apprehended on Dundas Street West, which suggests either a pronounced enthu-siasm for drink along that street or a greater-than-average application of the law.

That same newpaper carried a smaller story from the courts, entitled BOTTLE O' BOOZE: "At 4:15 a.m. PC 753 saw Denton A. Mullen in a lane with two ladies and a bottle. The bottle was half full, one of the ladies was entirely so. Mullen favored Magistrate Jones with an ora-tion beginning: 'I am a Canadian citizen.' Finally Crown Counsel JW McFadden asked him if he disclaimed all knowledge of the liquor, and he said he did. Station sergeant, however, declared that Mullen said that a friend had given him the liquor. Fined $100 and costs or 30 days."

Two days later, the *Telegram* reported from a hearing as to whether Casa Loma—Toronto's famous castle on a hill—should be turned into a hotel. Speaking against the motion was a local resident and fierce anti-drink advocate, the Reverend Ben Spence, who warned that customers of the hotel would visit the liquor stores of Toronto and haul their "leaky luggage" back to Casa Loma, where even worse would follow: "This is a dance hall. It may be a drinking place. Here we may have a combination of dancing and drinking. This is one of the most unholy and dangerous combinations we can have." (I can say from personal experience that the good reverend was not far off. Reverend Spence, by the way, was the uncle of Ruth Spence, who had written the definitive history of the buildup to Prohibition, and the grandfather of my friend Gary Nicholson, a known toper.)

And what of the taverns? Whoa, slow down! As part of their efforts to appease the teetotalling community, provincial governments were reluctant to loose the dogs of public drinking. If drinkers (mostly men) performed their loathsome practice at home under the watchful eyes of their families (women and children), surely they would drink less and drink more responsibly. In fact, of course, there is ample evidence that the availability of alcohol in the home led more women to take up drinking. To say nothing of the children.

But there was a market for public drinking, and surely the brewers were keen to resume selling draught beer to thirsty Canadians, so again, bit by bit, provinces grappled with the idea of selling beer by the glass. (We can assume that added pressure was felt after the end of Prohibition in the United States in 1933 and the subsequent opening of bars on the American side of border towns.) Some did this more quickly than others. As noted earlier, PEI waited sixteen years to permit public drinking, while Nova Scotia held out for an astonishing eighteen years, from 1930 to 1948. But wait for it: New Brunswick ended Prohibition in 1927 and authorized drinking in public places only in 1961, thirty-four long years later.

The absence of public drinking in Canadian life for so long—sixty-three years, in the case of Prince Edward Island—gave legislators an opportunity to reinvent the tavern. They tackled their responsibilities with gusto. Imagine having the power to define what a tavern could and could not be. I'm guessing that readers of this book would have made a number of different decisions from our lawmakers.

For starters, many jurisdictions decreed that taverns could not be called "bars" or "saloons," words that flirted with the concept of fun and sounded too American. For that matter, outside Quebec you couldn't even call them taverns, though a lot of people did.

In small-town Ontario, you can probably still hear people talk about going "down to the hotel" for a couple of beers. Back in 1934, when Ontario finally authorized public drinking, against the wishes of many, it allowed these beverage rooms to be located only in bona fide hotels, as well as private clubs, trains, and steamships. Free-standing restaurants were not initially permitted licences, nor was anything that might be construed as a straightforward tavern.

After much bureaucratic delay, and a few false starts, the province mailed out permits to approved hotels. The first was issued to the Norton-Palmer Hotel in Windsor. The following day, July 24, 1934, hoteliers awaited the postman's call, then began pouring the beer. The management of the Prince George Hotel in Toronto could only sputter as their permit failed to arrive. Only at 11:15 a.m. did the Royal York pour its first beer, to—as the *Telegram* confirmed—H.P. Thomson, F.J. Cook, and R.H. Portch, the first legal public drinkers since 1916. The *Toronto Star* noted that the Royal York claimed to offer twenty-six different varieties of beer from seventeen breweries. I challenge many bars to do as well today. Other hotels offered "an old stock, a stout, lager and porter." Drinkers were required to be seated and to have a table in front of them (note: "in front of," not to one side). Draught beer in most places cost ten cents for twelve ounces, or twenty cents for a bottle.

The following day, a *Telegram* reporter spotted no fewer than twenty-eight empty kegs in a lane behind Scholes Hotel on Yonge Street, each formerly holding twelve and a half imperial gallons. The reporter then laboured to estimate how much beer was consumed in the ten Toronto hotels that had opened the previous day. It was rather a lot.

Ontario was not being entirely original in its regulations governing public drinking. British Columbia was among the first to authorize sales of beer by the glass (in 1925), and the first to have a delay between ending Prohibition and allowing taverns, or something like taverns. The province hewed to the rule insisting that only hotels could house beer parlours (words like "bar," "barroom," "tavern," or "saloon" were specifically forbidden). There had already existed places selling "near beer" (beer of only 1.25 percent alcohol by volume, which isn't very near at all), and these establishments tried to remain in operation, resorting to turning themselves into private clubs. Under duress, the BC government authorized veterans' clubs, forerunners of the Legion beer halls, because veterans of the First World War were still annoyed to have returned home to Prohibition, and rightly so.

In much of Canada, food was banned from taverns in the mistaken belief that drinkers (mostly men) would grow peckish and return home for their dinners. No one said you had to be smart to get elected to public office. In British Columbia, there could be no food, soft drinks, or entertainment. Taverns were discouraged from being comfortable or welcoming, again in the naive hope that drinkers would prefer to be at home with their loved ones. The result, of course, is that the new beer parlours served no purpose beyond drunkenness, which they achieved admirably.

One of the laws that intrigued me when I began my life of public drinking in Ontario in 1965 (Friday, October 1) was the one that forbade drinkers from standing up with a glass in their hands. Seriously: if you wanted to move to another table, you asked the waiter to transport your glass to that table. (This being a work of serious nonfiction, I'm not allowed to make any of this up. Be assured this isn't one of those books like the one that got James Frey in trouble with Oprah after it was discovered that he had fabricated a lot of it.) Did this law stem from a moment of whimsy in the 1934 Ontario cabinet? Were they a little giddy themselves when they thought this one up?

It turns out that most provinces introduced this law, on the grounds that it was more difficult to land a blow while seated, though I've seen it happen a couple of times. (Once, in a Toronto tavern in about 1974, I saw a woman sock the guy sitting beside her in a booth. He dropped to the floor and stayed there some considerable time. There wasn't much reaction from other patrons; it was that sort of place.) Drinkers sat at small tables, presumably because a drinker was statistically less likely to find someone to fight in a smaller group. The drawback of drinking while seated, of course, is that unless you're a frequent patron of the toilet, it's difficult to know how drunk you've become. Many of the laws of the time had exactly the opposite effect their creators hoped for, which is a lesson for us all.

But, I hear you asking, wouldn't women have had a moderating influence on all these pugnacious men? Yes, of course they would, except that, for the most part, they weren't allowed in. In most provinces, they weren't even allowed to *serve* beer, even if they owned the joint.

When British Columbia authorized public drinking, there were two other provinces offering the same service. Quebec forbade women from entering taverns; Alberta allowed them only in rustic areas. It seems not to have occurred to BC lawmakers that women might turn up (they had not been keen saloon-goers in the bad old days before Prohibition), but turn up they did. BC was not as genteel as it is now, and some of the women who came to beer parlours were apparently not the wives of the head of the local chamber of commerce, if you get my drift. The Vancouver *Province* opined, "There is no doubt that the presence of women makes it more difficult to conduct beer parlors in a decent and orderly manner."

Was it the fault of the women or of the men? Who can say? Whoever was to blame, the BC Hotelmen's Association (and you will note it was not the BC *Hotelpersons'* Association) decreed in 1926 that, as of August 15 of that year, women would not be served in Vancouver beer parlours, which had a monopoly on sales of draught beer. It was illegal for the women of Vancouver to drink draught beer; even now, that seems harsh.

Were women livid at this turn of events? There were divided opinions. Some female prohibitionists were simply happy that fewer people could drink, even if it was them. There was a strong feminist streak in the prohibitionist movement, however, and some women were not happy. On the other hand, one letter to the *Vancouver Sun*, from someone who signed herself "A Worker's Wife," expressed the view that the decision to ban women was "wise," though she wished that beer parlours were permitted to sell beer to take away, so that her husband could bring her a cold bottle of beer on his way home.

(There was still much debate over public drinking in British Columbia at the time. One perfectly reasonable correspondent to the *Sun* wrote that he had heard so much about the issue that he had made a point of visiting a few beer parlours and had found them "orderly and respectable." The utterly sensible tone of his letter was tarnished only by the fact that he signed his letter "Jack the Ripper.")

Women in British Columbia were not going away, however, and a solution had to be found. That solution was the Ladies and Escorts room, a separate section that permitted women to drink without enabling acts of wantonness and sexual abandon. It was an innovation that eventually spread across much of Canada. (Interestingly, this accommodation was apparently never actually enshrined in law in British Columbia, though it was clear that non-adherence would not be well regarded. This seems to have been the case with numerous drinking laws, in BC and elsewhere. The provincial liquor boards made it plain what they would accept and what they would not.)

Unaccompanied men drank in a room restricted to their sex. Women, alone or with an escort, drank in the Ladies and Escorts room, which was usually a bit more civilized and less sparsely furnished. In most places, the rooms were sufficiently partitioned that one could not see from one into the other. The irony is that, if a man went to a tavern to meet women, he had to bring one along in order to enter the room in which women drank. It's no surprise that large-scale immigration was the only way to maintain the population of Canada in those days.

As a general rule, taverns—in Ontario, they were officially designated "beverage rooms," while in BC they were "beer parlours"— were required to present a circumspect exterior. Innocent, God-fearing people were not to be subjected to the sight of licentiousness within these dens of misdemeanour. Windows were securely covered, and bars had double sets of doors, lessening the likelihood that an exiting drunkard would reveal the unsavoury behaviour going on inside.

(British Columbia, when in 1925 it authorized hotels to serve beer, went in the opposite direction, specifying that "Persons from the street may have an unobstructed view of the premises where beer will be served at tables." This was presumably intended to prevent men from being able to hide out in bars, where their wives couldn't find them, as well as to present drinkers to the full shame of public view. It's difficult to say which approach better induces shame in the drinking person.)

Needless to say, there were regulations governing not only what you could call a tavern, but also how you could advertise it from the outside, and for many of us, these regulations have not entirely gone away. Some years ago, my wife and I were driving through Cazenovia, in upstate New York, when we spotted a bar with a notice outside advertising "booze and fun." Sometimes you just know you're not in Canada any more. What did we do? We did exactly what *you'd* do: we pulled over and went inside, proving that the Canadian authorities are quite right to ban such blatant enticements to commit sin. As recently as 2007, a Toronto drinking establishment attempted to get a licence under the name The Booze Emporium. Rejected, of course. It is now doing business under the name Prohibition.

Once a set of laws is in place, only superhuman activity will dislodge them, and in most provinces the laws that governed drinking remained in place, with only minor adjustments, for decades. By the late 1960s, however, the winds of change were causing at least a mild stirring in provincial legislatures.

I see two major agents of change. One was Expo 67, the world's fair that brought many Canadians to Montreal to celebrate the nation's centennial. Within the Expo site, there were numerous, relaxed drinking spots. I can remember drinking outdoors at Expo 67, an activity still strictly illegal in much of the country at the time. There was also an English pub and a Bavarian beer hall. There were apparently also pavilions highlighting the non–alcohol-related achievements of many nations, but many of us recall most fondly the newly available adventures in beer drinking.

Even if you didn't get to Expo but made it to Montreal, you were likely to encounter new ways of drinking. Everywhere you looked, you saw people having fun—including women. You saw women and men, drinking together. It is difficult now to remember how exotic that seemed at the time.

The other catalyst for change was the invention of the charter flight. Before the 1960s, air travel was an expensive holiday choice, reserved largely for the well-to-do. Jet-setters really were glamorous in those days. But in the sixties it became possible for groups to charter airplanes at great savings. At first, you were required to be a bona fide member of a respectable organization, or at least pretend to be one. Briefly, in 1970, I was a member of something called the Caledonian Friendship Society, which allowed me to fly from London to New York for a fraction of what it would have once cost. Whole airlines sprang up to cater to this new market of travellers. Hands up, anyone who remembers Wardair.

Suddenly, the sort of people who didn't formerly go on long-distance holidays were crossing the ocean. Students were flying. Everyone was flying. And Canadians were going to places where drinking was not regarded as a social disease. They were drinking in English pubs and German beer halls and French cafés and Greek tavernas. Then they came back to sordid beverage rooms that offered a pickled egg and no choice of brand of draught beer, where you sat at little Arborite-topped tables and couldn't run a tab or pay with a credit card, where you were treated like a social deviant who was not to be trusted.

How, indeed, were you going to keep them down on the farm? The gradual shifts in drinking legislation began to speed up. The minimum drinking age fell, the partitions between the Ladies and Escorts rooms and the men's beer parlours started to come down, and eventually we were considered mature enough to stand up with a glass of beer. People started to open mock English pubs and we all learned to say "cheers."

Finally, liquor stores began opening on Sundays, displaying their wares, and allowing customers to pay with credit cards, and Canadians at last entered the promised land of drink-related sophistication. The pinnacle of all this liberty and fun was reached in the early 1980s, when the Liquor Control Board of Ontario announced to its customers, "You are your own liquor control board." It wasn't true, of course; they meant to carry on controlling us as they had done for decades. It was just a marketing slogan, but it made us feel good for a day or two.

Heroes and Villains, Stubbies and Killer Beers: Beer in Canadian Life

Us Against Them: Canada and Our Neighbours to the South

Can't live with 'em, can't live without 'em. That, in a nutshell, describes our relationship with the Americans. How do Canadians define themselves? As not being Americans. They're crazy and we're not: that's the difference.

There was a time, which some readers may be old enough to remember, when Canadians were proud of two ways in which we were better than Americans: we played hockey way better and we made better, stronger beer.

We still play better hockey. Sure, Canadian teams don't win the Stanley Cup very often, but there are several good reasons for that, none of which I can remember. As I recall, it has something to do with the fact that a full 16.67 percent of those teams are called the Toronto Maple Leafs, which skews the figures.

But where would those American teams, the ones many of us hardly even recognize as hockey teams (there's really a team called the Columbus Blue Jackets?), be without their Canadian players? Playing to small crowds, that's where. Well, all right, many of them already are playing to empty seats, even with their Canadians. But think how much smaller those crowds would be without Canadians. (And how many people in those crowds are Canadians passing through—Leaf fans who haven't been able to afford to watch a game at home in several decades, for instance, or ex-pat Canucks who went in search of warmer weather in, well, Columbus?)

It's mildly interesting, too, that in most of the world hockey is a game played on a field with a ball and odd, rounded sticks. If reminded of *our* great sport, they call it "ice hockey" and complain that the one time they tried to watch it they couldn't follow the puck.

But this is a book about beer. If it's hockey you're after, the Canadian publishing industry produces countless books about it every year, and I recommend them all to you. Though, if you buy them all, you'll have little money left for beer.

What of our once-bold claim that we had better, stronger beer than the Americans? "Better" is a subjective term, but surely a Molson Export in 1965, say, was better than a Budweiser or a Miller High Life. "Stronger" is easier to quantify, however, and we were all mixed up back then. Historically, Americans have measured the strength of their beer in terms of alcohol by weight, whereas we have used alcohol by volume. This leads to different numbers. So, what we (and most Americans as well, for that matter) took to be a massive difference in buzz was only a slight, pretty much impercep-tible, difference. There was no shortage of American drinkers who came up to Canada years ago and got hugely drunk on what they took to be vastly more potent beer. They were generally impressed by our robust ability to throw back such massively powerful beers and remain conscious. Which tells you how much of drunkenness is psychological. (A customer of a London pub I once worked in was a drinker of vodka and orange juice. One day, one of his friends told me to leave the vodka out, just to see what would happen. This man had three or four glasses of orange juice and started to become noticeably, well, drunker, at least until his friend filled him in.)

The other big difference back then, depending to some degree on which province you inhabited and how close you were to the border, was that America seemed a beacon of licentiousness. Bring me your thirsty, your underaged, your victims of outlandish drinking legislation, the country to the south seemed to be calling. And young Canadians answered the call. Even if the American beer was swill, it was available to all. What we didn't know at the time was that many American states and counties had drinking laws that were even nuttier than ours. In Pennsylvania, you have to be twenty-one years old to buy non-alcoholic beer. And even today, an estimated eighteen million Americans live in dry counties or towns. Luckily, these areas tend not to be tourist hotbeds, and no wonder. (Not surprisingly, dry counties tend to have higher rates of drunk driving, given that everyone has to drive somewhere to drink.) The entire state of Kansas was dry from 1881 to 1948, twenty years longer than Prince Edward Island. In those days, people were truly grateful that they weren't in Kansas any more.

Author/pollster Michael Adams, in his book *Fire and Ice,* argues that Canadians and Americans are becoming more different, rather than more alike. That is certainly clear from our drinking legislation. Back in the 1960s, drinkers in most of Canada were required to be twenty-one (and sit up straight) to drink legally, whereas Americans had to be only eighteen or nineteen (and could slouch at will). Crossing borders was easier in those more innocent times, and the drinking traffic was all one-way.

Starting in the 1970s, Canadian provinces began lowering the drinking age and removing the punitive element from tavern life. Then, during the Reagan Administration, the American drinking age rose to twenty-one. Although alcohol legislation is a state responsibility, Reagan and Congress decided that Americans should be older before they drank, and threatened to withhold interstate highway funding from any state that didn't revise its drinking age upward. No state stood up to this federal bullying, though in recent years a number of them have started muttering quietly about revoking this bone-headed law, presumably on the grounds that the extra booze taxes might make up for the loss in highway cash. In any case, they would save money they currently spend enforcing a silly law.

And enforce it they do. There are many bars in the United States that deny entry to anyone under twenty-five, just to be on the safe side. There are even bars that demand ID from the author of this book. A quick glance at the author photo should demonstrate the unutterable absurdity of this ridiculous activity. Do they think I've spent all day applying latex makeup to make myself look like something from a horror movie, just to sneak into their bar?

Still, it works. No American under twenty-one has touched a drop of the intoxicating beverages since 1984, when this pernicious law was passed. [*Editor's note:* The author of this book is known to engage in irony. It is apparent that he feels that numerous underage Americans have found ways to contravene the legislation to which he refers. Not that we endorse the breaking of any law, domestic or foreign.]

Michigan law-enforcement officers in 2002 tried to get a conviction against a nineteen-year-old on the grounds of "consumption" and "possession" of alcohol. The young Michigander had indeed consumed alcohol—entirely legally, as it turned out, in Canada. At issue was the definition of "possession of alcohol," which, prosecutors maintained, extended to its presence in his bloodstream when he returned to American soil. A Court of Appeals sensibly threw the charge out, noting that "[T]he commonly accepted meaning of 'consume' as it relates to a beverage means to drink or physically ingest the beverage. For example, a person would not say that he is still consuming milk an hour after breakfast because the milk is digesting in his body. Similarly, a person does not 'possess' a beverage once it has been ingested and is digesting. One no longer has control over the beverage as it is digesting." A rare display of common sense, as well as an excuse to use the word "Michigander," which I've always liked. What's good for the Michigoose is good for the Michigander.

The most prominently reported instance of underage drinking in America of late was the repeated illegal conduct committed by the Bush twins—Jenna and Barbara. Lord, those were bad girls. Ironically, the No Child Left in Pubs Act of 1984 was passed when their grandfather was vice-president. Sadly, the twins, since reaching the age of majority, appear to have become law-abiding, dull Republicans. What a waste.

Actually, the 1984 law addresses "public possession" of alcohol, which means that in a number of states teenagers can drink at home. They can also drink for religious reasons ("God, I'm thirsty!"), and when the alcohol has been "prescribed or administered by a licensed physician, pharmacist, dentist, nurse, hospital or medical institution." Now, I'll defend my dentist to the death, but he's never served me a drink in all the years I've been going to see him. The last time he removed a tooth from me, he suggested—a little half-heartedly, as if he knew he was passing water in the wind—that I not go directly to the pub. Fat chance.

(There's another interesting twist to Reagan's come-back-when-you-grow-up law. His successor, George H.W. Bush, signed something called the Drug Free Schools and Campuses Act, which most of us have never heard of. This withholds federal cash from schools and universities and the like that don't behave in an overbearing manner toward their students and employees in the matter of alcohol and drugs. According to something called the Higher Education Center, these regulations apply to foreign study programs as well. So, if you're a student of Podunk College and take a semester studying in, say, Florence, where the drinking age is sixteen, you are obliged not to drink unless you are twenty-one, at the risk of having dear old

Podunk shut down by the feds. That illustrates just how crazy the Americans are.)

Anyway, the effect of the American National Minimum Drinking Age Act (to give it its proper name; I was just kidding before about No Child Left in Pubs) has been to enrich bar owners in Canadian border towns. Take Windsor, Ontario, across the river from Detroit. Who's crossing into Windsor? Nineteen- and twenty-year-olds looking for a drink, gamblers heading for the Windsor Casino, and guys who want strip clubs where the dancers take off more than they're allowed to in Detroit. Who's going the other way? Academics studying urban decay, motorists looking for cheaper gas, and people who want to drink in bars with no nineteen- and twenty-year-olds. Who would have believed that Windsor would become Sin City?

There is, of course, one more group crossing from Windsor to Detroit: beer drinkers. If you're looking for anything unusual to drink in Windsor, you're setting yourself up for disappointment. When last heard from, Windsor's only microbrewery, Walkerville, was battling the evil forces of bankruptcy, and Windsor's too far from most of the other Ontario craft brewers to get deliveries. So the serious Windsor beer drinker needs Michigan.

And Michigan does all it can to help. There's a Michigan brewery called Bell's, which is located a convenient 137 miles from the front door of the Windsor Casino. You'll be hard pressed to find Bell's excellent beers on the Canadian side of the border, so you have no viable alternative to undergoing the ritual humiliation of crossing into the USA and answering all those personal questions designed to differentiate you from an al-Qaeda operative. You may think you'll be home free if you announce you're going for beer, on the assumption that al-Qaeda operatives aren't supposed to drink beer, but isn't that the perfect cover for a terrorist, one that is likely to put the Homeland Security guys off the scent? "Jeez, how was I to know he was planning to blow up the Corn Flakes plant in Battle Creek? He told me he just wanted to drink beer."

Bell's is not a big brewery—in 2005, it was America's thirtieth-largest (though it has expanded since then), grabbing a full 0.03-percent share of the domestic market, compared with Anheuser-Busch's 49.47 percent—but it's a very good brewery nonetheless. According to the Bell's website, its beers are available in fifteen American states, which gives the company a potential market of more than 110 million customers. Take that, Canada's thirtieth-largest brewer, whoever you are. (possibly some guy making beer in his basement).

Bell's makes a beer called Hopslam Ale, which it describes as "a biting, bitter, tongue bruiser of an ale." It clocks in at 10 percent alcohol by volume, or double a Labatt Blue, and it's not even their strongest beer.

The Boston Beer Company, maker of the Sam Adams line of beers, was, in 2005, the sixth-biggest brewery in the USA, representing a whopping 0.69 percent of American beer sales. The Sam Adams beer you don't see every day is an occasional brew called Utopias, a beer that goes through wood aging, sometimes for up to thirteen years, and comes in a numbered, twenty-four-ounce, fancy-pants, copper-finished bottle for a suggested retail price (if you can find someone to sell it to you) of $130—each. The most recent vintage hit the human bloodstream at a hefty 27 percent alcohol by volume, or about 5.4 times a Molson Canadian. This is not a lawn mower beer; it is to be sipped as you might sip a port or brandy. This beer is so strong that it's illegal in twelve American states, and so rare that even empty bottles have been known to go on sale for a hundred dollars. *Now* do you want to talk about Canadian beer being stronger than its American counterpart?

Oh, how we scoffed, once upon a time, at American beer. Gnat's pee, bat's pee, horse pee—we said some very unkind things, things that maybe we shouldn't have said. Don't compare Budweiser with bat's pee if you've never actually tried bat's pee. (Have you? And, if so, how sick are you, and why should we trust your judgement on beer? Or anything else?)

The point is this: we used to think Americans were stupid because they drank lousy beer. Stupid Americans, we said. In 2008, *The Globe and Mail* ran a piece about Canadians' beer-drinking habits, in which reporter Marina Strauss reckoned that the second-most popular beer in Canada is Coors Light. Number one: Budweiser. Stupid Canadians. Oh, Canada.

When Canadians Knew Squat: The Stubby in Our Lives

Historically, beer bottles have varied in shape. Lager bottles were usually taller and narrower, while ale bottles took a shorter, rounder shape. These preferences were echoed in the choice of glasses in which these beers were generally served.

Colour has also varied. To this day, we see mostly brown bottles, but there are lots of green bottles and clear, colourless bottles. The colourless ones have the advantage of showing off the colour and clarity of the beer inside, but they also let in the light, which is a bad thing. Once, at a beer festival, I heard a beer enthusiast drilling his harried young daughter on beer knowledge.

"What are the enemies of beer?" he quizzed her.

"Light, air, and heat," she replied, obviously not for the first time in her young life.

"Correct," he acknowledged.

And she was right. Light, air, and heat will turn beer skunky, so keep your beer in a cool, dark place and hope the producer has made the bottle airtight. (And hope also that everyone in the bottling, warehousing, and distribution processes has been equally careful.)

So, then, colourless bottles should be regarded with suspicion. Green bottles are better, but brown ones are best. All things being equal, of course.

Glass, generally, has an interesting place in beer history. As we'll see in a later chapter, the mass manufacture of glass neatly coincided with the rise of clear, golden lagers from Pilsn, in Bohemia, a factor that was pivotal to the success of this new style of beer. Beer drinkers had seldom seen what they were drinking until affordable glass came along, and this clear, pretty pilsner looked nicer than the darker and murkier beers they'd known. Which was the chicken and which the egg is not clear, but the match of accessible glassware and eye-pleasing beer was irresistible.

Well, this is all a long way from the Great Canadian Stubby, but you can't write about glass in a vacuum. Or at least, I can't. Beerstorian Patrick J. Hunter informs us that the first Canadian beer bottle was not made until 1825. In those days, of course, bottles were blown by hand, one by one. Hunter then tells us that the first machine-made beer bottle in Canada was produced in 1906 by the Diamond Glass Company. Most Canadian breweries of the day continued in the European tradition of putting ale and lager in different bottles.

By the late 1950s, however, the brewing industry was in fewer hands, particularly after E.P. Taylor's assault on countless breweries. It was thus easier for the remaining breweries to address the issues that concerned them.

One of which was the bottle. The bottles then in use had any number of problems: some of them let in too much light and spoiled the beer; they were all heavier than they needed to be; and the variety of shapes of bottles made the entire process more unwieldy and expensive, especially since bottles were returned to central stores for refund. The Dominion Brewers Association decided the solution lay in a standard bottle. Committees were struck in 1958, and by 1961 the brewers were ready to test a prototype bottle: one that was brown, lighter, and more durable. It all led to the big day: March 1, 1962, by which time 288 million bottles had been made (by three companies) and distributed to Canada's breweries. A nation held its breath. The Dominion Brewers Association called its new creation the "compact" bottle. Canadian drinkers instantly dubbed it the "stubby," the name that stuck.

The downside of the stubby was that it was difficult to carry multiple bottles in one hand. The upside was that a case of twenty-four fit nicely in the trunk of a car. You could easily stack them two high, even in the fairly small cars that were popular in the 1970s after the energy crisis. (Whatever happened to the energy crisis anyway?)

The stubby became a great Canadian institution. It wasn't elegant, by any means, but it was cute, damn it. It was like us: unprepossessing and practical. And cute. It couldn't have been more Canadian if it had tried.

The brewers of Canada had agreed on the stubby, but brewers can be a fractious lot. Not surprisingly, it was the rise of American beers in the early 1980s that spelled the end for this Canadian artifact. In those pre-NAFTA days, it was difficult for American breweries to break into the Canadian market. Rather than try to beat the big three Canadian brewers, the Americans took a different approach.

For some years, Canadian breweries had been producing foreign beers under licence for the Canadian market. Labatt, since 1965, has brewed a bottled version of Guinness. It used to be fairly grim; their brewer's licence was more like poetic licence. I can't vouch for it these days. In 1980, Labatt formed an alliance with Anheuser-Busch to make Budweiser in Canada, a step that led to untold degradation of our beer life. At first, they packaged it in the stubby bottle, but it just wasn't the same for Bud lovers.

It seems to have been Carling O'Keefe, however, that changed the rules and eventually killed the stubby. In 1983, Carling became the

Canadian brewer of Miller High Life, that exemplar of high quality and full flavour.

Now, let's face it: the only charm associated with these American imports lay in the packaging. After two decades of the stubby, Canadians found long-necked bottles glamorous, and the only reason to drink Miller High Life was to be seen in the company of what, by now, seemed an exotic bottle. It would be unwise to underestimate the appeal of novelty. Or branding. You can travel around the world and see impressionable beer drinkers guzzling Budweiser from the bottle, for no better reason than they want to be associated with this global brand. (How many people on the planet pay money to wear clothing with the Nike logo, imagining it makes them appear athletic?) Drinking Bud from a glass doesn't count; it looks like any other light lager. You have to be able to see the distinctive label. (The other reason to drink it directly from the bottle is so you won't taste it much. It's true: if you can't smell something, you're less likely to taste it. If you're given a mediocre beer to drink, take it straight from the bottle. I'm here to help.)

Carling O'Keefe saw that marketing Miller in stubbies would defeat the purpose, so they arbitrarily broke the agreement they had made with the other brewers and sold Miller High Life in American-style bottles. Molson and Labatt squealed with displeaure. When that didn't work, they started putting their beers into the suddenly fashionable long-neck bottles, and a year later the stubby was gone.

The stubby lived on in our hearts, however, and there can be few Canadian basements that don't have an old stubby or two tucked away somewhere. In 2002, the Brick Brewery in Ontario obtained the rights to brew an old Carling beer, Red Cap Ale. Carling O'Keefe had disappeared in 1989 as part of a merger with Molson engineered by Elders, the Australian company that by then owned it. Red Cap had once been Canada's top-selling beer, but it had become a piece of history until Jim Brickman decided to resurrect it.

How do you position a beer that people vaguely remember from the distant past? You either try to make it hip and sexy, as Molson did briefly in the 1990s with Black Label (whose success lasted exactly as long as the expensive marketing campaign that supported it), or you make it self-consciously "retro" and stick it in a stubby—let the bottle do your marketing for you. Other Canadian microbreweries have made similar efforts to use the stubby. It seems unlikely the stubby will ever entirely leave us, and that's not a bad thing.

Domestic or Imported?

There are Canadians—some of them proud Canadians who paint their faces red and white when a Canadian national team is playing—who believe that imported beer is better than beers made right here. To be fair, this is not just a Canadian failing. Just about anywhere you go on this earth (I cannot speak for other planets), you will find people seeking out imported beer in preference to homegrown brands.

It's a globalized world we inhabit these days, and the beer drinker would be parochial indeed not to try the best brews of the world. And, as I write these words, I have recently returned from my supplier of exotic ales with no fewer than sixteen bottles of imported beer, from Belgium, Germany, England, Austria, and the United States. These are beers, by and large, that no one here is making, unless there are some Trappist monks brewing something wonderful in Saskatchewan and not telling anyone about it. Which wouldn't be kind. (And even if they made it and sold it, Canadians outside Saskatchewan would probably never see it.)

Our innovative domestic brewers are improving all the time, but no one is yet making a Westmalle Trippel in Canada, so we have to import it. There are numerous landmark beers of the world, only some of which we ever get to see here. Without question, imported beers enrich our lives. At their best, they also raise our standards.

But—and I'll say it again: but—it is one thing to get misty-eyed and all in a dither at the prospect of one of the great Belgian, British, or Czech beers, preferably served in a reasonably authentic manner; it is another thing altogether to assume that, just because a beer has travelled a great distance to get to you, it is by definition superior to your usual tipple. (Unless your usual tipple is not very good to begin with, but that's between you and your local provider.)

Particularly on draught, most of the imported beers available in Canada are not among the top echelon of global brewing. The few English ales that make their way here, for instance, tend to be beers one would seldom seek out in England, and are rarely, if ever, served in their optimal condition. The whole point of English draught beer is to drink it in its natural state—fresh, unpasteurized, and having undergone a secondary fermentation. (And certainly not injected with lots of nitrogen to make it "smooth.") Anything else is an unconvincing imitation.

Guinness lovers are constantly on the watch for the perfect pour of their favourite beverage, and the likelihood that you will hear Guinnessites complain about their pint increases the farther they are from the actual St. James's Gate Brewery in Dublin. Draught Guinness used to be a rarity in these parts. Part of the appeal of travelling to the US was always seeking out a bar that served the black nectar. Is Guinness the same as it was, even allowing for the fact that its makers now demand a colder serving temperature? You could start a fight or two among the cognoscenti merely by asking the question. Is it even as dark-coloured as it once was? I merely ask.

For a very long time, Guinness almost defined stout. Why would you drink anybody else's stout, even if you could get anybody else's stout? But times change, and nowadays craft brewers across North America are offering us alternatives to the Irish behemoth. Most Guinness-heads refuse to countenance these upstarts, won't allow them to pass their lips, but increasingly beer bars on this continent are banishing Guinness in favour of local variants. Members of the Guinness community are affronted to be told by a bartender that they might want to try something else instead, but if the alternative is going back out into the snow and finding another bar, some will actually relent. If they're lucky enough to be offered a St-Ambroise Oatmeal Stout, made by McAuslan in Montreal, they might not go back to their habitual choice. (Who am I kidding? Guinness drinkers have the keenest brand loyalty in the beer game.)

As noted above, the snobbery around imported beer is not just a Canadian tragedy. To walk into an English pub and see actual English people, who should know better, drinking Stella and Bud and Black Label is to wonder what goes on in people's heads. Still, there is the occasional backlash. C'est What in Toronto has thirty-five draught taps, all devoted to Canadian-made beers. (Guinness drinkers, please note: C'est What offers, when last I looked, five porters and three stouts on tap, but not your particular poison.)

Sometimes, patriotism can go too far. In the early 1990s, I had occasion to visit a roadhouse-type place in Anaheim, California. I did it so you won't have to. At the bar, I looked around for palatable beer, but the bartender cut to the chase. "This is an American bar," he told me. "We've got Bud, Bud Light, Coors, Coors Light. None of that imported stuff here." He clearly saw me as one of those Heineken-sipping, Saab-driving, girly-man Democrats who are unwelcome in Orange County, when in fact I was happy to drink American beer. I really wanted to drink American beer, just not those particular American beers. Really, what is it with manly men and their girly beers? (Most women I know wouldn't touch the stuff.) Bud Light? Why not just drink water and be done with it? As the

Wychwood Brewery in England asks in its ads, "What's the matter, Lagerboy, afraid you might taste something?"

But I digress, and not for the first time. There are two areas of growth in North American beer sales: imports and craft beers. In Canada especially, these segments are eating into sales of traditional Labatt and Molson products. Labatt is owned by a major importer of beers into Canada, so it is scarcely surprising that InBev is happy to promote its global brands at the expense of beers it hadn't even heard of a few years ago. Marketing of Stella Artois sends the message to Canadian beer drinkers that the stuff they've been drinking for years isn't up to snuff. If you drink to impress, you should be drinking Stella, not the other rubbish our company brews in Canada. (At the other end of the scale, discount buck-a-bottle breweries send the message that it all tastes pretty much the same, so why not buy the cheapest? Small wonder the domestic middle-of-the-road beers are suffering. And small wonder also that, in 2007, Labatt swooped down to buy Lakeport, the prime Ontario purveyor of cheap beer. If you can't beat it, own it.)

Breweries spend a lot of money on advertising, and what they choose to advertise at any time tells you what they're hoping you'll buy. At the time of writing, Labatt advertises, to different markets, Budweiser, Keith's, and Stella. Labatt Blue, once the superstar of beer sales in this country, threatens to vanish from our consciousness altogether. Squeezed between the cheap brews and the allegedly classier imports, Blue has nowhere much to go.

Molson, meanwhile, has partnerships with the likes of Heineken and Corona, two huge worldwide forces of beerdom. Honestly, when Corona comes across as a sophisticated choice for the discerning beer drinker, it's time to switch to gin. And where's Molson Export these days? Below the radar. Even mighty Molson Canadian languishes beneath Bud and Coors Light, despite its annoying commercials. I'll talk about beer advertising elsewhere.

My point—and I knew I'd get to it—is that some imports are worth making a fuss over, but most of them (and usually the ones that sell best) are designed to separate the honest drinking person from his or her cash, on the premise that said drinker will feel more cosmopolitan, more attractive, more likely to speak other languages, and considerably more able to leap tall buildings. Isn't that worth paying a little extra for? To be fair, many of the pubs that sell imported beers on tap offer domestic beers of such low quality that an import is just about the only way to go.

As I noted many chapters ago, beer is very heavy. This is another reason for seeking out fine local beers. Say you live in Kelowna, for example. Have you any idea how far your pint of Stella has travelled to get to you? Me neither, but it's a hell of a way. Now, this is meant to be a book about pleasure, and I'm certainly reluctant to start getting all preachy about your carbon footprint, but wouldn't you feel better about trying to find a Tree Brewing Hophead IPA, made right where you live? It's made on Richter Street, for crying out loud, probably right around the corner from you. You'd be keeping your dollars local, supporting a local business, employing local people, buying fresher beer, and drinking better beer as well. Talk about a win-win-win-win-win situation.

Now, put that Stella down. You don't know where it's been.

Home or Away: Where We Drink

Where do you drink?

It's a serious question. In Britain, historically, people drank their beer in the pub. It cost about the same as drinking at home, and the pub was usually warmer than home, even if only because a roomful of drinkers raises the temperature, whether there's a fireplace or not. And it was nice to get out of the house sometimes. Like, say, every evening.

Even relatively recently, it was estimated that three-quarters of British beer consumption happened in pubs. North Americans were generally just the opposite, drinking three-quarters of their beer at home. These figures are changing, particularly in Britain, where pubs are shutting down at a worrying pace. There are many reasons for this. Drinking-and-driving laws have kept fearful, law-abiding folk at home, which has taken a toll on country pubs. Smoking bans have had an impact as well. Most British homes have central heating nowadays, thus removing one traditional incentive to go out. Property values have soared, particularly in London, and pubs are worth more as residences. And supermarkets have used discounted beer and other alcoholic drinks as loss leaders to the point that it is now vastly cheaper to drink at home, especially if you're not picky about what you drink. Not to mention that British governments in recent years have socked the beer industry with ever-rising taxes.

North American drinkers, on the other hand, are doing more of their drinking outside the home than ever before, despite the effects of smoking legislation in many places. This is in large part the result of greater choice. The lingering effects of Prohibition left most Canadian communities with nasty taverns that discouraged respectable drinkers—especially women—from entering. The stamp of shame provincial governments impressed upon Canadian drinkers was that much more pronounced on drinkers who practised their vice in public places. That most provinces forbade public drinking for some time after the end of Prohibition also encouraged the habit of drinking at home.

The liberalization of drinking laws that swept—though perhaps "swept" is far too dramatic; "crept" is probably more accurate—across Canada in the 1970s and 1980s led to a growing number of fairly respectable drinking locales where middle-class drinkers could assemble without feeling they were engaged in vaguely criminal activity. Canadian society was becoming more secular in nature, so most Canadian urban drinkers could visit a pub without the spectre of "sin" entering into their decision.

From their arrival in Canada in 1953 until the arrival of fake English pubs in 1976, my parents did little of their drinking outside their own or someone else's home. They weren't hoity-toity by any means, but they had no affection for being treated like crap, which was standard fare in the beverage room of the time. The people who drank in beverage rooms were all too accustomed to being treated like crap, which was maybe part of the reason they were drinking in the first place. Why not be served by a gruff waiter who treated you as if he were your boss? You were used to it. Siddown, shuddup, drink your damn beer. Even the nice ones didn't say "Cheers!" as they dumped your little glasses of draught beer on your table.

So my parents gave parties and went to parties. For a few years they took up curling, which was a dandy excuse for a weekly party, a party that often went on till dawn and beyond. As a kid, I remember looking forward to a time when I'd have as much partying stamina as my parents. A few years ago I came to terms with the sad fact that I never had, and never would. They drank all right, my parents, but seldom outside someone's home, unless it was a restaurant or a hotel bar. When I took them to one of the places I inhabited, they looked around like anthropologists dropped into a savage society where they didn't know the rules but thought it likely they'd get eaten.

In their jurisdiction, the fake English pub arrived in 1976, and it was a godsend to my very real English parents. They could drink beer from proper pint glasses and eat food they recognized as English: shepherd's pie (occasionally, to this day, spelled correctly), fish and chips, variations on meat pies (though, as Canadians don't like the idea of kidneys, infrequently steak and kidney—and never steak and kidney pudding, the dish I will choose as my last meal before they hang me). It all made a very pleasant change from the pickled eggs and beef jerky that represented haute cuisine in the beverage room of old.

Shame, if not completely eradicated, was now at least concealed behind the bar—available if you wanted it, but no longer compulsory. I recall a visit I made to London, Ontario, with my parents in about 1963 or 1964 (I remember the approximate date because I was told I looked a bit like George Harrison, probably because of my crooked English teeth). An old family friend was in the country, visiting his daughter, and we made the journey to see him. A bang-up dinner was called for, and we made our way to what was presumably the ne plus ultra of local dining, probably a hotel restaurant. It was a grand place, with tablecloths and matching cutlery, so we knew we were in the presence of quality.

The subject of dinner was broached with our waiter, and one of the alpha males—either my father or the visiting Englishman—asked for the wine list. It was if he had asked for a selection of the finest pornography to pore over while we waited for our dinner. Unsure as to whether he should summon the police at once, the waiter explained haughtily that it was Sunday, and that he didn't know what life was like where we came from, but that in the God-fearing province of Ontario, people knew how to behave and knew better than to attempt to corrupt a decent working man such as himself with talk of alcohol on a Sunday, thank you very much.

All right, he didn't say all of that, not out loud, but it was clear that only some depraved alcoholic of the lowest breeding would even consider drinking on the Lord's Day, and in the finest dining establishment in London, Ontario, to boot. I don't believe that he audibly tutted, but the tut, though silent, hung in the air for some time. I don't know who was more embarrassed—the visiting Englishman, for inadvertently exposing his friends to a sort of public rebuke that might lead to a day in the stocks, or my parents, for revealing the sort of backward hellhole they had emigrated to. Still, the day wasn't a complete disaster. A girl had said I looked like George Harrison.

Hence the joy of my parents when fake pubs burst onto the scene; now they could drink in public without too much fear of being shamed by the staff. Not that they went every day, or anything like that, but they were happy to know they could. And all it took in their case was twenty-three years. I regret that they didn't keep journals. I'm sure their first years in Canada would have come across as not unlike the accounts of Susannah Moodie or other early English travellers to this country. Roughing it at the Ontario liquor store.

Public drinking is not the exclusive practice of human beings. Nature documentaries frequently show animals, often different species of animals, gathering at the water hole to drink and, presumably, to swap gossip in their own way. I might feel different if I were a hippopotamus (which is putting it mildly), but I think we do it better. For starters, we have beer. I write elsewhere in this book about the great interest elephants take in drinking beer, but they're largely dependent on humans to make it. Down at the watering hole, they're pretty much limited to water. Hence the name, although humans are apt to refer euphemistically to watering holes. Euphemisms are largely unknown to the animal kingdom.

I know pubgoers who maintain that they never drink at home, that indeed they never keep beer in their home. This seems strange to me. I know we all do an amount of compartmentalizing in our lives, but this seems an unduly rigid policy. I also know people—not as many, because how would I ever meet them?—who do all their drinking at home, like my parents in the fifties and sixties. Even stranger, if you ask me. What are they trying to hide?

As noted earlier, most Canadian provinces were reluctant to authorize public drinking when they began to repeal Prohibition in the 1920s and beyond. Fortunately, given the entrepreneurial spirt of humankind, the "blind pigs" that had operated during the dry years kept on operating. There was a human need to drink in groups in a congenial environment in which someone else cleaned up and washed the glasses. There: it's as simple as that. This is what separates us from the hippos mentioned a few paragraphs ago. It's what makes us who we are. I can't tell you how many times I've invited my cat down to the pub, always without success. I even offer to buy; I know he's usually strapped for cash. I've given up.

One of the earliest representations of beer is an illustration of ancient Sumerians, roughly five millennia ago, drinking beer from a common vessel through a kind of straw. Beer, then as now, was a social drink. We tell our friends we'll meet them later for a pint. We don't say we'll meet for *two* pints—one for me, one for you. Sometimes, we share a pitcher of beer, though usually not through straws.

American writer Ray Oldenburg has decried the shortage of local drinking holes in his country (read *The Great Good Place,* please), pointing out that society needs democratic places where people can assemble, places that are neither home nor the workplace.

Prince Charles played a key role in the establishment of an organization called Pub Is the Hub, an initiative that aims to preserve both pubs and rural communities by broadening the role of the pub within its community—by offering a post office, a shop, or dry cleaning services. Anything to keep the pub solvent and preserve its place as the community centre it's always been. The Miners Arms in Derbyshire hosts a computer skills workshop for the locals. The main bar of the Weir Hotel in Lancashire is used on Sunday mornings for church services and Sunday school. The Cock Inn in Oxfordshire works with a chemist in a nearby village who delivers prescriptions to the pub, so that locals can pick them up when convenient. The Old Spot in Gloucestershire offers, free of charge, space on its website, where its regulars can advertise their services. You can find anything from a French teacher to a chimney sweep.

And that's what a good pub does. You might find a friend, a job, a spouse, or a chimney sweep in a good pub. In the next chapter, you'll learn about a Halifax barmaid who saved a customer's life. Yes, I know it's cheaper to drink at home, and you might not have to go outdoors to smoke, and you can watch any television channel you like, but it's not the same as a pub. And you'll never know the barmaid who might just save your life, such as it is.

Support your local pub. If you don't have one, move.

Yes, but Isn't It Bad for You and Bad for the Planet?

No, of course not. Honestly, listen to yourself. Things that taste good are bad for you; things that taste bad are good for you: what nonsense. Which old wife have you been listening to? Did she tell you any other tales?

Beer is made of barley, hops, yeast, and water. All of these ingredients are good for you. For much of human history, water has been dangerous, but the water in beer has been boiled and is perfectly safe. The simple act of boiling water to make beer has saved countless millions of lives over the centuries. Beer's practically a wonder drug, for that reason alone.

Many people refuse to acknowledge this obvious truth. Say you cook up a batch of barley and eat it. Your friends will accuse you of going on a health kick, of becoming a vegan. Now, take that same batch of barley and *drink* it. Suddenly it's become some sort of poison? Of course not. It's barley: it's good for you. Hops are filled with antioxidants, and have traditionally been used as aids to easing insomnia and anxiety. People sleep on hop pillows. Hops are used in herbal concoctions that promote breast enhancement. Brewer's yeast? They sell it in health food stores. It's a disgrace that governments actually tax beer.

Study after study has confirmed that alcohol, in moderation, is good for us. Moderate drinkers live longer than teetotallers. (It only seems longer for teetotallers.) A 1985 study by Alexander Richman and R.A. Warren reported that regular beer drinkers took less time off work and spent less time seeing their doctors than other Canadians. As early as 1924, the great philosopher P.G. Wodehouse, in a novel called *The Inimitable Jeeves*, wrote, "It was my Uncle George who discovered that alcohol was a food well in advance of modern medical thought." Which reminds me of the line attributed to practically everybody: "Remember that beer has food value, but food has no beer value."

Even before Wodehouse's observation, card-carrying doctors were extolling the health benefits of beer. Philadelphia beer writer Joe Sixpack (he says that's his name and I have to believe him) found a case cited in the *New York Medical Journal* in 1886 in which Dr. Charlton R. Gulick reported his treatment of a man with pneumonia. It was not going well. "Electricity was first used, then quinine, and then digitalis. The use of the drugs was pushed to the fullest extent, and finally Duquesnel's Digitalin was used hypodermically, but this proved exceedingly objectionable to the patient, and lager beer was ordered. Within 72 hours marked improvement was observed."

In 1909, a Chicago publication called *The Medical Standard* noted, "Hot milk poured into an equal quantity of good ale or beer makes an excellent going-to-bed drink, and for puny, restless and scrofulous children." (Apart from anything else, this observation reminds us what a wonderful word "scrofulous" is, particularly when applied to children.) And in the early 1920s, American doctors rallied against the forces of Prohibition for the right to prescribe beer and other alcoholic products to their patients. The doctors lost in the Supreme Court, five votes to four.

The British beer world was shaken, late in 2007, when one of the members of the commission that, twenty years earlier, had set the alcohol consumption guidelines for the British government acknowledged that the figures had no scientific basis, that they had been "plucked out of the air." In response, an British gastroenterologist wrote to *What's Brewing* magazine about a study that suggested that eighteen units of alcohol a week seemed to be ideal. At that point, drinkers outlived teetotallers by a long shot. Above that mark, the gap closed slowly, to the point that a drinker had to consume sixty-three units a week to become as unhealthy as an abstainer. Just to attain the brief life expectancy of someone who avoided the demon alcohol altogether! Now, I'm sure that an abstainer who eats wisely and gets regular exercise can live a long and fruitful life. But why take that risk? Why dice with death, when there's a healthy alternative?

I mentioned earlier that hops were used in the natural healing community for breast enhancement. Oddly enough, I am told of a Czech saying that dark beer makes breasts grow larger. And there was a story in 2001 about a twenty-one-year-old woman in England, a student at Manchester University, who found that she couldn't afford to drink red wine on her modest student budget and switched to drinking beer. After a little time had passed, she discovered that she had not become fatter but that her bra size had gone from 34B to 36DD. This is anecdotal evidence, to be sure, but it's interesting.

Manchester University, by the way, seems a worthwhile institution. Its website boasts of "world-class research facilities," and I'm not surprised. A study done in 2005 at MU tackled the scientifically controversial issue of "beer goggles," that phenomenon by which people become more attractive to someone who has been drinking. It is impossible to overstate the importance of beer goggles in human history. How many of us would be here today had our forebears not spied one another across crowded rooms after a few flagons? Not many, if we're being honest. You may even have noticed this phenomenon in your own life, but don't feel you have to drop me a line with the details. Unless they're particularly good.

(I have been told—by a woman, for what it's worth—that the beer goggle syndrome does not affect women, that only men suffer from the illusion that other people have become significantly more attractive after a pint or two. Apparently, they did some sort of study. I bet they just asked a passel of women, all of whom denied ever having found a fellow more handsome after a couple of margaritas. It's like the surveys they do all the time that reveal that the trait women look for most in a man is a sense of humour. Pull the other one. I am living proof that women experience beer goggles. I got married, didn't I? And my wife, thirty-odd years on, continues to drink, hoping to find me as attractive as she clearly did one night long ago in the Morrissey Tavern. I admire just about everything about women, apart from their easy ability to lie to people who perform surveys.)

Now, the non-scientist might assume that beer goggles were simply an effect of drinking, but the non-scientist would be wrong. The unflagging researchers of Manchester University set about examining the beer goggle syndrome with scientific rigour, though where they found research subjects I cannot say. Well, I think I can. *Private Eye* magazine in 2006 cited, in its Quote of the Week feature, the *Sunday Times:* "Its students have a reputation for sex and drug-taking, yet Manchester University attracts more applications than any other College." (It's the word "yet" that triggers the *duh!* impulse.) We can be fairly sure there was no difficulty getting volunteers for the beer goggles study.

Anyway, it isn't just the quantity of beer consumed, though that's certainly a factor. Our dogged researchers isolated other forces: the distance between the viewer and the "person of interest," the level of lighting in the room (measured in candelas per square metre), the smokiness of the room, and something called "Snellen visual acuity," which is basically a measure of how good the viewer's eyesight is.

In other words, a myopic drunk, catching a glimpse of someone across a smoky, dimly lit room, is very likely to say "Wow!" or something like it. The Manchester team actually developed a formula to measure the effect of all this, though honestly I'm not sure how it's going to help. It looks like this:

$$\beta = \frac{(An)^2 \times E(S+1)}{\sqrt{L} \times (Vo)^2}$$

Well, this time I really have lost my way. Oh yes, this chapter's about the health of beer drinkers and the health of the planet. The fact is that, for many millennia, beer was a major source of nutrition for many of our ancestors. Grain, water, yeast: does that ring a bell? Depending on how much water you add, and whether you bake it or boil it, it's either bread or beer. Like bread, beer is a staple of a good diet, unless you're on one of those low-carbohydrate diets that were popular not long ago. (Keep telling yourself: Doctor Atkins died in 2003, weighing an alleged 258 pounds.) Beer contains no fat or cholesterol. It's good for your heart. It relieves stress.

As noted earlier, alcohol generally is good for you, but it seems that red wine and beer are better than most other alcohols, and beer is better than red wine for raising your Vitamin B_6 readings. The darker beers seem healthier than paler ones, for what it's worth.

And, of course, the medics all stress moderation, however you choose to define it. I always think a moderate drinker is someone who drinks roughly what I do. Any more, and you're a problem drinker. Any less, and I hope you're taking supplements to make sure you're getting the folate, magnesium, potassium, riboflavin, and niacin you need. I worry about you.

Not only is beer a healthy beverage, but it can actually save your life. On a 2008 trip to Halifax, noted later in this book, my wife spotted an item in the *Chronicle Herald* about a young woman named Jennifer Clarke, a beerslinger at a bar/restaurant on Spring Garden Road. Octogenarian Lewis Hurshman is someone who came to Gatsby's every day at 11 a.m., drank two Alpines over the course of three hours, and left. On Ms. Clarke's first shift of the week in question, she immediately noticed Mr. Hurshman's absence and called the police. They found him, alive but not well following a fall he'd suffered four days earlier in his apartment, and got him to hospital. Said Constable Jeff Carr, "She, in all likelihood, saved his life."

I don't know about you, but that story makes me all misty. Beer brings people together and keeps people alive. I hope Mr. Hurshman lives to drink many more Alpines and that nothing bad ever happens to Jennifer Clarke. Ever. You hurt Jennifer Clarke and you're answering to me.

Now, about the planet. Here in Canada, we are among the world leaders at returning our beer bottles for reuse, but we could still do better. Drinking Carlsberg that's come all the way from Denmark and doesn't taste much different from, say, Labatt Blue, is bad for the planet. Drinking beer that came from just down the road, on the other hand, is pretty good. For the planet, I mean. As recorded elsewhere in this book, brewing was once local, almost by definition. Beer was made locally and distributed locally by horse-drawn drays. The horses—and other livestock—thrived on a diet of the spent grains from the brewery. Talk about self-sufficiency.

In 2007, I met the owner of the Uley Brewery, in darkest Gloucestershire in southwestern England. Offered a tour of his brewery, I accepted, and in the course of the tour, I asked if he did any bottling of his beers. Chas Wright looked at me darkly, suggesting that I was an enemy of the environment for even asking. He pointed to a stack of casks and noted that they were the perfect beer containers, each one holding dozens of pints and almost infinitely reusable. If you care about the planet, walk to your local pub and drink draught beer—preferably (if you can get it) cask-conditioned ale that needs no artificial carbon dioxide. English cask ale, for that matter, has historically been served at cellar temperature, so it requires no, or at least less, refrigeration.

If you want to get inspired about all of this, I recommend a book by Christopher Mark O'Brien called *Fermenting Revolution*. The subtitle says it all: *How to Drink Beer and Save the World*. I'm already feeling nobler. A trip to the beer fridge can't be far away.

Perhaps because brewing is an earthy, no-nonsense process—none of this precious talk of terroir, no spitting out at tastings—the beer trade has generally been a planet-friendly pursuit. Brewers take perfectly natural ingredients and (usually) local water to create a beverage that lives in harmony with nature. The solids left over from the brewing process make nutritious food for farm animals.

The Great Lakes Brewery in Cleveland, Ohio, dispenses some of its spent grains to a local baker, who uses it to make bread for the brewery's restaurant, and the rest to local farmers, who feed it to livestock that winds up on plates there as well.

New Belgium Brewing in Colorado generates some of its power from methane produced by its waste-water program. It is also a major user of wind-generated power. After a year's employment, staff members are given a free bicycle. After five years, they get a free trip to Belgium to absorb a proper beer culture. You can't get more sustainable than these people, though I doubt they make their people ride their bikes to Belgium. *Outside* magazine in 2008 named New Belgium the best place to work in America among companies with 250 or more employees. It sounds pretty good to me.

Adnams Brewery in England won the Carbon Trust Innovation Award in 2007 for reducing the weight of its bottles by a third and opening a new, very green, distribution centre complete with solar panels and a plant-covered roof, among other clever design features. In 2008, it introduced a carbon-neutral beer called East Green, which the brewery's managing director described as "greener than any other beer on the market." Adnams is in the heart of the seaside town of Southwold, in Suffolk, and sponsors(free beer!) an annual volunteer cleaning of the beach. From across the common, at the Harbour Inn, you look at the town from a distance and see its three main landmarks: the town's famous lighthouse, the church steeple, and the brewery tower. Oh, and the beer's very good, too.

Many brewers are trying to use organic products in their beers. Crannóg Ales produces all-organic, draught-only, Irish-influenced beers on its farm in British Columbia. It doesn't have a map on its website, though the people there are happy to give brewery tours. You'll need to book ahead of time, and only then will they tell you where they are. Their goal is a totally waste-free operation, and what can be nobler than that?

Some ideas come along before their time. Alfred Heineken visited Curaçao in 1960, where he noticed a) beaches littered with beer bottles, and b) a shortage of cheap building materials. Eureka! Working with Dutch architect John Habraken, he created the Heineken WOBO (World Bottle), a square bottle that, when emptied, could be stacked and interlocked to build walls. Billed as "the brick that holds beer," the WOBO never took off when first produced, and there are today only two examples of this type of building, both on the Heineken site in Amsterdam. But maybe this is an idea whose time has come.

We used to think the only time for green beer was St. Patrick's Day, but beer has always been at least somewhat green, and in many ways it's getting greener. Always remember: the most sustainable way to drink beer is to drink locally produced beer, on draught, in a pub you can walk to, ideally with friends. Who knew saving the planet could be so enjoyable?

Ale or Lager?
East Is East,
and the West Isn't

It used to depend on where you lived in Canada. East of the Manitoba–Ontario border, you probably drank ale. West of that line, you probably drank lager. I recall being in Vancouver long ago, when craft beer was in its infancy and most beer drinkers had one or two fairly reliable mass brands to fall back on, and discovering that west coast pub staff appeared never to have heard of Molson Export. It was an ale. Like so much else in our national character, our beer habits have changed. In Vancouver today, you might well be looking for an ale, and a big, assertive, hoppy ale to boot.

What's the difference anyway? It's a perfectly reasonable question. Even if you tasted Molson Canadian (lager) and Labatt 50 (ale) in quick succession, you'd probably be none the wiser, which says more about Molson Canadian and Labatt 50 than about your palate.

Ale and lager are the two main families of beer. Ales include stout, porter, and most wheat beers. Lagers include such styles as pilsner and bock beers. Contrary to popular wisdom, ales can be quite pale in colour and lagers can be very dark. For that matter, pale ales are not always very pale. (And colour has nothing to do with strength or caloric content.)

Lager is made from the same ingredients used to make ale: water, malt, hops, and yeast. But different water, malt, hops, and yeast. Take water. Lager makers, broadly speaking, like soft water; ale brewers tend to prefer hard. (Pilsn, in the Czech Republic, where modern lager was born, has ineffably soft water; Burton-on-Trent, home of English ale, has water so hard you could injure yourself diving into it.) The lager guys speak affectionately of barley sown in the spring, while the ale guys like it sown in the winter. There are many varieties of hops, some of which suit lagers, others ale. Likewise, there are many strains of yeast, but they divide into bottom-fermenting yeasts (for lager) and top-fermenting yeasts (for ale). The lager yeasts work at lower temperatures and require a longer fermentation period. (The word "lager" in German means "to store.")

Yes, I hear you say, a trifle impatiently, top-fermenting and bottom-fermenting—what does it all mean? Lagers are inclined to be crisper in flavour, less complex, often more refreshing, whereas ales are usually bigger and bolder, or they should be. Think of lager as a white wine, ale as a red.

So, why was there a geographical divide in Canada when it came to these styles of beer? The eastern part of Canada was settled first, largely by people from the British Isles, but also by settlers from northwestern France, where ales were the popular tipple. These people were all in place before the lager revolution of the nineteenth century, and they knew what they liked to drink. Western Canada was settled, to a large degree, by new arrivals from continental Europe, where lager had taken over almost completely. They also wanted to drink what they were used to.

Victoria, of course, was traditionally an outpost of British emigrants, so when the brewpub/microbrewery revolution came along,

Victorians expected, and received, British-style ales. And they're drinking it to this day.

In recent times, this geographical split between ale and lager drinkers has become fairly meaningless. Postwar immigration changed a lot about Canada. No longer was it compulsory to come from the British Isles, and Canada received boatloads of people from countries—many of them southern or central European, but Caribbean as well—where, if beer was consumed in quantity at all, it was mostly lager (or, paradoxically, in the case of the Caribbeans, stout). The ale strongholds of Quebec and Ontario collapsed under the strain. The rise of craft beer, on the other hand, has heightened the awareness of assertive ales, many of them based on the hoppy pale ale model popular on the American west coast. British Columbia has been much influenced by this style.

To confuse matters even further, there are some who feel there is some sort of difference between ale and beer. Once upon a time, in a far-off kingdom called England, there *was* a difference, but it is believed that no one alive today can remember first-hand the distinction.

It was the wily continentals who started putting hops in their beer, roughly a thousand years ago. According to Martyn Cornell, in his book *Beer: The Story of the Pint,* there is evidence that this hopped beer had arrived in England by the 1360s, but its market consisted of European foreigners living in England, not so much the English themselves. This new product was called "beer," to differentiate itself from traditional, English, unhopped "ale." Soon, some domestic brewers were making this newfangled beer, despite strong arguments that it was unwholesome, unhealthy, and un-English (or "foreign muck," as the English have, over many centuries, characterized anything from anywhere else).

Hops act as a natural preservative and make beer last longer, so hopped beer was useful for both the army and the navy and thus won support from King Henry VI. But the distinction lasted, nonetheless, for years to come. Shakespeare, Cornell notes, was an ale man. References to beer in his plays are usually derogatory, while ale is almost always a good thing, "a dish for a king."

Gradually, English drinkers came to like and trust hops, and by the early seventeenth century unhopped ale was becoming a thing of the past, in part for the simple, practical reason that hopped beer lasted longer, but also because people had come to like the more bitter taste of hopped beer. Nowadays, the distinction is long ago and far away. All ale is beer, but not all beer is ale. I hope this is helpful.

For most of beer history, beer *was* ale. It appears to have been German monks who invented lager, possibly in the sixteenth century. Beer is more difficult to make in summer, the heat playing havoc with the process, and in many areas brewers took the summer off, just when the populace was crying out for their wares.

The monks, perhaps realizing that they'd just have to pray more if they weren't brewing, found a new technique to make beer that fermented at the bottom of the tank. This beer required a longer fermentation period, so had to be stored for a while, which meant that it could be brewed before the summer arrived and stored in tanks, ideally underground or in cool caves, ready to be served in mid-summer. Clever monks.

This was not lager as North Americans understand the term today. It was a darker, maltier brew, and there are lots of breweries, particularly in Germany, where these beers are still made and enjoyed.

What most Canadians think of as lager is a far more recent development, and it can actually be dated to October 5, 1842, when a man named Josef Groll—a Bavarian brewer who had been enticed to Pilsn (or Pilsen) in Bohemia, in what is now the Czech Republic—created his first batch of what we now call pilsner (or pilsener) beer.

In one of those coincidences you'd reject as too convenient in a novel, the Bohemians developed clear, golden beer at right about the same time they figured out how to mass-manufacture glass. For the first time in human history, ordinary people could drink their beer from clear glass containers, no longer forced to drink from earthenware or pewter mugs. They could actually see their beer. Hitherto, beer had been poured from one opaque vessel into another. If you drank at home but didn't brew, you took a pail to the pub and had it filled up, the equivalent of the modern "growler," available from most brewpubs.

Ale of the day was often cloudy, which didn't matter if the drinker didn't have to look at it. But this new stuff from Bohemia, and then other places, looked great in a glass. This is not superficial: visual appeal adds greatly to our enjoyment of anything we eat or drink. Go to Belgium and see the pleasing ritual of matching beer with the appropriate glass. (Heck, go to Belgium, period.)

Pilsner beer revolutionized the brewing industry in most of the world, though the British Isles resisted for more than a century. Germans with names like Pabst and Busch, who emigrated to the United States in the 1840s and beyond, took this new beer with them, and in time, clear, light-coloured, light-flavoured lager became virtually the only sort of beer brewed in that country—or practically anywhere else—though its flavour declined enormously from the high standards set back in Pilsn.

Lager has enjoyed a long spell of near-total dominance in the world of beer, and only the broad variety of beers championed by the craft beer movement has put a dent in that domination. And some of the best lager in the world still comes from Pilsn.

Tycoon Taylor Tinkered: Canada's Beer Villain

In *Fermenting Revolution,* author Christopher Mark O'Brien finds one guilty party responsible for everything bad that has ever happened to beer, and by extension everything bad that has ever happened to anything: the entire male sex. O'Brien points out that, for the first several millennia of beer, brewing was a female activity. Many of the early beer-related deities were female. Women made beer for their families; then, as we began living in larger communities, they became the first commercial brewers. It was a practically perfect world, and we all lived in peace and harmony.

Then it all turned ugly: men got involved. Within mere centuries, men were putting rice and corn syrup into beer, inventing insipid lagers and gimmicky beverages such as "lite" beers and "dry" beers, pasteurizing beer, and inventing massive marketing campaigns to gull consumers into spending their hard-earned groats on beechwood-aged, low-carb, great-taste-less-filling beer-like fluids with that great "cold" taste that makes a fellow irresistible to young women with large breasts.

You can argue that women eventually would have seen the vast commercial potential of beer and might have taken a similar route to world domination, but there's no question that the chest-thumping masculinization of beer and its testosterone-rich marketing, have persuaded many women that beer is just not for them. The Campaign for Real Ale in the UK has made efforts to recruit female membership, and in 2008, a nineteen-year-old British female entrepreneur announced that, after much research, she was launching a real ale designed specifically for women. Will women feel empowered by their own special beer, or will they feel they're being patronized and manipulated?

Anyway, even allowing for the argument that men are to blame for wrecking beer and turning it into a gigantic money spinner, some are more blameworthy than others. The prosecution calls Edward Plunket Taylor (1901–1989) to the stand.

To admirers of horseflesh, E.P. Taylor is something of a national hero. The owner of Windfields Farm, Taylor was the mogul behind Northern Dancer, the thoroughbred that won the Kentucky Derby and brought glory to our great nation. Like most self-respecting moguls, Taylor had his fingers in numerous pies. Judging by some of his photographs, he appeared to have had numerous pies in his fingers as well. (Moguls of the mid-twentieth century and earlier were expected to have a robust appearance. Today's CEOs work out and pride themselves on looking trim and fit. That's the difference between a CEO and a mogul.)

Taylor is celebrated for horses, the Argus Corporation, and inventing Don Mills, Canada's first so-called planned community. But what concerns us here is his interest in beer. Or, rather, his interest in buying and selling beer. Beer put E.P. Taylor on the map, and, like the British Empire, he tried to paint the map red. Red, as in Carling Red Cap Ale. Also black, as in Black Label.

Taylor was a clever young chap. At eighteen, he invented an electric toaster that heated both sides of a slice of bread simultaneously. He was not born rich, even though his father bore the grand name of

Plunket Bourchier Taylor, which sounds pretty plummy and upper class. Taylor's maternal grandfather, however, was a successful entrepreneur who gave young Eddie big ideas. At twenty-two, Taylor became a director of Brading Breweries in Ottawa, one of the companies owned by his grandfather.

It was 1923, and Prohibition raged. But not in Quebec. Brading was in Ontario, where it was forbidden to sell beer but perfectly legal to brew it and sell it elsewhere, and Quebec was just across the river. By 1926, it appeared likely that Ontario would go wet, and Taylor was ready. When Prohibition ended in that province on June 1, 1927, there were thirty-seven breweries in Ontario—most of them greatly weakened by eleven years of brewing low- or no-alcohol beers and bottling soft drinks to stay afloat. Nor was the end of Prohibition a ticket to instant wealth, as Ontario continued to ban taverns for another seven years.

Taylor saw that success in the beer trade depended on getting bigger. Acquisitions and mergers were the way to compete with Molson, Labatt, and National Breweries (in Quebec), Canada's three biggest brewers of the time. In 1928, Brading bought the Kuntz Brewery in Waterloo. In 1930, Taylor's holding company, the Brewing Corporation of Ontario, went on a buying spree, picking up Carling Breweries and a number of other companies. And Taylor was just getting started.

He held on to the breweries that were doing well and kept the brands that were successful. Everything else he simply shut down, to eliminate competition. The Great Depression made capital scarce, but it also made the small breweries even weaker and easier to acquire.

By the early 1930s, Taylor had set about changing Ontario's laws governing drinking outside the home. To this point, Ontario's drinkers were restricted to shopping in beer stores and government-run liquor stores, and liquor was easier to carry home than beer. The beer industry needed public drinking, so Taylor discovered a defunct organization called the Moderation League and brought it back to life, encouraging the consumption of beer, as opposed to hard liquor, as a beverage of moderation. On July 1, 1934, Ontario's beverage rooms opened. Drinkers cheered, and so did Ontario's breweries.

By the late 1930s, Taylor had started buying horses as well, but he never lost the taste for buying breweries. By 1945, after buying up and closing down the competition, Taylor was able to crow, "We have reduced the number of brands from several hundred to only nine today." A proud boast indeed.

Taylor was also on the cutting edge of taste in Canada. Eastern Canadians after the Second World War were still drinking ale, and usually fairly robust ale at that. Molson's Montreal brewery made nothing but ale at that time. Taylor somehow detected a market for lighter beers, and when he burst onto the Quebec brewing scene in 1952, he took a chunk of Molson's market share in that province with more "modern" brews with less flavour. Molson responded, according to Shirley Woods's account of the Molson family, by lightening up the recipe for Molson Export and introducing a new low-flavour beer called Molson Golden. So even Molson Golden is E.P. Taylor's fault.

The next year, Molson retaliated by opening a brewery on Fleet Street in Toronto, barging into E.P. Taylor and Labatt territory. What made this move even more pleasant for the Molsons was that the land on which they built their new brewery had been half-owned by Taylor. The real estate transaction was done through an intermediary in top secret, and Taylor had no idea who was buying the land until it was too late.

By this time, Taylor was buying up breweries across the country, giving him access to expanded markets, and Molson and Labatt had no choice but to join in. National brewing, once only a dream, became a reality. Historian Craig Heron points out that, at the end of the Second World War, there remained thirty-one companies producing beer in Canada at sixty-one breweries. By the mid-1960s, there were ten companies and fifty-one breweries; Molson, Labatt, and Taylor's Canadian Breweries accounted for 90 percent of Canadian production. By 1976, six companies were brewing at forty-three breweries, three of those companies now controlling 97 percent of the business.

In 1968, however, Taylor sold out to the giant Rothman tobacco company and exited the Canadian beer trade, leaving behind an industry that was not only pasteurized but homogenized as well, an industry in which three companies offered a shrinking range of increasingly similar products. (In 1987, long after Taylor's departure, Rothman sold what was now called Carling O'Keefe to an Australian company, Elders IXL. Two years later, Elders took over Molson and merged it with Carling O'Keefe, reducing the number of major brewing powers in Canada to two. In 1998, Molson bought itself back from what was by now called Foster's. Crystal clear?)

E.P. Taylor was not content with wrecking—sorry, rationalizing— the Canadian beer trade. He had, as a young businessman, forged alliances in Great Britain, and had been able thus to get financing in the early thirties after a major Canadian bank had turned him down. And it was to Britain he returned when he decided that Carling Black Label should become a global brand.

There was a time in Britain when the beer drinker could walk into a pub and choose from light and dark ales, milds, porters, and stouts, but not a drop of Carling Black Label. Amazing but true. E.P. Taylor, quite rightly, saw this as a cruel fate visited upon the British drinking man and woman, and resolved to change it. As early as 1953, he formed a deal with a small English brewer called Hope and Anchor to introduce Black Label to the UK market. From this quiet start, he applied what he had learned in Canada to the British brewing industry, buying up companies and shutting them down (including his old friends at Hope and Anchor). By 1967, he had taken over larger breweries as well as small ones, and now owned Bass Charrington (via a deal billed as "the brewing merger of the century"), controlling

11,000 pubs and a fifth of the British beer market. In *The Penguin Guide to Real Draught Beer* (1979), author Michael Dunn cites calculations that Bass Charrington had absorbed some 273 companies, of which, at that time, eleven were still operating.

As in Canada, the remaining large breweries in Britain followed suit in order to keep up, and beer choice declined at an alarming rate as the brewing barons closed down regional operations and forced tasteless national brands on the drinking public, of which Carling Black Label was merely one of the worst.

Just in time, a small group of English drinkers formed, in 1971, what was to become the Campaign for Real Ale, in an effort to save traditional British ale from extinction. CAMRA's success can be measured by their annual *Good Beer Guide*. In 1982, the guide listed 169 independent UK breweries, including thirty brewpubs. The 2008 edition, by contrast, examined no fewer than 630. As the international giants have effectively abandoned quality beer, hundreds of smaller breweries have stepped in to fill the gap. Most of them are not getting rich—certainly not by E.P. Taylor's standards; few of them maintain thoroughbred stables—but they're combining hard work and passion to make good beer. Bless 'em.

Oland the Family

Brewing has long been a family enterprise. From the Young and Theakston families in England to the Busch and Coors families in the United States, breweries have been handed down through generations. There have been any number of major brewing families in Canada—the Molsons and Labatts spring to mind, as do the Sleemans, though they took a bit of a breather between 1933 (when they got busted for running beer into Detroit) and 1988 (when John Sleeman resurrected the company using his grandfather's recipe book)—but there are few more influential families than the Olands.

Is it because the Olands are generally to be found in New Brunswick and Nova Scotia that Canadians unfairly seem to ignore them? Still, we know about the Irvings and the McCains, while the Olands appear to operate in near secrecy. Maybe they don't fight among themselves enough to get our attention.

The Canadian Encyclopedia, usually an invaluable source of information, is mute on the subject of the Olands, save for a tiny reference to a family member who served as lieutenant-governor of Nova

Scotia. And, as far as I'm aware, there are no books about the Olands, which almost guarantees that there are no interesting scandals.

Maybe we don't pay attention to the Olands because the ur-Oland, the one who put the clan on the map, was—gasp!—a woman. Susannah Oland was noted in her Dartmouth, Nova Scotia, neighbourhood for her brown ale. She was simply doing what women had been doing for millennia: brewing beer for her family and anyone who dropped by. A friend of her husband's commented that Susannah's brown October ale might have some commercial potential, especially in neighbouring Halifax. Why should this Alexander Keith guy get all the business?

Funding was found, and Susannah turned professional in 1867, a fairly big year in this country's history. Things did not always go smoothly for the Olands and their family. Susannah's husband, John, was fatally thrown from his horse in 1870, and the Olands lost control of the business for several years. Twice, the brewery burned down. It was destroyed again in the Halifax explosion of 1917, and an Oland and several employees were killed. And, of course, the arrival of Prohibition, followed by the Depression, didn't help.

Susannah had long departed this vale of beers by now, and the family split into two factions, one of which moved to New Brunswick and bought the Red Ball brewery in Saint John, while the other remained in Nova Scotia and, in 1926, rebuilt and reopened the Oland and Son brewery. Two years later, they purchased the Alexander Keith brewery and ran their business under that name.

Years passed, and both sides of the Oland family prospered in their respective provinces. The New Brunswick branch expanded and swallowed up smaller companies, changing the company name, in 1947, to Moosehead Breweries Ltd., which should ring a bell. The Nova Scotia Olands succeeded as the premier brewery of Nova Scotia, but grew nervous as the national companies started looking to expand into the Atlantic provinces. After rejecting one bid, they finally relented and, in 1971, sold Keith's to Labatt for a handsome sum of money. Sid Oland stayed on with Labatt after the sale, eventually becoming president. The Oland name lives on within the Labatt empire as well: the Halifax brewery is still called the Oland Brewery, and Labatt operates a division called Oland Specialty Beer Company But anyone called Oland or Labatt still toiling in those vineyards now reports to a Brazilian bloke, who reports to a cadre of Belgian blokes.

In New Brunswick, meanwhile, the fifth and sixth generations of Olands are still at the helm of Moosehead. Sadly, Susannah Oland's brown October ale from 1867 is nowhere to be seen, but her great-great-grandson and her great-great-great-grandson now run Canada's biggest Canadian-owned brewery and its oldest independent beer producer.

Back in 2005, chairman and CEO Derek Oland told *Canadian Business* magazine that Moosehead was not just a family company, that anyone in the company was in the running for the top jobs. Two and a half years later, he named his son Andrew to the job of president. Perhaps the sixth generation of Olands will bring back Susannah's brown October ale. Or perhaps they're just selling too much Cold Filtered Light to care.

You Can't Do That:
Beer and the Law

In most of Canada, the rule of thumb has always been that, if you suspect something alcohol-related is illegal, you're absolutely right. It's not quite as true as it used to be, but it's still a fairly reliable indicator. Which shows how smart the lawmakers of this country have been: anyone of a certain age instinctively reacts to any questionable activity by assuming it's the wrong thing to do. We know without being told that drinking while [fill in the blank] is not just illegal but morally bankrupt and worthy of exclusion from civilized society.

(This sense of depravity does not, of course, apply to the province of Quebec, where the experience of pleasure is not necessarily seen as evidence of moral baseness. It is a distinct society. You can dispute that all you like, but taste a Unibroue Fin du Monde or a Dieu du Ciel Péché Mortel and tell me you're not feeling a bit distinct. Though, after about three of them, you'll be feeling quite indistinct.)

If we're being completely honest about it—and I know it goes against the grain—many of us who began our drinking lives back in the days when drinking in anglophone Canada was an official sin have to acknowledge that there was some appeal in the old days to the feeling that one was breaking all the rules of decent society by entering a beverage room. It was almost like being in an opium den or sipping absinthe in a Paris garrett. It was as close to decadent as you could get in Canada in the 1960s.

Sin has its charms. Sitting in a smoky room, shuttered off from the respectable outside world, with a couple of small glasses of not very good beer made a fellow feel like Marlon Brando. What are you rebelling against? Whaddya got?

Nowadays, it's not quite the same. Sitting next to a large, plate-glass window, within view of decent, hard-working people with mortgages and RRSPs, in a no-smoking pub with ample vegan choices on the menu doesn't feel a lot like sin any more. It's practically a health spa. It's hard to rebel in a health spa; you really have to make an effort. I don't know what young people do. I suppose they get tattoos.

The banning of smoking in more and more jurisdictions across Canada has presumably revived the speakeasy, or blind pig. These illegal drinking operations were wildly popular during Prohibition, and many survived afterwards because most provinces and territories continued to ban taverns. Even when taverns returned to us, there was life in the speakeasy, because it offered longer hours and a more relaxed atmosphere than the post-Prohibition beverage room, where the sexes were often segregated and music was outlawed. The speakeasy never quite went away, though its days must have seemed numbered as the drinking age came down and licensing hours grew more liberal.

In 2006, according to the *Saskatoon StarPhoenix*, hotel owners in rural Saskatchewan became fed up with declining business in the wake of that province's smoking ban. Drinkers, they argued, were meeting illicitly in what they called "garage bars," drinking and smoking in back rooms of farm machinery dealerships and other such illegal and unregulated spots. It's comforting to know that sin still exists—and is being actively practised—in rural Saskatchewan. And you can be sure it's going on in other, possibly even more depraved, parts of Canada. Though many of us city-dwellers wouldn't know where to look for a farm machinery dealership.

Most Canadian drinking laws pertain to the age of drinkers, the hours in which public drinking may lawfully occur, and how large the book that gets thrown at drinking drivers ought to be. The laws of man are not carved in stone, so are open to change, but Canadians are at liberty to drink from the age of nineteen (eighteen in Alberta, Manitoba, and Quebec). Drinking hours are, predictably, all over the map, subject to local and provincial legislation. (Toronto frequently offers extensions to a few hand-picked establishments during major international events such as the Toronto International Film Festival; you can't have sophisticated people from other countries subject to laws we taxpayers are bound by.) And pretty much wherever you live these days, the book that is thrown at you if you're caught with any significant trace of alcohol in your bloodstream while operating a motor vehicle or a boat will be a very large hardcover book, capable of inflicting severe damage.

As noted elsewhere in this book, the laws invented by Canadian legislators as we emerged from Prohibition were often as bewildering as they were draconian. Anti-alcohol lawmakers—and there appears to be no other kind—in the English-speaking world have managed to assemble a dizzying array of regulations to discourage the rest of us from pursuing our interests. They've never been sure, for instance, if they want us to eat or not while we drink. Most Canadian jurisdictions barred anything but the most basic of snack foods from taverns after Prohibition, in the mistaken confidence that drinkers would become hungry and return home to a healthy dinner. At other times, food has been compulsory. For a time in the early 1970s, Ontario drinkers were required to purchase food if they drank on a Sunday. This led to the famous Ontario cheese sandwich that circulated throughout taprooms on the holy day, dutifully ordered and delivered, but never eaten.

Good Friday 2008 marked the first time that Nova Scotia bars were allowed to open on that auspicious day without selling food. Before that, drinkers were required to spend more on food than on alcohol on Good Friday, for reasons that must have made sense to someone once upon a time. (I assume the change of law had something to do with modern anti-obesity concerns.) At the time of writing, however, Prince Edward Island and Manitoba persist in keeping bars closed on Good Friday, to Christians and non-Christians alike.

At one time, Ontario pubs (as opposed to the more basic beverage rooms) were required to sell as much food as booze, a difficult proposition. Most pubs found ways to fudge the figures, by treating cigarette sales as food and suchlike, but one Toronto publican refused to play these dodgy games, even though she was, I believe, an accountant by trade who had just stumbled into the pub business without the faintest idea of what drinkers and drinking were about. She was regularly in trouble with the authorities despite her best efforts to boost her food sales, efforts that included raising the prices or reducing the size of the portions so that people would buy more. She left the hospitality industry years ago.

Before 1999, British Columbia restaurants were forbidden to serve alcohol without a meal. Not just a snack, note, but a meal. Two "average-sized" people sharing a plate of nachos did not qualify. (Would it have been all right for two rather small people? And how much would a really big person have to order?) A mess of chicken wings also didn't count, unless served with garlic bread and salad. Was the garlic bread intended to make drinking folk even more offensive and less attractive to respectable people? Can you imagine a bunch of grown-ups actually sitting down and hammering out these rules? "What did you do today, dear?" "Not much. Defined lunch." The same parcel of laws also limited the number of televisions in a licensed establishment and the size of their screens. I mean, really.

Election days in Canada were traditionally dry, apparently because, in days of yore, ambitious politicians were said to have plied their constituents with drink as an incentive to vote for them. (I believe that voting turnouts were bigger in those days, for what it's worth.) To this day, I can think of Canadian politicians I'd have to be very drunk indeed to vote for. Closing bars on election day always seemed a bit overbearing. What if you could prove that you had voted before you went for a beer? What if you could prove you were a foreigner and ineligible to vote? I used to know a wily purveyor of falafels and shawarmas in Toronto who helped to ease the pain of election day by filling a large soft drink cup with something that was clearly not soft. May his tribe increase.

(Similarly, there are said to be many Chinese restaurants that will respond sympathetically to a late-night request for "tea." This has probably led to some surprises for customers who really wanted tea.)

Many of the laws older Canadians grew up with are no longer on the books. Most Canadians nowadays can drink on Sunday, or standing up, or with strangers of the opposite sex, or on their front porch— all fairly harmless activities that were once forbidden. Though I'm given to understand that it's still illegal in Saskatchewan to drink while watching an exotic dancer. Whatever happened to human rights in this country? If you look the other way, can you take a sip?

Canadians didn't invent dopey drinking laws, and you can find lots of international instances online—though you will find some of them difficult to believe. Okay, I believe that Texas and Ohio ban Fat Bastard wine from their cellars; there are an awful lot of fat bastards in those states who might take it personally. In Ontario in 2006, the provincial liquor autocrats ordered in a Belgian beer named Delerium Tremens, which duly appeared on liquor store shelves until, mysteriously, it didn't. Had someone complained? We don't believe so. The story seems to be that someone with the power to do so decided that somebody—The Unknown Drinker—might take offence at the name. The LCBO continued to sell the beer, you understand, but you had to ask for it specially and hope someone would fetch a bottle from the back for you.

In the USA, it is illegal—blame the Bureau of Alcohol, Tobacco, Firearms and Explosives for this—to advertise any alcoholic beverage with the word "refreshing." It is, paradoxically, entirely legal to advertise Miller Lite with the words "great taste."

It appears to be illegal to tend bar naked in Illinois. We know this because, in September 2008, thirty-three-year-old Janet Brannon was arrested after Jersey County sheriff's deputies did a routine check on the Cabin Tavern in Delhi, Illinois, at 4:49 p.m. on a Thursday afternoon. Ms. Brannon was charged with misdemeanour public indecency, though there is no evidence that anyone complained.

In North Carolina, it's easier to buy a shotgun than a keg of beer, in that you require a permit for one and not necessarily the other. In Utah, civilians can't buy a keg of beer, period. It was not until March 2009 that Utah legalized home brewing. This leaves only Alabama, Kentucky, Mississippi, and Oklahoma as states in which making your own beer is a criminal offence. Saloons were barred in Kansas until 1987, and in the 1970s that state's attorney general made sure that alcohol was not being served on trains passing though Kansas or on planes flying over it. Which must have kept him busy.

These laws sound sadly plausible. But can it be true that Nebraska says bars can't serve drinks unless they are simultaneously making soup? Or that you can't run a tab in Iowa? Or that you can't serve beer and pretzels at the same time in North Dakota? Or that you can't serve alcohol to a fish in Ohio or a moose in Fairbanks, Alaska? When it comes to drinking laws, I never rule anything out, but even so . . . (And I don't believe for a moment the story that the *Encyclopedia Britannica* is outlawed in Texas because it contains a recipe for home-brewed beer. That's ridiculous. It's banned in Texas because it's a book, or even worse, a bunch of books.)

The long arm of the law knows no national boundaries. In 2008, an Australian driver was fined $750 for providing a seat belt for a thirty-can case of beer but leaving his five-year-old child unprotected. Further evidence that nobody's perfect.

A large amount of Canada's alcohol legislation is devoted to the sale and distribution of alcoholic beverages, and again, there are discrepancies across the land. As a rule, Canadian provinces and territories operate centralized alcohol agencies that control the sale of intoxicating beverages. The exception is Alberta, which privatized its alcohol sale and distribution in 1993 and 1994 under Premier Ralph Klein. Defenders of this move argue that prices are lower now, and choice greater, while detractors argue exactly the opposite.

Alberta was already a distinct society in that its hotels are permitted to sell beer to be consumed elsewhere, and have been since 1934. This is civilized. The new privatized liquor/beer/wine stores, however, must do their primary business from the sale of alcohol, so there is no beer or wine in corner stores. You can sell booze or you can sell food, but you can't sell booze *and* food. Quebec has its own government liquor stores (known as SAQs), but allows the sale of beer and wine through corner stores and supermarkets.

Ontario controls the sale of liquor, wine, and some beer through its government stores, though the majority of beer sales are conducted through stores that are owned and operated by the three major breweries: Molson (a.k.a. Coors of Colorado), Labatt (InBev of Belgium), and Sleeman (Sapporo of Japan). Although Ontario's beer stores are the domain of (very) private enterprise, some 60 percent of Ontarians persist in believing that they are government-run, possibly because the stores have all the charm of the passport office— which, come to think of it, might be a slur on the passport office.

More worrying to some patriotic Ontarians than the charmlessness of The Beer Stores, as these emporia are imaginatively named, is having the sale and distribution (and pricing) of our most popular alcoholic beverage in the hands of non-Canadians. In 1985, David

Peterson's Liberals came to power in Ontario, largely on the basis of not being the gang of Tories who had run the province since the dawn of time, but also on the promise that beer would be sold in corner stores. Once elected, however, Peterson lost interest in the cause. When a namby-pamby bit of legislation finally arrived in the Legislature, the premier was not even on hand to see it defeated. In 2007, it was the Tories who campaigned in part on beer in corner stores, but the other planks in its campaign platform put them under. It should be noted that there are, in rural and northern Ontario, special instances of privately owned liquor and/or beer agency stores located in general stores. There are also numerous private stores selling the wines of particular Ontario wineries, some attached to supermarkets.

New Brunswick decrees that all alcohol be sold through government stores and, like most other provinces, mandates a minimum price for beer. This lowest allowable price is set at a patriotic $18.67 for a twelve-pack, which means that New Brunswickers who live within reach of the borders of Quebec or Maine do much of their beer shopping out of province. Chagrined at the loss of an estimated $12 million every year, the provincial government in 2009 went into the brewing business. Like you, I was disappointed to learn that the premier and his cabinet were not actually cleaning out the mash tun and fermenting tanks themselves, but had farmed the entire business out to Moosehead, and were selling the beers (a lager and a light lager) at lower prices than their competitors and giving them prime location in their ANBL stores. Shaun Fraser of Moncton's very good Pump House brewery was less than impressed at having to compete with his own government.

The odd thing about this move was that these official New Brunswick beers were still selling for considerably more than cross-border beers, so it's difficult to see what impact they would have on consumers. Maybe they're really good. As one local drinker said on the day the new brands were launched, "It's better than Alpine.

Less of a skunky aftertaste." That wasn't "no skunky aftertaste," just "less." The official website of the new product boasted that the beer was made of malt (barley), hops, water, and yeast. Having tasted it, New Brunswick beer and wine writer Craig Pinhey contacted the ANBL to point out that he had detected a strong corn syrup flavour. Shortly thereafter, the information on the website was changed.

Wherever you are in Canada, you will find unrest in the drinking community about the sale and distribution of booze. Yes, things by and large have improved, but many of us own calendars, and we know that this is the twenty-first century. Much of the debate over liquor sales takes an ideological perspective. The free-market people see no reason for government to play any role in selling us our liquor and argue that private enterprise could do the job better and more cheaply. They particularly relish the notion of firing all those unionized employees and replacing them with minimum-wage retail drones. (I've been a retail drone myself, so there's no slur intended.)

Yes, say others, but governments will never let go of an operation that brings in untold billions of dollars every year. Ah, but surely those billions are earned from punitive taxes on alcohol, not so much from the actual retail operation. What with all those unionized employees, it's hard to say whether the actual stores make much money. It is argued that Alberta continues to take in as much as it ever did before it privatized its liquor operations. Plus, of course, it made rather a lot of cash from selling off its stores. One observes as well that Alberta privatized shortly after its unionized liquor employees went out on strike.

One advantage the provincial liquor boards have over an independent retailer is the ability to buy in volume. The Liquor Control Board of Ontario, for instance, is one of the biggest purchasers of alcohol on the planet which gives them a competitive edge. On the other hand, the LCBO is buying in such enormous quantity that it has little interest in picking up smaller purchases from smaller suppliers.

Its beer-purchasing decisions are often bewildering, though its pricing of those beers it does import is usually very good. Ontarians will find a far wider range of global beers across the American border, but at higher prices.

Whenever the subject of privatization of liquor sales is bruited, the provincial boards go into overdrive to inform us how valuable they are. I have observed service and supplies improving whenever prominent citizens step forward to agitate in favour of breaking up the government monopoly. It's worth bringing up the subject at regular intervals just to keep them on their toes. In Ontario, we are reminded that the C in LCBO stands for "control" rather than "cash cow," as they hasten to tell us how many underage drinkers are refused service every day in a Ontario liquor stores, challenges you can be sure would not be made in some money-grubbing private store staffed by retail drones. (The weakness of that argument is that a whole lot of underage drinkers are challenged every day in privately owned bars, at the insistence of owners who don't want to lose their licences.)

Alberta has privatized, and the sky appears not to have fallen. You could argue that Alberta has enjoyed an economic boom since privatization, but some would suggest that the boom has more to do with another valuable, highly taxed fluid.

Wouldn't a Dow Go Good Now? When Beer Kills

It seems just a handful of chapters ago that I was telling you how healthy and nutritious beer is, and I meant it. I really did. But this is a Canadian book, and we must present the negative side as well as the positive—not for long, you'll be happy to know.

Yes, beer can turn on you. Beer in excess can damage your liver. Mind you, lots of other things can damage your liver as well, some of them prescribed by your doctor. The statin drugs, designed to make you live longer by improving your cholesterol figures, can damage your liver. Simply being alive can damage your liver.

Beer can make you feel so good about yourself that you begin to feel immortal. Sometimes, this is all right, as long as you restrict yourself to making passes at inappropriate people, practising karaoke in public, or speaking freely to your boss at a company function. Behaviour of this sort can lead to humiliation and unemployment, but will seldom kill you.

What *can* kill you is drinking enough beer to make you think you're in great shape to drive. Or, because you now feel immortal, you believe you can fly, or swim, or ski, or just about anything but sit still and drink your beer. There's a saying in the American southwest: "Beer kills you, but it does it slow." But sometimes it does it more quickly.

Beer can kill in many ways. In 2006, according to the *St. Louis Post-Dispatch,* an unnamed woman shot her husband "four to five times"—which seems unprofessionally vague in a respectable newspaper—because he handed her a warm can of Stag beer. I'm not sure I've ever had a Stag beer, but it sounds like the sort of beer you want really, really cold. Even so, "four to five" shots to the chest seems high. One might suggest that drinking beer in the company of armed people with anger issues is unwise and bad for your health.

And as recently as 1902, a Brooklyn cigar maker died after drinking a poisoned beer in a saloon, the motive being robbery. The suspect, according to police, had "a bad reputation." Lesson: do not drink beer with disreputable people carrying cyanide. Five years later, *The New York Times* printed the sad story of a group of Kentucky men who were killed when a "big" copperhead snake got into a keg of beer. Four men drank the beer and quickly expired, and not much hope was held out for two others. I have to say that I don't entirely understand this story, or what exactly killed these men, but it certainly shows that you have to be careful when you drink beer. It's also another reason, in case you needed one, to fear snakes.

In 2008, an American man with a number of forty-ounce bottles of beer in his knapsack perished while attempting to climb a chain-link fence when the chest strap of the knapsack caught around his throat. And it's not just us humans who are at risk. In 1991, a beer spill sent thousands of gallons of Coors into a Colorado creek, killing an estimated three thousand fish. Fish are used to being surrounded by fluids: think what Coors could do to people. Mind you, if you have some Coors on hand but you don't like killing fish, they say that beer is useful for doing away with head lice.

Speaking of beer, animals, and danger, you should be advised to keep your beer away from elephants. Think of the person you know who loves beer the most. Now, imagine that person as an elephant (fun, isn't it?). Asian elephants love beer, and, since they are forbidden from drinking in bars like the rest of us, they have to resort to more desperate measures to get it. Assam state, in northern India, has the awkward combination of many wild elephants and a population that makes rice beer. In 2004, at least twenty-two Assamites were killed by rampaging elephants, many of which were either looking for beer or were getting rowdy because they'd found it.

In another story from northern India, six elephants were fatally electrocuted in 2007 when they uprooted an electricity pole while on a drunken spree. This story even earned the attention of Paris Hilton, who was reportedly mounting a campaign to encourage Indians to hide their beer better from extremely large, heavy drunks with tusks. Said the heiress, "It is becoming really dangerous. We need to stop making alcohol available to them." Hang on—it's talk like that that led to Prohibition. Nevertheless, I'm delighted to find a way to bring Ms. Hilton into this book. They said it couldn't be done.

(Elephants aren't the only animals that like beer. I've never known a cat who liked it, but someone recently told me about a border collie who developed a great taste for beer and was actually caught in the basement draining the dregs from bottles. And it's not exactly beer, but in 2008, we learned about the Malaysian pen-tailed tree shrew, a tiny critter that guzzles fermented nectar (up to 3.8 percent alcohol) from flower buds of the bertram palm without even getting woozy. The clever bertram palm has evolved this means of pollination, which presumably takes place when the tree shrew pees. And it's not just the pen-tailed tree shrew, either. They have footage of something called a slow loris bellying up to the bertram palm as well. The bertram palm—feel free to call it Bertic—seems to be a kind of tavern for small Malaysian animals. Nature is a wonderful thing.)

The most famous case of Canadians being killed by beer—and I'm back to humans here—happened in Quebec in the 1960s. The Dow Brewery traced its beginnings to 1790, when a Scots brewer set up a business near Montreal. In 1952, the original Mr. Dow being long gone, it became a major part of E.P. Taylor's Canadian Breweries and expanded into Ontario and the Prairies, but its heart was always in Quebec.

Dow liked Quebec, and Quebec liked Dow. Anglophone Quebecers responded positively to the advertising question, "Wouldn't a Dow Go Good Now?" For francophones, it was merely "Dites Donc Dow!" which actually sounds more Chinese. Dow Ale was Quebec's most popular beer until the spring of 1966, when Dow started losing its customers in the worst possible way. Beer drinkers in the Quebec City area started turning blue, which is never a good sign, and complained of nausea, stomach aches, shortness of breath, and weight loss. (When beer drinkers lose weight, breweries start to worry.)

Eventually, sixteen of these beer victims died, having suffered damage to the heart muscle and the liver. It emerged that what these men had in common was a taste for beer, of which they had consumed something like eight quarts a day. It gradually came out that the beer to which they had been so fiercely loyal was Dow Ale, brewed in Quebec City and Montreal. The popular theory today is that the difference between those two breweries is that the former had started adding cobalt sulphate to the beer to enhance and maintain its head. What's good for the head is not necessarily good for the liver. Lesson for home brewers: downplay the cobalt sulphate. Perhaps leave it out altogether.

Killing sixteen customers counts as a negative among beer marketing experts. Insult them by running inane commercials that make users of your product look like idiots, fine, but stop short of killing them. Even turning them blue looks bad. After all, the beer didn't kill all the sufferers; a number of people turned blue but survived. But they were probably in no hurry to have another Dow Ale.

This was, to say the least, a ticklish situation for Dow. There was no actual proof right away that there was something in Dow's beer that turned people blue and killed them, but there was suddenly a public perception that suggested it. Dow responded by shutting down temporarily and pouring nearly a million gallons of beer into the St. Lawrence River (more bad news for the fish). They also took out ads in the papers to explain what they had done and why, making the point: "One thing is certain—the beer was perfectly good." They wanted us to go on loving them, and they argued that they were taking the heat on this story only because they were the most popular brewer in the province, which is why they were showing leadership by killing fish—no, I mean by dumping their beer and scrubbing out their tanks and kettles. (It can't have helped that Dow shared a name with the corporation that provided napalm and Agent Orange for the US military during a war that drove a lot of people to drink.)

Not surprisingly, Dow's defensive approach didn't cut a lot of ice with the beer-buying public, and the company never properly recovered from the disaster. As a result of this culling of the drinking herd, brewers stopped using cobalt in beer, ale drinkers stopped dying en masse, and Dow eventually went away. Even if a Dow would go good now, you're out of luck.

Hey Mabel! Marketing Beer

What if there were no beer advertising? Imagine a world with no television commercials, no young women in tank tops inspiring you to leave the comfort of your home to get to the pub to buy a pint of beer, which in turn will inspire young women in tank tops to think you're exactly what they've been pining for all these years—not that there have been *that* many years, of course (although, it goes without saying, everyone involved must be of legal drinking age).

What brand of beer would you drink if there were no commercials? Would you even drink beer at all, without all the cultural signposts we associate with beer marketing? And would you drink beer if hockey didn't exist? Well, of course you'd drink beer, because it's terrific and makes your life better. And think how much more you'd have done with your life if you hadn't wasted all that time thinking about young women in tank tops, only because they were there every time you watched a hockey game. It's possible there would be no such thing as young women in tank tops but for beer advertising. Do they even exist in real life?

Imagine a world in which beer brands rose or fell on their own merits (or absence of same). A world in which beer drinkers actually discussed the taste of beer and made their choices accordingly. (Actually, it sounds like an evening with beer geeks, which comes with its own set of charms and dangers.)

But that is not the world we live in, which is a blessing for ad executives—and young women in tank tops. Millions of dollars are spent every year to encourage you—and, yes, I mean *you,* as long as you're male and under twenty-five—to drink particular brands of beer.

I once heard a radio comedy sketch (and I would tell you whose sketch it was, but I can't recall—I've asked Roger Abbott and Dave Broadfoot about it, and they both said that it sounded like an Air Farce sketch, but they didn't remember it) about a man going into a beer store and asking for beer. The fellow behind the counter asked what brand he wanted, and the man said he didn't know. Well, asked the fellow behind the counter, do you go up in hot air balloons? No, said the man. Okay, do you enjoy backyard barbecues with young women in bikinis? Never tried it, said the man. And on it went. Do you play hockey with the boys? Do you listen to rock bands? Whitewater rafting? All negative. Finally, the fellow behind the counter said, "I'm sorry, sir. We have nothing here for you."

Beer commercials are all lifestyle ads. You are the sort of guy—and you *are* a guy, let's face it—who plays in spontaneous road hockey games, or would if such things happened in real life. And here's the beer that's brewed specially for your sort of guy and your sort of lifestyle. And if you don't have a lifestyle, you can borrow ours. And if this lifestyle doesn't appeal, we might have another one next season, when we hire a different ad agency because this campaign didn't work. In the meantime, have one of our beers.

Who drinks the most beer? Young males. And who's the least committed to brand loyalty? Same guys. That, at least, is helpful to beer marketers. They don't have to pitch to two different groups of people.

They can concentrate on young, heterosexual, mostly white guys of legal drinking age; no one will admit to trying to appeal to youngsters.

In the mid-1970s, Molson ran an ad for its Stock Ale, in which older guys sat about carving things and enjoying "the original Blue." This may be the last occasion on which men over twenty-five were addressed in a beer commercial. (Ironically, I was not much over twenty-five at the time, but was already drinking Molson Stock—old before my time.) Women are still waiting to be addressed. Except, possibly, lesbians. A few years ago, Molson made an ad that featured two women kissing. It was originally rejected by the authorities for linking beer and sexual attraction, but was later given the thumbs up because it celebrated diversity. That said, I'm not sure the commercial ever aired. I never saw it.

And what about taste? Beer marketers speak of the two components of their product: the "liquid" and the "package." People who describe beer as "liquid" are probably not going to waste a lot of time talking about flavour, which is, let's face it, not the distinguishing feature of the big beer brands you see advertised on television. When marketers do talk about flavour, it's usually absurd. We've already noted the comic "tastes great" claim of Miller Lite. More recently, we've heard about beer having that "great cold taste" or "great smooth taste." If you say it often enough, people might actually begin to think that "cold" is a taste, or that "smooth" is a taste. "How's your beer taste?" "Pretty cold."

For that matter, the markerters of Bud Light and (shudder) Bud Light Lime boast of their beers' superior "drinkability," apparently pitching their products at those beer drinkers who have trouble swallowing more rugged beer, at any temperature.

There are movie buffs who advise you never to go to a movie advertised on television. It's not a bad rule for beer lovers, either, unless lifestyle is a bigger factor in your purchasing decision than flavour.

As noted in an earlier chapter, what the big breweries choose to advertise tells you plenty about their priorities. InBev clearly prefers to put its money on Stella and Bud rather than on former Canadian giant Labatt Blue. When InBev chooses to promote a Canadian brand in Canada, it's generally Keith's, with the result that Blue sales have tanked precipitously.

Molson Canadian, Blue's traditional rival, hit the jackpot with the "I Am Canadian!" campaign of 2000, which cleverly spotlighted the brand name while subtly attacking Labatt for being foreign-owned. When Molson then merged with Coors of Colorado, the "I am Canadian" boast lost its steam, and subsequent commercials concentrated on a smart-ass American (actually played by a Canadian) insisting that Canadians were crazy to think there was anything distinctive about Molson Canadian, then being punished in imaginative ways by maple-leaf-festooned beer lovers. Or, at least, Molson Canadian lovers.

Many years ago, in New York City, I heard Abbie Hoffman and Paul Krassner on the radio, talking about advertising. What they had realized is that the key to understanding advertising is to know that whatever the advertiser is pushing is generally, in fact, the weakest component of his product. So, if a commercial insists that a product is long-lasting, it may turn out to be fun for the whole family or new and improved, but what it will probably *not* be is long-lasting. So, when you buy it and it breaks after a week, you'll congratulate yourself for buying the long-lasting one and not the one that would have broken before you even got it home. This rule has stuck with me all this time, so when I hear that Molson Canadian is distinctive, I chuckle a bit. (Another instance that proves Hoffman and Krassner's point might be the 2008 election ads that assured us that Stephen Harper was a warm, cuddly human being who loves playing the piano with his kid.)

Given that there is so little difference among the big, most advertised brands of beer, advertisers are forced to invent new and exciting ways of promoting their brands. As often as not, they come back to the infallible young women in tank tops. But, every now and then, we get something new. In recent years, that new something has most often been temperature. The drive for cold may have originated with the development of ice beers: obviously, you're not going to serve ice beer at room temperature.

You might think that serving beer cold is a simple matter of putting it in the fridge and leaving it there for some length of time before consuming same. If you're technologically advanced enough to figure out the workings of your fridge, you could actually lower the temperature of the appliance and thus make your beer colder. But technology comes to the rescue, because beer drinkers are obviously too stupid to keep their beer cold.

A few years ago, the technical whiz kids came up with a new draught beer tower that could serve beer at a temperature below freezing. Ice actually formed on the outside of the tower. Man, that's cold. In 2005, Labatt announced a new can called the Labatt Blue Cold One that kept beer colder longer, even if the drinker's hot, sweaty hand was clutching it tight. If you drank it quickly enough, you'd never have to taste it at all. There's no better way of masking the flavour of your beer than numbing the drinker's taste buds.

Given all the money breweries have spent on coldness, it follows that their advertising must reflect these new advances, so we see commercials for beer in cans or bottles that change colour when the package is cold enough. And that, my friends, is how stupid beer drinkers are—or, at least, how stupid the ad agencies think we are. If you can't reach into your fridge and tell whether your beer is cold enough to drink, you may be too stupid to drink it.

It is easy to criticize the people who make beer commercials. Who among us hasn't done it? But it is the case that the regulations governing beer commercials in Canada are such that you'd almost be crazy to want to produce one. Well, except that there are massive amounts of money to be made from it, and they're more fun to make than insurance ads.

The regulations, as always, vary slightly from province to province, so for a national campaign, many rules have to be taken into account. There are a few basic rules. You may not pander to underage drinkers, though practically every brewery that has ever paid for a beer commercial has pushed that envelope a bit. There are, believe it or not, limits on how much you can use sex to sell beer. Any suggestion that choosing a certain brand of beer will help you get lucky is forbidden. Yes, I know, I've seen those ads too. "I'm so mad at my boyfriend."

You may not show anyone actually drinking. If characters in a commercial are holding a glass, that glass must be full. And remain full. If characters are shown performing athletic activities, it must be clear that the consumption of beer happens only after such activities have ceased and the puck has been put away for the night.

Characters may not be shown doing obviously dangerous things. In 1998, Labatt aired a commercial showing a group of young men hurtling along busy streets while racing shopping carts. In its mid-year report of complaints from members of the public, Advertising Standards Canada (no jokes please: we do *too* have advertising standards in this country) noted that no fewer than twenty-one Canadians—not all of whom were necessarily employees or board members of Molson—had complained about this commercial. ASC upheld these complaints on the basis of Clause 10: "Advertisements must not display a disregard for public safety or depict situations which might encourage unsafe or dangerous practices, particularly when portraying products in normal use."

Were Labatt executives upset by this ruling? Not a bit. They had expected it, and were happy to have managed to get almost eight weeks of exposure for a successful commercial before it got shut down. It wasn't Labatt's only ad in the first six months of 1998 to be rejected by ASC. It had run another commercial in which a male taxi driver watched with pleasure as an attractive female passenger in the back seat lasciviously changed her clothes before arriving at a club. At the end of the ride, the driver waved off the fare. This ad was deemed "sexually exploitative" and in violation of Clauses 3(i) and 3(iv) of the ASC Guidelines. Only eight people complained about that one.

At one time, it was forbidden to use celebrities in Canadian beer commercials. This policy may have been abandoned as a result of a series of O'Keefe commercials in the 1970s that starred a popular (and heavy-drinking) journalist named Paul Rimstead. The other breweries cried foul: Rimstead was a celebrity. No he's not, replied Carling O'Keefe, he's a journalist. You can't be both. It's possible that this undignified squabble about who qualifies as a celebrity led to the rule being scrapped.

Canadian beer marketing is inseparable from hockey. Even though we drink most of our beer during the off-season, when are we glued to our television screens? And when do the summer beer campaigns begin? During the playoffs. Without hockey, beer marketers would have almost nothing but decks and docks and women in tank tops. Beer companies have paid large sums of money to be associated with *Hockey Night in Canada,* which is an effective way of mainlining into the arteries of young male Canadians.

Think of the hockey-related commercials: the impromptu hockey game in Toronto's financial district; the Canadian who gets angry with the stupid American who makes fun of Canada, so he hauls the guy's jacket over his head in order to pummel him (though, of course, we don't see any actual pummelling; that would be Clause 10 again, with its concerns about safety); the guy who keeps his Labatt 50–drinking pals waiting because he's working on his shot; the guys who can't get into the bar because the hockey team's in there, but who then find the Stanley Cup in the back of the taxi; any number of commercials that show a bunch of hoser couch potatoes staring at a television screen during a game; the guy who ignores a "booty call" because he's watching the playoffs. The list is endless; think of your own favourites.

Most beer marketing is aggressive and in-your-face: drink our beer and you'll have great sex, damn it! Here comes our slogan again! But one of the most successful campaigns in recent years has been an American campaign to promote Pabst Blue Ribbon. Blue Ribbon—or PBR as its adherents prefer to call it—is a retro beer that was a big seller decades ago. In the 1970s, there was a country song called "Red Necks, White Socks, and Blue Ribbon Beer," which celebrated the redneck lifestyle.

Like many other once-successful brands, PBR fell into decline as newer generations rejected Dad's beer. And it wasn't very good anyway. Eventually, Pabst, one of America's oldest beer companies, closed all its breweries and had its beer made under contract by Miller. Then, in 2002, it was discovered by young drinkers, notably by hipsters. Presumably, they were being ironic. Part of the charm of PBR for them was that it was off the cultural radar—there hadn't been a Pabst Blue Ribbon television commercial for years. Sales soared.

What was Pabst to do? If they started promoting PBR as a hip beer, they would wind up killing it off. Instead, they carefully—and stealthily—used their resources to support indie music festivals and whatever else hipsters like. Result so far: success. I see a similar phenomenon in Canada. What is the Canadian beer most like Pabst Blue Ribbon? Labatt 50. It's your granddad's beer, with its ugly old label. But if you're sitting in a bar and someone you think might be a hipster comes in, pay attention. Chances are he's about to order a 50. Not because it's terrific beer or because he's seen a commercial for it. That's the point: he's probably never seen a commercial for 50, unless he's an aging hipster who remembers the "Me and the Boys and Our 50" campaign of the early eighties. I bet Labatt 50 sales have jumped in the last handful of years, and only a hipster could tell you why. Has Labatt unleashed a stealth campaign for Labatt 50 to mirror the sneaky Pabst campaign? I don't know, but I wouldn't be surprised.

Users of YouTube are familiar with the many ways one can fritter away the hours. One of those ways is to search for beer commercials.

Many of them are there, even some of the older ones. Drinkers of a certain age will groan with a perverse pleasure at remembering the beer slogans of yesterday:

It's a Canadian game.
That's why hands across the country reach for a Blue.
Blue smiles along with you.
50: you can't say beer any better.
Cuttin' out, I'm movin' outta here.
Okay, okay, I'm workin' on my shot.
Comin' home to your world, comin' home to 50.
A whole lot can happen out of the Blue.
It's time to call for a Blue.
My name is Joe, and I am Canadian.

Our beer commercials are as much of our social fabric as Bobby Gimby's annoying song for our centennial year or Stompin' Tom Connors's "Hockey Song" or Gord Lightfoot's "Canadian Railroad Trilogy" or Murray MacLachlan's "Farmer's Song" or anything by Anne Murray or Rita McNeil. It doesn't mean I necessarily want to drink the beer, but I defend to the death their right to advertise it.

Barkeep! Gimme Another Light Dry Low-Carb Ice Beer with No Aftertaste!

For many millennia, humans drank local beer, made from local ingredients. Agricultural and technological restrictions limited the number of choices brewers had at their fingertips. Beer is made from fermented grain, so brewers used whatever they could get: usually barley, wheat, oats, or rye, often in combination. These choices would determine the flavour of the beer, as would other flavouring agents—bog myrtle, juniper berries, ginger, and assorted other fruits, herbs, and spices.

The big breakthrough, as noted already, was the arrival of hops in the brewing world around a thousand years ago, an event that changed the taste of beer forever. Early in the eighteenth century, possibly by accident, someone overheated a batch of malted barley and inadvertently invented porter, a dark, smoky beverage that quickly became the beer of choice for the thousands of porters who hauled things around London. Eventually, porter was overtaken by its close relative, stout, though it has made a comeback in recent years.

Germans made dark lager (dunkel) for years, but it was only in the early nineteenth century that modern lager beer came into being. This was a huge breakthrough in both the appearance and flavour of beer. You could point to such developments as pasteurization and the invention of screw-top bottles or pull-top beer cans as further examples of innovation in the beer world.

But surely there was never a more innovative brewing period than the late twentieth century. Charmed were we who lived in such an age. [*Editor's note:* Here he goes again. If you think you're detecting the author's sarcastic streak, you probably are.]

It took an American, roughly ten thousand years after the arrival of beer on planet Earth, to invent light beer. It took another American to call it "lite" beer. It is said that one Joseph L. Owades, a biochemist, developed something called Gablinger's Diet Beer in 1967. The recipe fell into the hands of the Meister Brau company in Chicago, which brought to market a beer called Meister Brau Lite. Not long thereafter, Miller took over Meister Brau, rejigged its "lite" beer, and created Miller Lite in 1975, which succeeded where Gablinger's and Meister Brau had not.

Miller decided to use the word "lite" because there were other beers on the market that already called themselves light. Schlitz had run a campaign with the slogan "Real gusto in a great light beer." Schlitz wasn't saying its beer was lower in alcohol or calories than other beers, just that "light" suggested a nice colour and possibly a refreshing nature. (Remember that Americans are not permitted to use the word "refreshing" to promote an alcoholic beverage.)

Europeans had made lightish beers for diabetics and the calorie-conscious, but hadn't thought of spending millions of units of the local currency to promote beers of interest to a small minority. It took an American to do that.

Oddly enough, according to beer writer Fred Eckhardt, light beer was made possible because of malt liquor, an American designation for a beer with greater-than-normal strength. Malt liquor had been around since the thirties, but it really came into its own in the sixties. The trouble with strong beer, traditionally, is that it comes with a strong flavour, so it's not to most tastes. The pioneers of malt liquor developed a process whereby beer could be made stronger while the flavour was reduced. (It has something to do with enzymes that reduce unfermentable dextrins, which might sound good, but it's the dextrins that give beer its flavour. I don't understand it either, but I bet Fred Eckhardt does. And humourist Dave Barry would almost certainly suggest that the Unfermentable Dextrins would be a terrific name for a rock band.)

Now you had a product that could be chugged back without difficulty and give the drinker a bigger, faster buzz. Colt 45 was the first brand to make a national impression, beginning in 1963. Brewing light beer essentially involved making malt liquor and watering it down, producing something wet and beer-like that has even less flavour, lower alcohol, and fewer calories.

Now for something interesting (as opposed to all the boring stuff you've just been forced to read). What's the difference between the United States and Canada? I'll give you a hint: it's beer-related (so it's not about guns or health care or invading countries on the off chance they have weapons of mass destruction).

Actually, I can think of a couple of things. One is that we insist that the alcoholic strength of beer appear on the label, while Americans (or at least the Bureau of Alcohol, Tobacco, Firearms and Explosives) insist, for the most part, that brewers do not even hint at the strength of their beer. This kept the makers of malt liquors from advertising the ultra-strength of their product, though Colt 45's label, with its illustration of a kicking horse, might have got the message across. (Kick: geddit?) The same policy also kept makers of light beer from advertising what was distinctive about it. Hence the Miller Lite campaign, in which famous former athletes bickered over whether it "tastes great" or is "less filling."

The other interesting difference is that what Americans mean by light (or lite) beer is not what we mean. A Canadian light beer is one that ranges between 2.6 and 4 percent alcohol by volume. An American light beer is one that contains fewer than one hundred calories in a standard bottle. (See, I told you it was interesting. We're concerned about strength, they worry about calories. It's a bit like movie ratings: we warn people about violence; they get all excited by sex and nudity, not to mention smoking. As I write, *The New York Times* is running a full-page ad for a movie whose warning reads, "Mature thematic material involving sexuality and smoking." American movie warnings also often include something they call "teen partying." I'm always grateful to be warned about teen partying.

Aided by what *Advertising Age* apparently deemed the eighth-best advertising campaign of all time, Miller Lite swept the USA. Americans couldn't get enough of less. By 1992, light beer was the most popular beer style in America, as drinkers decided that Budweiser, Coors, and Miller High Life just had too much flavour. Miller owned the market for a while, but eventually lost it to Bud Light and Coors Light. All these years later, we can see how effective light beer has been in reducing the weight of Americans.

Needless to say, Canadians couldn't wait to drink bland, lower-alcohol beer, and Labatt obliged in 1977 with Labatt Special Lite. Today, Coors Light is the second most popular beer in this country, to which a beer lover can only respond, "Huh?"

Brewing professionals outside North America were not as quick to jump on the lite beer bandwagon. The Belgian monks did not rush out a Westmalle Lite; they are, after all, doing the Lord's work. British brewers were already making beers that were low in alcohol— full-flavoured milds and bitters that weighed in at 3.8 percent and lower, so they didn't need to go out of their way to introduce anything called Lite. In fact, when the geniuses at Anheuser-Busch introduced Bud Light to the British market, it provoked nothing but head-scratching. It soon vanished.

But here's another reason to be a proud Canadian. In 2008, InBev invented a product called Stella Artois Légère, that same smooth-tasting premium lager they advertise as dating back to 1366 (actually developed in 1927), but with less of what you like in beer. And who got to taste it first? We did. Yes, friends, because we are so discerning and entirely lacking in gullibility, InBev tested Stella Légère on the Canadian market. We may be only the twentieth-best beer drinking nation, but we had Stella Lite—sorry, I mean Légère—before the Czechs, the Germans, the Irish, even the hoity-toity Belgian drinkers. Fair enough, the hoity-toity Belgians are used to big, substantial, knock-you-on-your-bum beers, so a Stella Légère might seem a bit effete and watery to them. Still, we had it first.

Labatt, usually the innovator in the Canadian market, was not the first to bring us dry beer, a style originally concocted by the Japanese brewery Asahi in 1987, closely followed by Kirin. Molson had the edge in this case, as it was already brewing dry beer for Kirin under contract in Vancouver, mostly for the American market. This way, Kirin could advertise that the beer was imported, which was true only in the sense that it was imported from Canada. This wheeze is not uncommon. If you buy, say, a Löwenbräu in the United States, it will be "imported" all the way from a Labatt brewery in Canada. Hey, did we say it came from Germany? No, we only said it was imported. Shut up and drink your beer.

Dry beer sounds like an anomaly. I know what a dry martini or a dry wine are, but beer is traditionally wet. Now, I don't know if you've ever taken part in a focus group, but if so, you'll understand why certain products come to the market. Someone comes up with a cockamamie idea, which then gets run past a focus group, a random gathering of demographically appropriate people. In my experience of these things, you don't know when you arrive what sort of product you'll be discussing, and it usually takes some time to figure out what the marketers are getting at.

The trouble with Canadian focus groups—and I can't speak for elsewhere—is that we're too damn polite. Someone has promised us fifty dollars to turn up and give our opinions; the least we can do is speak highly of their product. Well, wouldn't *you?* I was once in a focus group that was being pitched low-alcohol wine, an appalling and unnecessary idea. You should have heard these people. Would you buy this product? You betcha! Would you take it to a barbecue? Can't wait!

The more you hear about dry beer, the more you know there were focus groups involved. Brewers insisted that consumers had told them that what they didn't like about beer was its aftertaste. If you said the same thing about wine, you'd be scoffed at and labelled an ignoramus, but you can say anything about beer and be taken seriously.

So, brewers rose to this new challenge. Drinkers—particularly young women, I'm afraid—said they didn't want aftertaste, and the customer's always right. Dry beer was not unrelated to light beer and malt liquor, in that the best way to ensure the absence of aftertaste is to reduce the actual taste. Longer fermentation succeeded in reducing those dextrins we spoke of earlier. Voila—less taste, and practically no aftertaste.

Operating secretly, Molson inflicted Molson Special Dry upon Canadians in 1989. Not surprisingly, it was a big success, bigger than Molson had expected. Labatt executives gnashed their teeth, and, hoping not to be left behind, hurriedly brought out Labatt Dry. The Labatt product was the usual 5 percent alcohol that is considered normal in Canada, but Molson's product carried an extra half point— and Molson was first, which counts in gimmick wars. Consumers merely groaned when, a little later, Labatt brought out Labatt Dry Light, followed by Blue Dry and Wildcat Dry.

In the meantime, the American market was moving on. Miller found success with Miller Genuine Draft, a non-pasteurized beer served, oxymoronically, in bottles. (An increasing number of British breweries are making bottled beers that undergo a secondary fermentation in the bottle, making them very much like draught beers, though I'm not aware that any of these breweries market them as such. An English brewer of my acquaintance mocked the concept of bottled draught beer, observing that draught beer, by definition, is "drawn" from a larger container—i.e., a cask or keg. I guess he's never heard of marketing gimmicks.)

Obviously, Miller Genuine Draft (MGD to its friends) was bound to enter the Canadian market via its licensing partner, Molson, so Labatt had to try to get in there first. Which it did in 1992 with—wait for it—Labatt Genuine Draft. Now it was Molson's turn to gnash, and the grinding sound could be heard across the land. Not only had Labatt beaten Molson to market, it had stolen (in Molson's view) the name and much of the packaging, which is where the lawyers came in.

Legal battles notwithstanding, Labatt got there first and sold more beer, if "beer" isn't too grand a word for it. The numbers couldn't last, of course; the public would soon need a new gimmick. For a full account of what happened next, read Paul Brent's *Lager Heads,* but here's a summary.

Labatt was looking for something new, something no one else was doing. It came up with ice beer. Not that people hadn't linked beer and ice before. The Germans have made something called Eisbock for some time, using a process that freezes the beer, then removes the ice (because the water freezes before the alcohol), thus making the beer stronger. This is not what Labatt was up to. Well, we think it wasn't, but the technology was so top-secret and beyond what any brewer in human history had even imagined that we may never know.

Labatt claimed to have spent ten years, and much money, to set up its breweries to produce this new beer, and they patented the process, hoping that other breweries would have to come to them (and pay a licensing fee) to be able to make their own. The process sounds like essentially what German brewers and the Niagara Falls Brewing Company had been doing to make Eisbock, but it was presumably more technologically advanced.

The Labatt operation was conducted in great, almost military, secrecy. Only vital personnel had any idea of the project. The advertising agency higher-ups had to sign a six-page confidentiality agreement before they even heard what the product was. Every possible precaution was taken. Well, almost. It is possible that Labatt had produced some mock-up beer cans for this new product and then simply chucked them out afterwards, rather than destroying them. Whatever the case, Molson found out. And by now you can guess what the inevitable plan was: Molson Canadian Ice Draft. Honestly, you couldn't make it up.

Labatt went into overdrive to beat Molson to launch, preparing a series of commercials that featured actor Alexander Godunov, looking like someone who knew something about ice and beer. Godunov was a last-minute replacement for Labatt's first choice, Rutger Hauer, who wanted to rewrite the scripts. Molson had a name for a beer, but no actual ice beer to sell, so Labatt got there first. And we know how important *that* is. Once Molson finally did get something called ice beer on the market, the lawyers were called on once again. In the world of Big Beer, lawyers are at least as important as brewmasters, and are probably much better paid.

Labatt had the better Canadian sales, as well as the satisfaction of starting a trend. Within a year of Labatt's launch, there were thirty-eight ice beers in the US, and Labatt had received not a penny in licensing fees for its patent. The ice beer battle went on. In 1993, Labatt came up with something called Maximum Ice, which clocked in at a whopping 7.1 percent alcohol. Molson cried foul, took the high moral ground and agitated for government restraints, then launched its own Molson XXX at an alarming 7.3 percent. Ah-oo-gah!

All these new and exciting beers of the era had more gimmick about them than flavour, but the big brewers weren't finished yet. Responding to the popularity of the Atkins diet in the early twenty-first century, Anheuser-Busch introduced a beer called Michelob Ultra in 2002, a low-carb beer for weight watchers. For once, it was the Sleeman brewery that made the first Canadian leap into this new trend, followed by Labatt, Molson, and Alberta's Big Rock. As with any new gimmick, the beers took off briefly then settled down as drinkers slowly realized that they didn't like them much.

If you're seeking beer-related amusement, I recommend a website called RateBeer.com, where beer enthusiasts from many lands post their ratings of beers they've tasted. These people tend to fall into the "beer geek" category of human beings, which simply tells you that they feel strongly about their beer. The beauty of computers is that they make it easy to generate lists. So, if you want to find the best beers from Azerbaijan, or the best *bières de garde,* or the best Latvian IPAs, it's all there (always keeping in mind that these scores are based on people's opinions). You can also find a list of the fifty worst beers in the world. The last time I checked, this list contained ten ice beers, ten light beers (plus one "light ice" beer), seven malt liquors, seven low- or no-alcohol beers, and five low-carb brews. Interestingly, there were no dry beers on the list, perhaps because they've all but disappeared from public awareness.

Listen, if you get called up for a focus group and it turns out to be the next new gimmick for beer, give them one new and surprising word: "flavour." I'd do it myself, but they stopped inviting me years ago.

Geeks and Angels, Spitters and Burpers: Becoming a Connoisseur

Are You a Beer Geek?
(There's No Right Answer)

If you're reading this book, and you've come this far, chances are you're someone who enjoys a glass of beer. Either that, or you're stuck at someone's cottage on a rainy weekend, you're bored witless, and this is the only book you could find. In which case, I'm very sorry.

I believe we've established that beer is, on the whole, a good thing. I hope we can at least agree on that. That said, there are different sorts of beer enthusiasts. There are those who don't much care what kind of beer they drink as long as it's cold. A cold beer, a hot day, a barbecue, a deck, the nineteenth hole, fishing off a dock by a lake. Excuse me: I'm just a young woman in a tank top short of a beer commercial.

Beer is a great drink for Canadians. It takes someone who has gone through (yet another) winter to appreciate the joys of summer, and it is in summer that we drink most of our beer. Not that we don't enjoy our beer the other eleven months of the year, but summer is what commercial breweries live for. Historically, the big brewers have launched new product lines or new marketing campaigns with the May two-four weekend in mind. Catch us then, they reckon, and they've got us at least for the summer, which is the long term in the beer marketing world.

Some beer enthusiasts talk about something called "lawn mower beer," the kind of beer you look forward to drinking after you've done your yard chores. It's likely to be an uncomplicated brew, served cold and probably straight from the bottle or can. Its purpose is to refresh and restore, to make a person feel righteous about getting the chores done and cheerfully hedonistic at the same time.

Most Canadian beer drinkers of a certain age know these lawn-mower beers well; when we were young, there wasn't much else, even though the winters were longer then and you could sometimes go two or three years at a time without summer. This is not to say we didn't think about our beer at all. Many of us reckoned we could tell the difference between, say, an Old Vienna and a Black Label, and maybe we could. Many of us continue to insist that it was better back then (we say that of everything, of course, from popular music to hockey; it'll happen to you, too, so don't look so smug), that the big brewers didn't use as much corn syrup and other cheap adjuncts when we were young. It's possible that we're right. After all, who wouldn't rather listen to Little Eva than Lil' Kim? (I'm not about to try to describe either of these entertainers to generations at extreme ends of the scale.)

I have written elsewhere about the forces that drove provincial governments to liberalize drinking laws in the 1960s and 1970s. While we were off seeing the world and drinking in English pubs and German *Bierstuben,* we noticed that not only were our new settings more pleasant than the beverage rooms we were used to, but the beer was tastier than Blue and Export. We might not have realized this right away, because we were still distracted by different customs, different glassware, different accents, and different languages. Perhaps it was only when we got home and resumed drinking the beers of our youth that we twigged to the undeniable fact that they weren't as good as some of the stuff we'd had elsewhere—though, being know-nothings, we usually weren't even drinking the best stuff when we went abroad. Still, if nothing else, we began to realize that there wasn't just one taste of beer. This may seem obvious today, but it was something of an epiphany all those years ago.

In that era, there were many people who drank the same brand of beer all the time. There were, and I believe still are, people who were fiercely loyal to either Molson or Labatt. If you were a Molson guy, you regarded Labatt products as utterly unacceptable (unless there was nothing else available), and vice versa. Often, these prejudices came about as a result of sneaking beers from your dad's cache; it was the taste you were used to, and you stuck with it. (Similarly, families passed on car biases. Some homes were General Motors homes, others Ford loyalists, and so on. We didn't know much then about foreign cars, except for a few sports cars.)

This loyalty to Dad's beer all changed, of course, and young drinkers wanted to drink anything but what that doddering old fool drank. Which left them in the cagey hands of beer marketers, who were all too happy to tell them what to drink instead. The range of flavours was still so limited that only the ad campaigns made any meaningful distinctions among the beers on offer.

The so-called craft beer revolution in North America can be traced to a man named Fritz Maytag of the appliance family. Living in San Francisco in 1965, Maytag became an admirer of a local brew called Anchor Steam Beer, just in time to be informed that the brewery was shutting down, unable to compete with the mass beers. Maytag brought the brewery and slowly began restoring it to life, finally bringing out his first beer in 1971. Maytag has expanded since then, but has resisted becoming bigger than he's comfortable with, though he has branched out into wines and spirits, most notably a first-rate gin called Junipero (apparently pronounced you-NIP-ero). Maytag's example inspired a generation of brewers who learned from the Anchor experience and, one by one, opened their own businesses.

When craft beers slowly began to arrive on the North American scene, it was a relative band of pioneers who braved the strange world of beer that didn't taste like Bud or Blue. But once drinkers discovered this new universe, they were unlikely to go back to the bland side. The revolution in Canada began in British Columbia, with the first brewpub and the first microbrewery in modern Canadian life. (There had, of course, once been lots of brewpubs and microbreweries, but they hadn't survived the twin evils of Prohibition and brewery consolidation. Post-Prohibition legislation effectively stifled any such innovation, and independent brewers in most provinces had to lobby to change laws before they could even start their businesses.)

Every day, some beer drinker in Canada goes into a bar and asks for his everyday beer, only to be told that the bar doesn't stock that particular beer, but why doesn't the beer drinker try, say, one of these? Much of the time, that beer drinker won't pay much attention to this new beer, and sometimes the beer drinker will turn up his nose and wish he could have his everyday beer. But sometimes, the beer drinker—and female beer drinkers are often more likely to be adventurous—will take note of a new set of flavours and write down the name of this tasty beer. Maybe she'll go looking for it again, and the craft beer revolution attracts a new freedom fighter.

We met a man once, a few years ago, in a pub in Hamilton, Ontario, called the Winking Judge. This guy, an older, blue-collar kind of guy, was a poster boy for craft brewing. He had come into the pub one evening and asked for the beer he usually drank, but either Al or Bill (the pub owners) told him to try an entry-level, not-too-scary craft beer. That worked out all right, and in a short time he was drinking full-flavoured beers and had become a Winking Judge regular. If craft brewers could afford to do television commercials, he's the man you'd want up front. Though I'm not sure I want to see him in a tank top.

I don't expect to live long enough to see archaeologists rooting around old Molson and Labatt breweries, trying to ascertain what almost beer-like activities once went on in these ruins. The big guys are doing fine, or at least somewhat fine. They're making bigger profits than all the craft breweries put together, though they're not showing a lot of growth, which is important for megacorporations (in 2007, Budweiser in the USA marked its twentieth straight year of declining sales, according to *Brew Magazine*). It's the craft brewers who are showing growth, both in Canada and the US. Craft beers still account for a very small part of the market, but it's growing.

The archetype of the craft beer enthusiast is a middle-aged (at least) male with a paunch, and probably a beard. These guys remember the bad old days of Canadian beer and will tell you about them at the slightest provocation. (Some of them even write books on the subject.)

There are today, however, young people who were born in a more enlightened era, whose first beers were craft beers, who have possibly never even tasted corporate beer. They are usually polite enough to listen to their elders telling the old war stories about what the government-run liquor stores used to be like, and who the waiters at the Embassy Tavern were. Some of these young people are even women, bless them.

Some people become interested in craft beer as part of a larger interest in quality-of-life issues. These are people who care about what they put into their bodies. They may be local food activists. They eat better bread, better cheese, better everything. They may have an interest in the slow food movement, not buying into the frenetic nature of North American life. They think food and drink are more than mere fuel, that they should be savoured at a human pace, preferably in good company (I would include hundred-mile diet people in this, except that almost nobody anywhere lives within a hundred miles of both barley farms and hop fields; think about that before you rush to embrace this otherwise worthy endeavour).

A word of warning: once you start drinking better beer, you'll find it hard to go back to the stuff that's advertised on television. There's the danger that you'll become too picky, which can lead to disappointment when you venture optimistically into a pub that serves nothing but lesser brews. You might begin to annoy your friends if you keep dragging them to places that don't serve the beers they know.

If you write a book about beer—not that I recommend it, you understand—people you drink with will become terribly self-conscious about what they order. I'm always happy to make suggestions, but I'm not a beer Nazi. I want my friends to be happy, and I encourage them to drink what they enjoy. Let's face it: the great majority of people don't much like the taste of beer, and they never will, so they prefer a sweet, corn-syrupy beer that will neither surprise nor offend, that will refresh and deliver a buzz. Don't you have some secret vice you'd prefer the rest of us not know about? (Feel free to drop me a line.)

I'd like more people to drink craft beer for purely selfish reasons: to reward quality brewers and encourage them to do even more, and to give publicans an incentive to offer a better range of beer to their customers. I have come to know a number of my local brewers—a finer group of decent, eccentric people you'll never wish to meet—and I'd like to see them prosper. Or at least make a living. I have never, to my knowledge, met the president or CEO of Molson or Labatt, but I frequently happen upon some of my local brewers making deliveries to, or performing quality control exercises in, pubs.

It's a bit like a pyramid scheme. If I encourage you and nine other people to switch to good beer, I am better off (unless you snag the last pint just before I turn up). If you then encourage ten people to switch to good beer, *you* are better off. The difference between this and a pyramid sceme, though, is that nobody loses. Even if you're the last person to sign up, you still win.

But do you want to become a beer geek? Geekery of any sort tends to be a male preserve. People who collect odd ephemera or memorize train schedules or re-enact American Civil War battles or learn to speak Klingon are usually guys. This appears to be related to the figures that reveal that autism is far more prevalent in the male of the species. That, and the fact that women have better things to do than be geeks.

At least beer geeks get to drink beer, which is a step up from most other forms of geekery. Plus, you don't have to wear pocket protectors or make Star Trek costumes, and sometimes you actually get to meet women. It's beginning to sound better and better, isn't it?

Of course, you may already be a beer geek. Take this simple test:

1. Do you know what IBUs are, and are they good or bad?*
2. Do you own more than seven T-shirts bearing the insignia of assorted breweries and/or beer festivals, and do more than three of those have dopey puns on them? (Anything involving the word "firkin" counts double.)
3. Have you gone on brewery tours while on holiday, to the mystification, and possible annoyance, of travel partners?

*IBUs, if you don't know, are a standard measure of the bitterness of beer, standing for international bitterness units. Beer geeks, by and large, enjoy wallowing in hops, which generate bitterness. Such people are usually known as hopheads. Many beer geeks will protest that, in fact, they like a *well-balanced* beer, in which the malt is not oppressed by the hop presence, but you would do well to stand back at a beer festival when they tap a fresh cask of something ultra-hoppy. Commercial breweries tend to be cagey about the IBU levels of their beer, but Budweiser is believed to be about 11 to 12 IBUs. Labatt Blue, surprisingly, seems to be nearly double that. Garrison Imperial Pale Ale, from Halifax, clocks in at something like 70 IBUs. Hoppiness tends to become apparent at about 20 to 30 IBUs (depending on the malt impact), and some of the big IPAs and Imperial IPAs weigh in at 100 IBUs or more, which is seriously mouth-puckering (though some people say that 100 IBUs is technically as high as you can go and that some craft brewers are making their numbers up). Beer blogger Stan Hieronymus has argued that people should not be permitted to drink beers whose IBUs are higher than their IQs.

Hopheads can be easily recognized. When they sip a beer, almost any beer, they report, "Not enough hops." In a vain attempt to satisfy them, a number of brewers have upped the hop profile to an absurd degree, hoping they'll hear the magic words, "Thank you. That's enough hops." Hopheads wept in 2006 when the S.S. Steiner warehouse in Yakima,

4. When someone mentions Michael Jackson, do you automatically think of the late English beer writer and become confused when you find yourself instead in a conversation about the late pop star?
5. Have you ever drunk cheap wine at a social or business gathering because the beer selection was so poor?

If you answered yes to most of these questions, or if you fell short of a perfect score only because you've never found a travel partner, you are almost certainly a beer geek. See you at the next beer festival.

Washington, burned to the ground, taking with it some 4 percent of America's hop harvest. Since then, there has been a global hop shortage, which I will discuss a bit in the next chapter. This shortage has provoked much fretting in beer circles generally, but has caused hopheads to weep and wail in an almost biblical manner.

Even Anheuser-Busch—which has been reducing its hop profile in recent decades to mollify those Americans for whom even Budweiser has too much flavour—was said to be leaning toward making Bud just the teensiest bit more hoppy, because even Bud drinkers had begun to hear about hops. Even more worrying was their introduction of something called Budweiser American Ale, which they promised would be "hoppier" than regular Bud. This suggested that they actually planned to put hops in the beer rather than just wave a hop cone several feet away from the brewing kettle during the boil. If they add even a single hop to a batch of the new beer, it could play havoc with the international hop market, and wreck the lives of hop lovers everywhere.

The Future of Beer: Can I Afford to Drink It? (Can You Afford *Not* to Drink It?)

After ten thousand years of non-stop consumption, it seems fair to assume that beer is pretty much on the map by now, that it's not going away any time soon. Even Prohibition didn't stop beer. As the commercials assure us, drinking beer is as Canadian as pulling your enemy's jersey over his head and pounding the daylights out of him, as Canadian as shopping cart racing, as Canadian as hearing choirs when you order a pint of beer.

But is the future uninterruptedly rosy? Put it this way: so far, I haven't heard anything negative about the future of yeast. Yeast, as far as I'm aware, is something you can relax about. There's enough to go around.

It's everything else that's a potential problem. I have quietly mentioned (so as not to raise panic among the beer-drinking population) the hop crisis. Well, let's not call it a crisis; crises are so worrying. Let's call it the hop syndrome. Suddenly, hops became scarce in

2006–2007. Growing demand among craft brewers, bad harvests, just plain bad luck—all these factors, and more, not only drove up the price of hops but made certain varieties of hops all but unobtainable. Part of the problem, we are told, is that we had been paying too little for hops in recent years, that hop growers had been switching to other, more profitable crops as a result. Faced with this syndrome, small brewers were forced, in some cases, to alter their recipes to accommodate the hops they were able to find. American brewer Jim Koch, of Sam Adams fame, had secured more hops than he planned to use, so he made them available at cost to numerous craft breweries, thereby assuring himself at least temporary sainthood.

The rise in hop prices, of course, offers the hope that farmers will see the value in our friend *Humulus lupulus* and devote space to it. Ontario has great swaths of land that have been long devoted to tobacco, a plant whose worth has shrunk in recent years, and there is evidence that at least some former tobacco farmers are switching to hops. I wish them well.

The news from the American northwest has become more cheerful. It was noted that hop growers in Washington, Oregon, and Idaho— the North American heartland for our aromatic pal—were expected to harvest 8,352 more acres in 2008 than 2007. Phew.

The big breweries experienced no major problems, given that they hardly use any hops—no, I mean, because they're so big that they have their future supply guaranteed. But where does the hop syndrome go from here? It's anyone's guess. The hop is a finicky plant that will give you a sub-par harvest at the drop of a hat, so the ravages of climate change could be an issue.

Climate change is already being blamed for barley shortages. *ABC News* reported in 2008 that Australia and New Zealand were both experiencing conditions—too hot and too dry—that threatened to harm barley harvests. Droughts are becoming less unusual in the developed world. In 2007, Georgia governor Sunny Perdue

(Canadian politics would be more colourful if our leaders had better names) led a public prayer for rain on the steps of the state capitol, in defiant opposition to the Atlanta Freethought Society. Perdue was merely following in the footsteps (or kneesteps) of the governor of Alabama and the prime minister of Australia, both of whom encouraged the power of prayer in the face of crippling drought.

Barley, of course, is not the only grain running short. Wheat (a major element in wheat beer), rice (a major ingredient of Budweiser; Anheuser-Busch is the single biggest purchaser of rice in the United States), and corn (a major ingredient of the budget-reducing plans of many mainstream brewers who use it as a cheap adjunct to reduce barley costs) all ran short in 2008. Corn, in particular, is in danger because we're now using corn to make ethanol to fuel our cars, so as not to be dependent on the oil barons of the Middle East and, erm, Alberta. Still, if we start using corn syrup in our gas tanks rather than in our fermenting tanks, we beer drinkers might actually be better off.

And then there's water. Most of beer is water, of course, and if you live in, say, St. John's or Prince Rupert, you might think that water is limitless. After all, it falls on you more days than not. Statistically, it's probably raining as you read this, which is why you're indoors with a book. And the climate change experts predict that most Canadians will likely get more rain in the future, not less.

Like many Canadians, I live a short distance from a fair-sized body of fresh water. As lakes go, mine is officially designated as a "great" one. So, all in all, water doesn't appear to be a problem.

But not so fast. Water levels are falling in the Great Lakes, leading Canadian conspiracy theorists to suspect that the Americans have put a giant pipe into Lake Erie and are pumping the water directly to Arizona golf courses. Glaciers are melting, which means that water supplies will diminish. Water is evaporating, wetlands are drying out, and less snow is falling on the Rockies. Much of the United States is drying out—heck, much of the world is drying out—and our water will be in demand, so we can expect to pay higher prices for it. (We have oil in Alberta, but does that mean we pay less for gas?)

Brewers in Canada and around the world cite all these factors and more to justify rising beer prices. Glass and aluminum prices are going up. No, it's not that brewers are putting glass and aluminum in their beer, but they are putting their beer *in* glass and aluminum. There has been some confusion about this.

Fuel prices, driven by American foreign policy and sharply rising demand in China and India, show little sign of falling, corn-based ethanol or not, so the costs of shipping barley to maltsters, of shipping malt and hops to breweries, of shipping beer to stores and pubs, of driving the beer home from the beer store, are all rising. (Another reason to drink local beer on draught in a pub you can walk home from.)

Rising beer prices have led to shady practices, according to *The Wall Street Journal*, which reported in 2008 that American bars and restaurants had been surreptitiously changing their glassware without telling their customers. The new beer glasses, with thicker bottoms, measure a whopping fourteen ounces, rather than the traditional American "pint" of sixteen ounces (yes, the American ounce is slightly bigger than ours, but still). One Oregon bartender dubbed these glasses "falsies." Reporter Nancy Keates actually enticed the vice-president of purchasing for a restaurant chain called Damon's Grill into saying, "Someone who comes in and wants a beer doesn't want a huge glass. Fourteen ounces is enough." That's easy for her to say. Other bar managers insist that any of these smaller glasses must have been an ordering mistake, that possibly these smaller glasses—if they exist at all, which seems unlikely—must have been brought in by customers. Which, I'm sure, happens a lot. Gosh, if I had a nickel for every time I've taken my own smaller glass to a pub and inadvertently left it there . . .

(This, of course, is not just a beer issue. Numerous food producers have quietly shrunk their package sizes rather than raising prices, hoping that consumers won't notice.)

All of this—and don't think that taxes on beer are ever going to come down—means higher beer prices in our future, unless farmers take advantage of the shortage of hops and barley and start planting more. And if beer prices go up and your income doesn't, you might have to consider what you can give up in order to support your beer needs. Since drinking and driving don't mix well, perhaps you could give up driving. And since you can hardly smoke anywhere any more, quit smoking. If you think about it, there are lots of things you could give up. As Henny Youngman may have said, "When I read about the evils of drinking, I gave up reading." [*Editor's note:* The author of this book will stop at nothing to make a joke, even if it is not original. It has been established, however, that reading informs, entertains, and lowers blood pressure, all at remarkably reasonable prices. And books contain no cholesterol or trans fats.]

And perhaps we'll discover oil wells in our backyards. In the meantime, keep buying lottery tickets, available in many convenient locations across this great country.

Get Real:
The Day I Met a
Beer Angel

If you've read my earlier book, *Notes on a Beermat* (excellent value and fun for the whole family), you will no doubt recall my mention of a man I met one day forty-odd years ago, when I was employed at a London pub called the Argyll Arms, just off Oxford Circus. Being young and foolish (I've changed: I'm not young any more), I knew little about beer except that I much preferred English beer to the Canadian stuff I had escaped from, but I didn't know much about the English beer itself. I don't think it had even occurred to me to ask why most of the draught beers we served came effortlessly from devices that were activated by turning a little tap or pressing a button, while one beer, Bass Ale, came from a hand pump that required a bit of effort to operate.

Anyway, the man I met there one day was one of our Bass-drinking customers, and he took advantage of a quiet spell to speak to me about beer. It's funny, the people you meet just once. Most of them you forget straightaway, and others you remember. He was an older chap, though when you're young, of course, everybody over thirty looks half-dead.

Patiently, he explained that the pint he was drinking was proper English beer, the way it was intended to be drunk. It was unpasteurized, unfiltered ale with no artificial carbonation, and had undergone a secondary fermentation in the cask. If the term had been available at the time, he might well have called it "real ale."

I always tell young people—not that they pay the slightest bit of attention—that they should listen to what older people tell them, a view, oddly enough, I grow more certain of the older I get. Sure, most of it is rubbish, but at the time you're not sure which bits of what you're hearing are rubbish and which bits aren't. Anyway, there I am, in a handsome London pub, listening to this older man—sometimes now I imagine him wearing an old tweed jacket and a cloth cap; other times I see him looking like Henry Travers, who played Clarence the angel in *It's a Wonderful Life*—and there's a young and foolish part of me that's saying, "Yeah, Gramps, get on with it," but there's another part of me that thinks I ought to pay attention. And, fortunately, I do.

I mention Clarence the angel because I sometimes think this man at the Argyll Arms was sent to me that day to make me think about beer. He probably knew I wouldn't change my ways overnight and become a missionary for good beer, but he hoped to plant a seed. I imagine him, later that day, in another pub with someone likeminded: "Had a pint at the Argyll Arms earlier on. Talked to a fairly thick young bloke behind the bar, gave him my standard talk about proper beer. Oh, you could see he was thinking, 'Yeah, Gramps, get on with it,' but I think I might just have got through that thick skull and given him something to think about. Not 'alf hard work sometimes, though."

A couple of years after my conversation with the man at the Argyll Arms, four Englishmen went on a drinking tour of Ireland. It was 1971. Sitting in a pub in County Kerry and bemoaning the state of modern beer, they formed what became the Campaign for Real Ale (CAMRA), now a flourishing enterprise with something like ninety thousand dues-paying members. CAMRA produces a monthly newspaper, puts on one of the world's biggest beer festivals every August, publishes an annual guide to beer and pubs in the UK, lobbies government, and acts as a general thorn in the side of those evildoers who would deprive the British drinker of good, honest ale. The struggle is ongoing, but the visitor can travel to most parts of Britain today and find a well-maintained glass of cask-conditioned ale in the majority of pubs, something that was becoming difficult to do in the early 1970s.

At least the British had a tradition of drinking cask-conditioned ale—real ale. Presumably, we once knew such beer here in Canada. There would have been a time when beer was, pretty much by definition, real ale, back before we became sophisticated enough to wreck everything. But nobody in these parts remembers it, so what is traditional for the Brits is new to us. "Real ale," of course, is a difficult concept to get across. It suggests that everything else is somehow "fake," which isn't necessarily true. Still, cask-conditioned ale, at its best, has an indisputably "real" quality to it. You know it when you taste it.

When microbreweries made their way onto the scene in North America, very few of them attempted to create cask-conditioned ale. Let's face it, things were tough enough without trying to make something pub owners didn't know how to maintain or sell and customers were hardly asking for. Real ale has a finite shelf life, particularly once it's been tapped, and it requires careful handling. Small wonder the big British brewers were keen to do away with it in the sixties and seventies. Thanks to science and technology, they had beers any fool could serve up, beers that didn't go off, beers that could be trucked hundreds of miles without a moment's concern. There was a lot more money to be made from modern beer.

The drawback, needless to say, is that it didn't taste as good. Still, that's what advertising is for. And there was a new generation of beer drinkers—the biggest generation ever—who didn't want to be drinking the tired old low-carbonated beer their dads and granddads drank. They wanted modern, cold beer. And even if they didn't, that's what they'd be offered.

And it nearly worked, too. All it took was the most successful consumers' interest organization in British history to stand in the way. It has to be conceded that almost none of the big, globalized beer corporations that operate in the UK go anywhere near real ale these days. Cask-conditioned ale is coming almost entirely from middle-range and smaller breweries, but there are a hell of a lot more of them than there were in 1970.

Why should we care in Canada? Because real ale is coming our way as well. Not all beers lend themselves to being served this way, but English-style ales most emphatically do. The Wellington Brewery in Ontario was offering cask-conditioned ales to pubs in the mid-1980s, at a time when neither pub owners nor beer drinkers knew what it was. Victoria, with its English name and heritage, was more open to real ale when the Spinnakers brewpub landed on its shores. Even so, cask ale has not driven Coors Light out of the marketplace. And, although sales of Labatt Blue are down, we cannot honestly attribute this to the astonishing rise of cask ale.

Nevertheless, the signs are promising. Americans, who severed their ties with Britain late in the eighteenth century, are beginning to try this "new" style of beer. We're starting to see cask beer festivals arising in places like Chicago, New York, and Toronto. San Francisco is climbing aboard, and so on. Even Buffalo is onside. People are holding meetings, which is a sure sign of progress. The temperance movement started by holding meetings, to be sure, but cask ale meetings are more fun, if only because you get to drink beer. (If they don't let you drink beer, don't attend the meeting. I belong to a group imaginatively called CASK!; we always drink beer.)

Yes, I hear you say, but why should I care? You should care because, when done properly, cask ale is utterly delicious. It's fresher than any beer you've ever had, the lower carbonation makes it wonderfully quaffable (no gas!), and you're reducing your carbon footprint by drinking beer with no carbon dioxide added. This is virtuous beer. And it's craft beer at its best. It requires craft from the brewer and the publican, and aren't we all about craft these days? Cask ale is the antithesis of high-profit, mass-market, freeze-your-tastebuds corporate beer.

Being a grown-up means that you think about what you ingest. If you really think about your quality of life, you don't just hoover down cheap, prefabricated food and beer. No sir, you take a moment to appreciate that someone—maybe even you—has put some thought into making something that brings you pleasure, something that tastes good and might actually be healthier for you than those corn chips and a Bud.

So, if you go into a pub and you see one of those old-fashioned, vaguely phallic hand pumps on the bar, ask your server if it's attached to something. Expand your mind. If the pub's doing its job, you may be in for a treat. Mind you, if the pub's not doing its job, you might hate it and think I'm more of a fool than the man I met in the Argyll Arms all those years ago thought I was. I do kind of think of him as Clarence the angel. And I believe that, when I drink a pint of cask-conditioned ale, somewhere a beer angel gets his (or, very possibly, her) wings.

Beer Festivals: Why You Should Care

If having a glass of beer seems like a good thing, if meeting a friend in a bar seems like a good thing, you might want to try a beer festival some time. Lots and lots of beer, lots and lots of friends—or at least, "friends ye haven't met yet," as Irish pubs often promise.

The premise of beer festivals is quite simple: you turn up and drink beer. Why? Because, as someone in a book I read not long ago said, beer makes people happy. Beer festivals are fairly relaxed events without a dress code. Many festival-goers wear T-shirts sporting witty (and, it must be said, often unwitty) slogans, often to do with beer, drunkenness, and sex—sometimes all three. People sometimes get drunk at beer festivals, which is inevitable when you put a lot of people in proximity to a lot of beer, but no one really minds too much unless you start spilling beer or breaking things.

The granddaddy of beer festivals, needless to say, is Oktoberfest. By which I mean, of course, the real Oktoberfest, the one in Munich. The one that takes place mostly in September. Don't tell me the Germans don't have a sense of humour. You can imagine them laughing up their lederhosen when North Americans turn up in the middle of October looking for Oktoberfest. Only the Germans have a word for *Schadenfreude*.

Oktoberfest dates back to 1810, when Bavaria's Crown Prince Ludwig married Princess Therese von Sachsen-Hildburghausen, an event worth celebrating if only because of the bride's impressive name. There were no von Sachsen-Hildburghausens in my high school; I would remember if there had been. Back in 1810, the party began on October 12 and ended on October 17, but today it's longer and earlier and features parades and rides and, oh yes, beer: fourteen large tents full of the stuff, operated by the local breweries. And countless *Freunden* ye haven't met yet—six million or more in a good year, drinking nearly seventy thousand hectolitres of beer and eating almost three hundred thousand pork sausages and nearly sixty thousand pork knuckles. Again, I defy you to tell me the Germans don't know how to have fun (no one, to my knowledge, has surveyed the pigs).

Other beer festivals pale by comparison, though most offer a wider range of beer styles and fewer oom-pah-pah bands. The Campaign for Real Ale in Britain sponsors around 150 beer festivals across the country, from Hove to Huddersfield, from Banbury to Basingstoke, but the really big one is the Great British Beer Festival, founded in 1977 and held every August nowadays in London. The GBBF attracts sixty-five thousand lovers of ale, who consume 350,000 pints of both British and imported beers. I love it to bits. I've never encountered pork knuckles there, but there's usually a purveyor of excellent pork pies in a dazzling range of flavours. The Empire may be a thing of the past, but an English pork-and-Stilton pie makes me a better person, cholesterol be damned.

You'll find the biggest choice of beers anywhere at the Great American Beer Festival in Denver every October. Nearly two thousand American beers, from four hundred breweries, are available to be sampled, so bring your taste buds. The weird thing about the GABF is that beer is served in—wait for it—one-ounce measures. This is not a typo. I said one-ounce measures, and I meant it. (Keep reminding yourself that the American ounce is relatively huge, the equivalent of 1.04 of our imperial ounces, so the serving is much bigger than you think. Well, all right, maybe not *much* bigger.) This, needless to say, improves your odds of trying all 1,969 beers (the numbers seved in 2008), but it doesn't make for a relaxing experience. You can't really sit down with a beer and gather your thoughts. It does, on the other hand, make you concentrate on what you're drinking. And the festival is listed in *1,000 Places to See Before You Die* (US and Canada edition), so there you are.

The GABF, to my knowledge (such as it is), is the only major festival to apply such strict rules about quantity. Oktoberfest drinkers down their beer by the litre. British festival drinkers have a choice of a pint, a half-pint, or a third of a pint, which gives the drinker a chance to taste many beers in smallish measures but still be able to sit down with a pint of something special and a pork pie. Most North American festivals dole out the beer in roughly four-ounce measures, though many brewers, being decent people, pour closer to five or six. Don't tell the authorities.

There are other interesting differences in festivals. Oktoberfest drinkers pay nothing to attend but pay for what they drink and eat. British beer festivals charge a nominal sum to enter (to cover rental of the hall, cooling equipment, and the like), after which you pay for what you consume. American festivals tend to charge a much higher admission fee, after which the beer is free, though that last bit may be changing (human psychology tells you that, in such a case, most members of our species will make damn sure they get their money's worth, which can lead to large-scale drunkenness, even at an ounce per serving). Canadian festivals are often a compromise: charge a fair bit to get in, then charge you for the beer as well.

That said, there's no admission charge for Mondial de la Bière, held in late May or early June every year in Montreal. Trust Montreal to have the most relaxed beer festival anywhere. You can roam in for an hour, taste a few beers, leave fairly sober (or not), and get on with your day (or not). Which is not to say there is no security presence at Mondial. There is no shortage of big guys in black outfits, whose main job appears to be to make sure you get a plastic bag to put your tasting glass in as you leave. I'm sure they get busier as the evening wears on. Given that there are no admission tickets, it is difficult to know how many people attend Mondial, but event organizers estimate that seventy-five thousand of us turned up in 2008. (Given that I went for at least part of all five days, I'm probably five of those people.)

There are a few rules that should be observed when it comes to beer festivals. One is that the best time to be there is a weekday afternoon, assuming you're given that option. It's a festival, for heaven's sake, so take some quality time off work, though you might want to be careful about lying to your boss: newspapers often run photographs of beer festivals, and it will do you no good to be seen in your wacky beer-drinking hat, swilling ale, while you're allegedly at your mother's funeral (anything applied to your head or face is likely to be photographed by the local press).

Evenings particularly, and weekends as well, tend to be extremely busy—and noteworthy for the sort of people who attend beer festivals in order to get in some quality shouting. They can often be seen from afar because, as a rule, they wear alarming hats of one sort or another. When you see them en masse at a beer festival, you might think them unemployable, but my guess is that they have jobs that require them to be quiet all day, necessitating a rambunctious release by evening. I'm guessing also that they shout well into the night, so they're seldom to be seen at festival opening time, even on weekends.

Mondial opens at 11 a.m., which is an excellent time to start tasting beer, especially on a Wednesday or Thursday. But even on Saturday and Sunday, Mondial is not too busy at opening time, though that soon begins to change. And if it rains, it can get crowded indoors.

Another rule about beer festivals I heard at Mondial is that, if the person serving beer at a brewery booth is a paunchy bloke with a beard, the beer's probably pretty good. If the beer is served by a very attractive woman, it's all just marketing. Indeed, this is often the case. Booths staffed by stunning young women in suggestive outfits are usually flogging bland, corporate beer, and the women— charming as they may be—are there to separate randy young (and occasionally not so young) men from their hard-earned beer tokens. If you try to engage these young women in conversation about their grain-sparging practices, you might be disappointed. They might call security, and I'm not sure I'd blame them.

At the risk of appearing sexist, I can report that this rule does not entirely apply at Mondial. It's in Montreal, see? You've been to Montreal? Then you know what I'm talking about. My friend Mary McMillan, at Mondial 2008, pointed to a young woman in a cowboy hat serving at a nearby booth and said, "She is so-o-o-o cute!" Now, Mary, as far as I'm aware, is a woman of a conventional lifestyle, inexplicably married for some decades to a high school friend of mine whom you'll meet later, and is not given to outbursts of that sort (she might have had a sample or two when she said this). The high school friend and I felt obliged, under the circumstances, to observe the young woman in question and concede, albeit grudgingly, that she was indeed as cute as a large container filled right to the top with buttons. She was a peach, no question. And she was not the only one. Some of them were selling beer from excellent breweries, and if I'd known how to say "grain-sparging practices" in French, I would have done so.

You expect a certain *je ne sais quoi* in Montreal, and you get it at Mondial. There's a very good cheese stand, an excellent frites stand, and all sorts of other delicacies to supplement your beer drinking. The hungry beer festivalist is seldom treated so hospitably. Anglophone drinkers, a long way from their high school French, might not always comprehend what's going on or what people are saying to them, but everyone seems ridiculously friendly. Here's a case in point: one evening, I had visited a Montreal brewpub and had had a very good time (I am not naming the brewpub in question, because I don't want to get the pub—or this particular employee—in trouble). The next day, the server who had taken care of us at the brewpub was on duty at the beer festival. Now, I don't remember having tipped outrageously the previous day, but he wouldn't take my beer coupons, waving me away each time, finally saying, "Today you are my guest." That's *je ne sais quoi*. And it's no wonder we don't have a word for *je ne sais quoi* in English.

Mondial takes place at the old Windsor Station in downtown Montreal. It's half indoors, under an arched glass roof, and half outdoors, in an open space between the station and the Bell Centre. I'm guessing it gets pretty crowded indoors if it rains on a Friday or Saturday evening, but by that time the sensible beer drinker, if such a creature exists, is sitting comfortably in a pub.

Beer festivals, like conferences and conventions, are better when they're away from home. It makes sure, for starters, that you're not at work, so you get the best opening hours away from the wage slaves. And it makes a holiday out of it. And when you're in a strange city and you've spent a few hours drinking four-ounce samples of beer, mostly standing up, you're ready for something completely different. Or, at least, drinking larger measures of beer sitting down. Attending a beer festival is a fine way of finding out where people drink, and Mondial is no exception. There are lots of fine places to drink in Montreal, and you'll read about some of them later.

But back at Mondial, the allegedly "cute" young woman is still plying her trade, and beer drinkers from near and far are throwing back the beer—sorry, I mean they're studiously tasting the beers and making detailed notes. The beautiful thing about tasting beer, of course, is that you don't have to spit it out, unless you really don't like it. Those hoity-toity wine buffs (or cork dorks) consider themselves morally superior to the beer louts, but who does all the spitting? Tell me that. *Dégoûtant,* if you ask me. Start spitting at a beer festival and you'll be asked to leave.

Unlike most beer festivals on the planet, Mondial is organized by a woman, Jeannine Marois, so you know the washrooms will be acceptable—in contrast to, say, Toronto's Festival of Beer at Fort York (is there a hyphen in porta-potty?). She has also been instrumental in introducing cheese workshops, an international beer cartoon competition, and a posh Friday-night dinner.

The other element that makes Mondial so enjoyable, particularly for a beer drinker from Toronto, is that it is held in Montreal. That fact alone introduces a broad spectrum of, how do you say it, *joie de vivre.* And there we are again: we don't have a word in English for *joie de vivre,* either.

Speaking of which, part of the excitement of attending Mondial, for the anglophone, is figuring out what's in the beer. Many beer lovers know that hops are *houblons,* but what is *seigle?* What about *chanvre?* (Rye and hemp, respectively.) Am I prepared to drink a beer described as *plutôt ambrée de robe,* which might conceivably mean "rather ambered of gown"? (Of course I am; I'm not afraid of surprises.)

The single recurring complaint about Mondial is the price of beer. Coupons cost a dollar (in 2008), and a four-ounce sample costs anywhere from one to five coupons—most commonly two to three, though the big, strong beers can be four or five, and occasionally more for very strong or obscure ales. An enthusiastic beer taster can very easily go through forty coupons in a session, which on average might constitute a mere three and a half pints of beer (though most of the samples are larger than advertised, trust me), some of which would be in the 8 to 10-percent-alcohol range. So, pricey, yes, but you're paying no admission charge, you're drinking beers you won't see in your dreary day-to-day life, and you're under no obligation to purchase the official Mondial tasting glass ($8 in 2008) or the T-shirt ($16). In fact, you're not obliged to buy anything at all, or even turn up. Staying at home is always the biggest bargain. Think of all the money you'd save if you never got out of bed.

Staying in bed is an option some members of Toronto's beer community exercise during the annual Festival of Beer, held, until recently, every August at historic Fort York. I can see their point. Saturday, which invariably sells out in advance, is a zoo—or, at least, the monkey cage of a zoo. Actually, a zoo that crammed that many inmates into a monkey cage would face charges of animal cruelty. If you're curious to see how drunk people can get on four-ounce samples, I recommend Saturday at Toronto's Festival of Beer. If you think it's a bit of an effort to get that drunk on little glasses of beer, I can tell you that there are many people willing to make that effort. Remember that Toronto is the city whose motto is "Thank God It's Monday" (it sounds better in Latin). People in Toronto work hard. They're goal-oriented. And if their goal is to get drunk four ounces at a time, they're willing to do whatever it takes.

That said, Thursday or Friday afternoon can be quite pleasant, though nowadays the festival doesn't open on those days until 4 p.m., giving the agoraphobic drinker less time before the workaholics check in. (See my earlier comments on the importance of organizing your working life around the schedules of beer festivals. I'm unaware that anyone has said, on his deathbed, that he regretted spending so much time at beer festivals and not enough at work.) In 2007, the organizers added a day (Thursday) to the mix for a premium VIP day, and shortened the Saturday and Sunday schedules. All four days now offer six hours each of drinking time, at prices that vary from $45 (Friday to Sunday) to $50 (Thursday's VIP treatment) if purchased in advance (2009 prices).

The admission price includes a commemorative sampling cup

(made of the highest-quality plastic) and five beer tokens, worth a dollar apiece. Patrons are allowed to bring in one (1) unopened bottle of water of no more than one (1) litre. The water rules have rankled festival-goers in the past, given that the festival is held usually in blazing sun with little shade. We all know about the importance of rehydration when drinking in hot weather, but the rules are the rules. I recall attending the Buffalo Brewfest some years ago, when it was held in the outfield of the baseball stadium on a hot, sunny afternoon. A forklift truck appeared and hauled in a skid of bottled water, gratis for the punters. And they complain about the American health care system.

It being Ontario, of course, humans under nineteen years of age are forbidden even to read about Toronto's Festival of Beer, let alone peek over the fence to observe the goings-on inside. By comparison, daytime tipplers at Mondial are likely to behold a gaggle of toddlers from the nearby daycare centre being led through the beer festival attached to what I am told is called a fabric caterpillar. With horrifying early experiences like that, it is not surprising that the people of Montreal grow up to be so fun-loving and well adjusted.

No one has ever said that about the residents of Toronto, and the difference is reflected in its beer festival. Now, everything I have to tell you about Toronto's Festival of Beer must be tempered by the fact that, in 2008, the last three days of the festival were sold out in advance, before even a sip of beer had been poured, which apparently means that more than thirty thousand people poured in (and, more literally, out). I had won (!) a ticket for the expensive Thursday-evening session by answering a skill-testing question that my friend Mr. Google was instrumental in my getting right.

I noticed that, amid the fine print on my pass, were the words, "Holder agrees to voluntary search." I naively imagined that this was a disclaimer that allowed them to give me a going-over if I appeared troublesome. Upon my cold-sober arrival, a young woman went through my bag with an element of thoroughness. I knew the rules, so my bottle of water was within the law. I worried a bit about the three small tins of cat food I was carrying; you're not allowed to bring in food. My luck held up though, and she didn't confiscate the cat food, which would have got me in deep trouble at home the next morning at feeding time.

But this was not the end of it. Another young woman then gave me the kind of frisking I haven't experienced since I spent a day at a major conspiracy trial of Black Panthers in New York City in the early seventies. I haven't been this intimate with a young woman since I was a newlywed. Still, it was good to know, as I walked into the festival grounds, that I had my annual prostate exam out of the way.

There were people wearing SECURITY T-shirts, which you would expect, but there were a bunch of other people with headsets, wearing yellow T-shirts emblazoned with the words ALCOHOL ENFORCEMENT. I initially took this to mean that they were on the premises to make sure people were drinking—it was a beer festival, after all. Wrong again: these guys were looking for infractions of any sort, violations of any alcohol-related nature. This being Ontario, there are count-less violations to choose from, one of which entailed drinking from anything but the mandatory tasting glass, or plastic (and if you lose your tasting plastic they'll charge you $20 for a replacement). These guys were also keeping a sharp eye on the people working the booths. They all had to be Smart Serve–trained (see page 204), of course, and they had to be wearing their approved credentials—ideally, with their photograph on their badges, though I was told the computer that dealt with the photographs was down. It's a wonder they didn't suspend beer sales until the computer came back up.

The most contentious issue, at least among the people I spoke to, was that people working the booths were forbidden to drink. As one brewer said to me, "It's a beer festival, for Christ's sake." I doubt that the president of InBev was working the Labatt booth, or that the brewmaster of Molson Coors was working his booth, but the micro-brewery booths were where you'd find the owner/brewmaster, and these people all know each other. A beer festival is an opportunity for them to taste each other's beer, but not in Toronto. One exhibitor was given an official warning and a threat of expulsion when a booth worker was spotted tasting a beer new to her company, one she hadn't tried before. So much for her ability to speak knowledgeably to the customers.

There was a time when Toronto's Festival of Beer was a chance for adventurous brewers to cook up something special, a surprising one-off just for the festival. In 2008, most of the adventurous brewers stayed home. Ken Woods of the Black Oak Brewery had his Double Chocolate Cherry Stout and said he'd have something cask-conditioned the next day, and the Great Lakes Brewery had an interesting green tea beer and a high-powered Special IPA, but for the most part it was beer you could find at enterprising local pubs or in the liquor store. Still, there is the appeal of being able to try something for a buck. It's unlikely I'd order a Nickel Brook Green Apple Pilsner in a bar or buy a six-pack at the Beer Store, but for one measly beer token I can have four or so ounces of it, enough to tell me that it's a nicely refreshing beer with a bit of a crisp Granny Smith quality, and my curiosity is satisfied. Now let's see what a dollar will buy at the Walkerville Brewing Company booth.

There is an interesting conundrum that organizers of beer festivals must confront: what do you do about the huge global brewers? Oktoberfest serves only beers made in Munich, so don't go looking for Carlsberg or Budweiser. The CAMRA festivals in the UK specialize in cask-conditioned beers, so the brewing behemoths eliminate themselves by not brewing any. The Great American Beer Festival has no quarrel with the big guys, and even has such judging categories as American-Style Light Lager so that the giants can win valuable prizes and boast about them (the long-suffering GABF judges award prizes in no fewer than seventy-five categories, from Wood- and Barrel-Aged Strong Beer to Leipzig-Style Gose; the awards ceremony takes approximately as long, and is as tiring, as a triathlon.) Toronto's Festival of Beer doesn't give out prizes, but increasingly embraces the corporate beer machine. There was a very large Budweiser display in 2008, complete with Bud Girls, right next to the stage. Sleeman had a huge area with a beach volleyball setup, where you could actually play volleyball with two very comely women in almost imperceptible swimsuits (it isn't often that the young women in tank tops, for which the beer industry is renowned, are upstaged). Molson had a long set of booths from which was played, at sanity-threatening volume, something that may have had its origins in music, causing aural distress among adjacent exhibitors.

What Toronto's Festival of Beer lacked, in one man's view, was much in the way of interesting beer. There was no cask-conditioned ale when I was there, for instance, though there would be one (1) the following day. On the streetcar home, I thought of seven consequential Ontario breweries that were not exhibiting; the following day, I thought of six more. But the great majority of attendees were probably not much bothered by the absence of Church Key, Grand River, or County Durham. One sight of the blonde beach volleyball players almost drove Beau's All Natural Brewing Company out of my mind, too.

It is what it is, as people say. There's no point criticizing Toronto's Festival of Beer for what it isn't—a proper beer festival. There's no beer judging here, and considerably less quality beer than used to be the case. But there's a lot of loud music and pretty girls, and the best ALCOHOL ENFORCEMENT team you'll ever see. It's a party that also offers a slightly greater variety of beer than such loud-music/girls-in-tank-tops parties usually include.

And, until they moved to the CNE grounds in 2009, it was an opportunity to see historic old Fort York, built long ago to protect us against the beastly Americans, which most Torontonians seldom visit. If not for Fort York, we might have to pronounce "en route" *enn rowt*, as the Americans do. Once a year, we could pay tribute to this historic spot and drink beer at the same time. And to be there on Thursday or Friday at rush hour and drink beer while watching the traffic going nowhere on the Gardiner Expressway high above you was a great pleasure.

Canada's oldest beer festival can be found every September in Victoria, BC. Its co-founder, Gerry Hieter, says it's the oldest, and he appears reliable (it seems to be a year older than Mondial, and about three years older than the Toronto fest). It's a very enjoyable two-day festival, held a manageable walk from downtown at the Royal Athletic Park. The great majority of British Columbia breweries turn up for this foamapalooza, along with breweries from Alberta, Saskatchewan, and the western USA, plus, in 2008, one brewery apiece from Ontario and Quebec. It doesn't quite justify the grand nomenclature of Great Canadian Beer Festival, but it's more pan-Canadian than the others.

And here's a nice twist: the Great Canadian Beer Festival welcomes craft beers only, so there were no Bud Girls on hand, no Sleeman beach volleyball girls. There were some young women in dirndls, I couldn't help noticing, but I can live with young women in dirndls. Well, not "live with," exactly, but you know what I mean.

Now, you might suppose that the absence of the Behemoths of Brewing, the Titans of the Taphouse, the Monsters of the Mash Tun, along with the inevitable young women in tank tops hired to promote them, would mean that the GCBF might struggle to sell tickets, or that the only buyers would be the paunchy middle-aged guys in brewery T-shirts who characterize the craft brewing movement. But you'd be wrong. (This book exists to explode preconceptions.)

Both days of GCBF 2008 were sold out ($20 for Friday, $25 for Saturday), and tickets for the Saturday session had vanished practically instantly upon going on sale. And were all seven thousand of us ticket holders grey-bearded geezers? Were we 'eck as like, as they say on *Coronation Street*. The older folks you see shuffling along the streets of Victoria obviously hadn't acted quickly enough to get tickets, for the overwhelming majority of the attendees were young, and many of them women. I have joked, at other festivals, that beer fests are the only place you see men lining up for the facilities while the women nip in and out of theirs without a care. Not at the GCBF, where I witnessed with my own eyes women invading the gents' toilets to avoid the queues at their own. Perhaps that reflects the imbalance of facilities at the Royal Athletic Park, but it certainly reflects the number of women attending the GCBF. Who needs Bud Girls?

So, a festival without Molson, Labatt, or Sleeman can be done, and it can still attract a youthful market (Unibroue, owned by Sleeman, was there, but no one can object to that). That said, I was reminded of another rule of beer festivals: the length of the lineup at a brewery booth is not necessarily indicative of the quality of the beer on offer therein. Another rule came to mind: beware of uniformed staff at beer booths. Matching brewery T-shirts are fine, but lederhosen seem a bit dodgy, unless the brewery in question is located in Bavaria. This may seem inconsistent with my earlier acceptance of dirndls, but I don't care.

The GCBF does a number of things right. Many beer festivals have a fairly central stage upon which bands of varying skills play music that is hard to avoid. The Victoria festival of 2008 had small music tents in three of the four corners of the park, in which mildly amplified musicians performed an assortment of styles of music. Drinkers were free to enjoy the music or not. In one of the central tents sat a very enjoyable German brass band. They played a bit, sat a bit, played a bit, went off looking for beer, then came back and played a bit. I liked them very much, if only because most of them were older than I.

The security presence at GCBF was minimal. A few Victoria police officers roamed around the grounds, but the only time I saw any of them forced to interact with the patrons occurred when one was asked to pose for a photograph with a group of guys decked out as the Village People. He cheerfully obliged.

I don't mean to suggest that no drunkenness occurred. Exactly one hour and twenty-three minutes after the festival opened on Friday afternoon, I heard one young man shout to a friend in the gents', "I'm fucked!" I've had a lot more practice; it's been a long time since I've achieved that state on four-ounce samples of beer in less than an hour and a half.

The weather in 2008 was pretty much perfect on both days, mostly sunny and warm. The organizers provide two large tents, presumably to offer shelter from rain or shade from the sun. It was the shade we needed on this occasion, though I'm told the weather's usually good, that the sun generally shines on the GCBF. And so it should.

One really good thing about beer festivals is that you get to meet the brewers. How often do you get to meet the important people at Molson or Labatt? If you're lucky, you'll meet the sales or marketing people—actually, come to think of it, they *are* the important people at Molson and Labatt. At the Victoria festival, I was introduced to a genial fellow named Steve Cavan, president and CEO of the Paddock Wood Brewing Company in Saskatoon. I innocently asked him how long his company had been around, which caused him to scratch his head and allow as how that was a difficult question. About half an hour later, I acknowledged that it had indeed been tough.

You never know who's going to end up running a brewery or how they're going to get there. Steve Cavan, originally from Ontario, wound up teaching classics at the University of Saskatchewan and doing a little home brewing on the side. Now, there are two reasons to brew at home. One is that home-brewed beer is cheaper than store-bought. The better reason is that you enjoy the process and take pleasure in developing new recipes and making the sort of beer you can't buy at the store. Steve was the second kind of home brewer.

Frustrated at not being able to buy the specialty malts and hops he wanted, Steve tried to import them from the USA and England, but the big companies wanted to do business only with other companies. So Steve made himself a company. Once he was getting the good stuff, he found himself bringing it in for other home brewers and becoming a distributor. Having researched many different styles of beer, he then expanded to making up customized all-grain kits for home brewers: tell me what you want and I'll try to replicate it as well as I can, and all you have to do is add yeast and water.

This being Canada, of course, Steve found out he had to get permits just to make up stuff that wasn't quite beer yet, which is when the paperwork really started. Once you start soaking barley, you're on the hook. Twice, through all of this, he decided it was too much work and tried to pack it in, but both times people talked him out of it. He had become too important. Eventually, he made the leap to become an actual brewer, while continuing to sell brewing supplies and make brewing kits.

Every bit of expansion involves cash you haven't earned yet, so Steve has taken on investors and enlarged his business. Paddock Wood, named for a centre of hop growing in Kent, is now available in Manitoba, Alberta, and BC, and he told me he has an eye on Ontario and Quebec, though not until he's expanded yet again. Once he's achieved a major expansion, he hopes to use his current space to make what he describes as funky beers—lambics and other weird brews. Even the Chinese are taking an interest in Paddock Wood.

In 2006, Steve left the university to devote himself full-time to his out-of-control brewery, but now finds himself leaving most of the actual brewing to someone else while he deals with the paperwork that comes from dealing with (so far) four provincial alcohol systems. Paddock Wood is making a very good Czech-style pilsner (a lot of breweries are making something that parades as a pilsner; Steve's actually making one), a dark lager, a very good IPA—all of which could be had at the Victoria festival—and an oatmeal stout I haven't met yet. Steve is not just a good brewer but also an excellent evangelist for good beer. May he thrive.

Most of the brewers themselves were on hand for the event, and it was a pleasure to see so many American breweries represented, even though most of their beers are not even available in BC. One Washington State brewer said he comes to the show because he enjoys it. And what better reason to attend a beer festival?

Montreal, Toronto, and Victoria are probably the three best-known beer festivals in Canada, but they're certainly not the only ones. Across the country, lovers of beer are organizing opportunities for you—yes, you—to attend a beer festival and taste a greater variety of fermented grain products than you'll see anywhere else in your town. Some of these are pub owners who put on special events such as cask-ale festivals. Support these people, and support the breweries that support these people. An awful lot of work goes into mounting something like this, and if they appear to be in a state of panic on the big day, they probably are. Be gentle with them, buy a T-shirt, taste a few beers, and meet some new people. In Victoria, I overheard a young beer drinker summing up his day for a friend: "Met a few girls and a few people." Look, he probably didn't mean it the way it came out. He'd had a nice day in the sun.

Name That Beer: What's This Stuff Called Again?

A lot of things were said in the 1960s, many of them barely audible, perhaps with a smidgin too much use of words like "groovy" and that sort of thing. Still, some of it made sense, or at least some sense. There was, for instance, the speculation that half of the rock bands created after about 1964 existed solely because someone had thought of a name that cried out to be a rock band. It seemed a waste not to use a name like Cat Mother and the All-Night News Boys, which was apparently a real group. (They spent three weeks at Number 2 on Toronto's CHUM Chart in August 1969, never able to get past first Zager and Evans then the Archies. Still, there's no shame in coming second to a swell song like "Sugar Sugar," is there?)

They say that if you can remember the sixties, you weren't there, and I'm happy to say I can't recall Cat Mother and her kittens—or, for that matter, Bubble Puppy, also on the charts that summer. It's interesting, and a little deflating, to see what was actually popular in that era, when we thought it was all really groovy music from far-out bands.

But I digress, probably not for the last time. It is easy to make similar judgements about some beer names. Did the fellows at McGuire's Irish Pub and Brewery in Pensacola concoct a big, strong beer and search around for a name, or did a long night in the pub provoke the name McGuire's I'll Have What the Gentleman on the Floor is Having Barley Wine, which led to the creation of a 12-percent beer that would live up to the name?

We'll probably never know, but ultimately, it doesn't matter. Once upon a time, back when brewing was local, there wasn't much need for fancy names. English brewers called their beers Mild, Bitter, and Best Bitter. Sometimes, the bitter was billed as Ordinary Bitter, which today must bring a chill to the heart of an advertising executive, if he has one. If the brewer made a porter, he would call it Porter. How imaginative.

Naming a beer after its style made sense: it informed the customer what she was getting. As brewing became more complicated, it was necessary to add the brewer's name to the beer, so Morland's Bitter or Morrell's Bitter. In today's globalized and heavily marketed world, there is more competition than ever before, as well as an increasing demand for wacky, off-the-wall beer names.

A brewer who wants to give an impression of being a stable, traditional company might stick with old-fashioned names. Even an offbeat beer might have a simply descriptive name, like Bourbon-Barrel-Aged Chocolate Vanilla Stout. It's an unusual beer, but you have some idea of what you're getting. You can't complain when you detect vanilla or bourbon in your stout.

Canadian brewers, by and large, are fairly conservative when it comes to naming their brews. Some of this may be based on fear of their provincial authorities. I've already mentioned the Ontario liquor board's fear of a beer called Delerium Tremens, but you must remember the official motto of Ontario: You Can't Be Too Careful.

For a Toronto beer festival in 2007, the Black Oak Brewery produced a one-off beer that responded to the standard complaint of beer geeks that beer is never hoppy enough. It was called Hop Bomb "S.T.F.U." Pale Ale. I'm given to understand that the first and last words of the acronym were "shut" and "up." We can only speculate what the middle words might be, but I don't expect to see this beer in regular circulation.

There is frequently pressure on brewers to tone down their names. Southern Christians complained when the Dixie Brewing Company began marketing a dark beer called Blackened Voodoo Lager. Wisely, the company realized that the people complaining probably wouldn't buy the beer even if they called it Jesus Is King Lager, so they carried on. No doubt, some critics have attributed Hurricane Katrina to the obstinacy and devil worship of the New Orleans brewery.

A group of us found ourselves in the Pizza Plant restaurant and pub in Buffalo in 2007, at one point evenly divided between beers called Hop Heaven and Hop Devil. From what I recall of the event, there was little actual theological debate over our choices, and I don't believe anything especially bad has happened to any of the Hop Devil drinkers, nor anything especially good to the others.

A man called Greg Schirf relocated to Utah in 1974, and a decade or so later started the Wasatch Brewery. This alone was a dodgy prospect in a state that is 70 percent Mormon, so theoretically teetotal (the only time I went to Salt Lake City, I fell in with a splendid family of Presbyterians, who seemed to be quite "out there," which tells you lots about Utah). Schirf dealt with this dilemma with humour, actively advertising beers called Evolution Amber Ale ("intelligently designed just for intelligent beer-drinkers") and Polygamy Porter ("why have just one?"). Schirf also promoted his porter with the slogan "Take some home for the wives." The more the complaints rolled in, the more the beer rolled out.

Canadians are less likely to imagine devil idoltry on beer labels, to our credit. If you tried to call a beer God, This Beer Is Strong, the provincial authorities would land heavily on you, not for the sacrilege but for boasting about the strength. It would be seen as encouraging the consumption of alcohol.

The Crannóg brewery in British Columbia produces a red ale called Hell's Kitchen and something else called Back Hand of God Stout. The Great Lakes Brewery in Ontario makes a Devil's Pale Ale (apparently brewed for 66.6 minutes with 666 kilograms of malt and 6.6 kilograms of hops, with a strength of 6 percent), and there's also an Ontario brewery called Church Key, located in what was once a Methodist church. Even in straitlaced anglophone Canada, I'm not aware that any of these developments have triggered mass protests from the faithful.

The Québécois operate in their own distinct way. Many Quebec breweries do things in an old-fashioned way, naming beers not necessarily for their style but for their colour: *blanche, blonde, ambrée, dorée, rousse, noire.* This can be confusing for the drinker. A blonde beer can be a pilsner, a pale ale, or a Belgian-style golden beer (which, of course, can also be a *dorée*). *Noire* can be a stout or a porter. Life is difficult enough for the drinking person without having to figure these things out.

Other Quebec breweries revel in imaginative names. There is a brewpub called Le Trou du Diable, which might do battle with a brewery/brewpub called Le Dieu du Ciel. (I suppose it ought to be observed that Le Trou du Diable—The Devil's Hole—takes its name from some natural phenomenon that occurs at nearby Shawinigan Falls. I haven't witnessed this myself; I merely point it out because I know you're curious.) Dieu du Ciel, in particular, combines excellent beers with interesting names, some of a religious bent—Corne du Diable (Horn of the Devil) and Péché Mortel (Mortal Sin)—and others merely whimsical—Aphrodisiaque and Vaisseau des Songes (Ship of Dreams). Unibroue also dallies with religious themes: Maudite (Damned) and Don de Dieu (Gift of God).

Quebec also seems interested in death. Unibroue offers Fin du

Monde (End of the World—well, it *is* 9 percent), while Dieu du Ciel brews Dernière Volonté (Last Will) and Rigor Mortis Blonde.

The recent taste for hoppy beers has produced a rash of beer names that reflect the hoppiness of the beer, hence Hophead, Hop Addict, Hopping Mad, Hop Wallop, Hopocalypse, Goldihops, Tricerahops, Uberhoppy, Hop Suey, Hop a Doodle Doo, Hoppimus Maximus, Hoppily Ever After, Hop Whore, Hop God, and so on. Possibly the best name for this sort of beer is one invented by Buffalo Bill's Brewery in Hayward, California: Alimony Ale, billed as "irreconcilably different" and "the bitterest beer in America." Ironically, a beer this bitter makes you pucker up, which is maybe the cause of the whole problem.

It is strong beer that tends to get brewers looking for odd names. British brewers frequently make a strong ale for winter, often calling it something as adventurous as Strong Ale. But there were those who became a bit bolder with the stronger stuff, giving it names like Tanglefoot, Bishop's Tipple, Old Thumper, Kneetrembler, and Gravedigger. These have been joined in recent years by Olde Homewrecker, Old Stoatwobbler, Old Disreputable, Olde Codger, and (I'm guessing it's a reference to fowl) Old Mottled Cock. One of the best known of the "old" beers of Britain is Theakston's Old Peculier, named for a long-since-vanished ecclesiastical position in Theakston's hometown of Masham, in North Yorkshire.

In 2008, the Orkney Brewery, picturesquely located somewhere off the coast of Scotland, was taken to task for brewing a beer called Skullsplitter, a highly regarded strong (8.5 percent) ale that has been brewed for some twenty years without incident. The name was felt by underoccupied busybodies to be inciting violence, despite the lack of evidence that any such violence has occurred. The brewery countered with the argument that their beer was named for local hero Thorfinn Hausakluif, the Seventh Viking Earl of Orkney, so there.

American craft brewers, in recent years, have mushroomed. In 1978, the darkest hour before the dawn, the United States was down to forty-one companies operating eighty-nine breweries; in 2007, the country claimed 1,449 commercial breweries, most of them small. This number, according to the Brewers Association, includes 1,406 small, independent, and traditional craft brewers. That's a lot of different brands of beer, all needing names. (Putting those numbers into perspective, the US held a whopping 4,131 breweries back in 1873, back before everything went kerflooey.)

They're also increasingly making extreme beers: beers with more hops than ever thought possible, beers with more alcohol than science ever thought possible. Extreme beers seem to call for extreme names, and as often as not, they get them: Fourth Dementia Olde Ale, Hairy Eyeball Ale, Arrogant Bastard Ale, The Beast (16.4 percent!), Old Ruffian, Old Horizontal, Dark Lord Imperial Russian Stout, and many more.

And it isn't all about strong beers. Like winemakers, brewers have learned the value of animal-related names (some would argue that the brewers got there first), so there's hardly a critter you can't find attached to a beer, particularly dogs. Thirsty Dog Brewing Company has a porter named Old Leghumper. Hair of the Dog Brewing Company has a barley wine named Doggie Claws, though most of its beers have simpler names: Ruth, Adam, Rose, and Fred. In 1994, this brewery made a beer named Dave (a tribute to the owner of the Toronado bar in San Francisco). In 2008, five twelve-ounce bottles of Dave went on the auction block for charity in Oregon, selling for prices that ranged from $478 to $707 each, an average price of $563.20.

There are even beers for nudists: New Belgium Skinny Dip, DuClaw Bare Ass Blonde Ale, and Stevens Point Nude Beach, all of which should be—but are probably not—available for sale at Vancouver's Wreck Beach. Jewish beer drinkers might keep an eye out for He'brew beers from the Shmaltz Brewing Company, brews that include Rejewvenator and Jewbelation Eleven. They're all kosher, needless to say.

As noted earlier, brewers in English-speaking Canada have displayed caution in naming their brews. When a brewer named—honestly—Perry Mason ran an Ottawa Valley brewery called Scotch-Irish, he established a military theme with Sgt. Major's IPA, which he followed with Corporal Punishment and Major Misconduct, the last of which might just be the best, most Canadian, beer name of all.

Beer vs. Wine

Let's be honest. If you want to be admired and respected, if you want to get ahead in the world and get the best jobs, you'll take up wine. Talk breezily about Pinot Noirs and Malbecs and Grands Crus, and your boss will give you a raise (hell, you probably *are* the boss). Potential romantic partners will look at you longingly. Wait staff will cower deferentially in your presence.

But, in the end, you'll still have to spit. That's the difference. Wine buffs spit; beer enthusiasts burp.

Even today, when beer appreciation has advanced by burps and farts, when pundits can, without being ironic, describe a beer as having a gooseberry nose and a lemon meringue pie fruitiness and a dry finish redolent of toasted day-old poppyseed bagels, when beeristas drool at the prospect of possibly someday getting their mitts on a bottle of Westvleteren Abt 12 (generally available only at an out-of-the-way monastery in West Flanders), beer drinkers continue to be dismissed as nacho-inhaling couch potatoes or psychotic lager louts.

You're absolutely right: it isn't fair. A few of us have acceptable, if not flashy, table manners, don't wear stripes with checks, do wear matching socks (mostly, and then only because we buy identical pairs in bulk), and don't live in our parents' basements. Many of us don't riot in the streets if our local team wins a championship. (*Editor's note:* The author of this book lives in Toronto, so he has little experience of winning championships. His point, however, is well taken.)

Things have reached the point that some beer people are accusing other beer people of getting too highfalutin. Hundred-dollar dinners with beer and food pairings and dress codes rub some people the wrong way. Some people feel self-conscious about sniffing their beer before they drink it. Aging beer in sherry casks sounds a bit effete for some beer drinkers, who wonder if they'll be expected to raise their pinky as they drink the stuff (answer: no).

Whatever happened to the innate democracy of beer? Nothing, that's what. The price of cheap wine and cheap beer is still about the same, alcoholic unit for alcoholic unit. But as soon as you start upgrading your wine, you're quickly spending a fair bit more money, while beer drinkers can upgrade for relatively little. How often do you see a $25 bottle of beer, or even six-pack? Not often. How high does wine go? Higher than you can imagine.

I wrote earlier about Sam Adams Utopias, the 27-percent-alcohol (i.e., double the strength of most wines) extreme beer that sells, if you can get it, for somewhere in the ballpark of US$130. But Utopias is cheap compared to the beer unveiled by Carlsberg in 2008. The Danish giant issued a heap of hoopla about something called Vintage No. 1, which comes in a 375-millilitre bottle (roughly half the size of Utopias) and costs—sit down, please—2,008 Danish kroner, or roughly $425 in Canada (if it were for sale in Canada). It's a mere 10.5-percent alcohol, but it's aged in French and Swedish wooden casks, the latter in case you like your beer to taste like your book-shelves. They made only six hundred bottles of the 2008 batch, so you've probably already missed it. And, given that they're not exporting any, you've almost certainly missed it. Which is a pity, because the next one is probably going to cost 2,009 Danish kroner, which is forty-odd cents more.

But even so, a very quick glance at my province's liquor board website offers me a bottle of 2000 Château Le Pin Pomerol, which I'm sure is fairly good, for a mere $5,899, which probably includes the twenty-cent bottle deposit. Getting change back from six big ones represents value in my book, though for that I could get a twelve-pack of Carlsberg Vintage No. 1, with enough left over for a six-pack of Utopias. Or I could buy a Canadian microbrewery. Not just the beer, but the whole damn brewery.

So, beer lovers don't have to worry that we're going the way of the wine industry. We don't have the clothes for it, to begin with. Yes, there are brewers putting pomegranates and vanilla beans in their beer, but not many of them, and you don't have to drink it if you don't want to.

Are there advantages to being a wine person rather than a beer person, apart from what I said earlier about being more attractive to the opposite sex (or the same one, if you prefer) and getting better jobs and intimidating sommeliers? Studies show that wine enthusiasts make more money than beer drinkers, on average. Well, they need to, don't they? At nearly $6,000 a bottle of that LePin Pomerol stuff, they need to be raking it in.

Studies also suggest that wine drinkers are healthier than beer drinkers. Fine, I'll accept that red wine has its share of antioxidants, but wine drinkers are healthier mostly because they're richer. If you were rich, you'd take care of yourself, too. Wealth is a serious incentive to live a long time. Both wine and beer are healthy beverages, and both act as stimulants to the appetite. Charles Bamforth, whom you'll meet in a couple of pages, cites a study in which one Dr. Morten Gronbaek pored over 3.5 million Danish supermarket cash-register receipts (I bet he actually got some unpaid students to do the grunt work) and found that people who bought wine also bought fruit and vegetables and other healthy food, while beer purchasers were picking up potato chips and the like.

And look what happens when we drink outside the home. The wine drinkers are in restaurants or wine bars, so when their appetites get stimulated they wind up eating "nouvelle cuisine" or "*cuisine minceur*," or, as we say in English, "small servings." Which frequently include vegetables. The beer drinker gets peckish and orders a plate of nachos with a side of wings, and maybe a few sour-cream-and-bacon-stuffed potato skins, just in case. Who's getting fat, and why? Maybe if we spat it out—the nachos, I mean—we'd be as healthy as the wine guys. Not to mention that the wine guys go running and spend time at the gym while we're at the pub.

(The general healthiness of wine drinkers is less apparent in the UK, where a 2008 government report decried the high levels of alcohol abuse in the country. The worst offenders appeared to be not the football hooligans and lager louts, but "middle-class wine drinkers." Many English pubs offer a 250-millilitre glass of wine; three of those and you've consumed a bottle, by which time all the *cuisine minceur* in the world won't help.)

Part of the reason, of course, that the beer louts aren't in the fine restaurants is that most fancy-pants eateries treat beer—and beer lovers—with contempt. Ask for a beer in a good restaurant. Go ahead. "We 'ave, erm, Budweiseur, monsieur, or we 'ave Coors Light," you are likely to be told. The smartass thing to do at this point would be to ask for a bottle of Baby Duck. You will be regarded with *horreur* by the *garçon*, at which juncture you note that you just assumed that if they served nothing but mediocre beer they would probably do a good line in mediocre wine. Mind you, you won't get a good table next time you go back, especially if you're still wearing that ragged old brewery T-shirt.

This is not always the case, and a few quality restaurants recognize that beer can be a decent partner for food. Beerbistro in Toronto offers very good food, often prepared with beer, and suggests possible pairings. (They also have wine for the hidebound.) The Spotted Pig in New York City has a Michelin star, but it also offers not just good beer but cask-conditioned ales. As other defenders of beer have noted, the wine drinker will usually have one bottle to last at least most of the meal, whether or not his appetizer has anything in common with his entrée, whereas the beer person can enjoy, say, a wheat beer with her starter, a spicy IPA with her main dish, and a stout or porter with her chocolate dessert. Well, at least if the restaurant allows her to (some jurisdictions allow diners to bring their own wine, but most draw the line at beer, even barley wine).

Beer has a greater variety of flavours than wine, so the beer drinker has more flexibility when matching beer with food. Wine writers begin to hem and haw a bit when recommending wine for practically any Asian food or Mexican food, cuisines that almost cry out for beer. The right beer is a perfect match for chocolate, and you can pick your beer for dark or milk chocolate, bitter or sweet.

And, despite everything you grew up believing, the perfect marriage for cheese is not wine, but beer. One American wine writer has dismissed the combination of wine and cheese as "a train wreck in the mouth." Fair enough: some people enjoy train wrecks. Both cheese and wine tend to coat the mouth, but the carbonation of beer cleans out the palate and prepares it for more cheese. (Cheesy lips can damage the head on your beer, but it's an imperfect world.) I should report that my wine-guzzling copyeditor argues that sparkling wines and high-acid whites cut nicely through the fat in cheese. Let him write his own damn book.

Beer writers are prone to observing that what beer and cheese have in common is grain: beer is fermented grain and cheese is made of grain that has been processed by a cow, sheep, goat, or any number of other animals. This might sound tenuous, but we are what we eat, and, when we eat animals or animal by-products, we are what *they* eat as well. Linking beer and cheese reminds us that both are going through an exciting period of rediscovery, particularly in North America, by imaginative artisans bent on finding new flavours and ways of enhancing old flavours. Some cheesemakers are even putting beer in their cheese, though I'm not aware of any brewers doing the opposite. Look, if you can make a milk stout . . . well, maybe not. I have had some very good beer-and-cheese soup, welsh rarebit made with beer, and even beer-and-cheese-flavoured potato chips. And, of course, if you see bread as simply solid beer, what's nicer than a cheese sandwich washed down with a glass of beer?

Brewing is a more complex process than making wine, and breweries are more technologically advanced than wineries. California beer writer and teacher Charles Bamforth amuses his students by pointing out that Jesus turned water into wine because turning it into beer was technically too difficult. In his book *Grape vs. Grain,* Bamforth also observes that brewers work hard all year round, while winemakers have a very busy spell immediately after the harvest, then sit around for the rest of the year.

Another point Bamforth makes is that nobody accuses winemakers of inconsistency if the 2009 vintage tastes different from 2008. Oh, they say, it was warmer, or windier, or damper, or dryer, or cooler, or the moon was in Sagittarius, so it tastes different this year. End of story, no apologies. Brewers, by contrast, work hard to ensure that, whatever may have gone wrong with the barley harvest or the hop yield, their beer tastes exactly the same as it always did. It's one thing to develop the perfect recipe; it's something else to duplicate it every time.

Given all the spitting and all that trampling of grapes by barefoot peasants, it's difficult to believe that wine is the socially superior drink. According to Tom Standage, author of *A History of the World in 6 Glasses,* wine snobbery dates back at least to the ninth century BC in ancient Assyria. A very rich king named Ashurnasirpal II threw one of the great parties of all time, for which he obtained some ten thousand skins of wine. This had to be imported for the occasion, so it cost ten times as much as the native beer—which made it, by extension, superior. It's the old anything-imported-must-be-better-than-anything-domestic notion, especially if it's ten times as expensive. Even the Assyrians were falling for it, nearly three thousand years ago.

The Greeks enjoyed a better wine-growing climate than the ancient Assyrians, so wine was affordable for far more of the populace. For the Greeks, wine proved their superiority to the beer-drinking barbarians around them. The Greeks were so posh that they mixed their wine with water and discussed philosophy and politics while speaking flawless ancient Greek, which is more than most of us can manage (except for Saskatoon classics prof-turned-brewer Steve Cavan). The Romans and Egyptians didn't speak a lot of ancient Greek, but they adopted the wine snobbery they had picked up from their Greek neighbours.

And the wine snobbery continues, even among people who would be hard-pressed to explain Plato in their own language, let along ancient Greek. In North America, only fifty years ago, a lot of today's wine buffs thought Black Tower was pretty sophisticated, so, if the truth be known, they merely got a head start on the rest of us. We're catching up, though it has to be admitted that the great majority of beer drinkers on this continent are still drinking the beer equivalent of Black Tower, Blue Nun, and Mateus.

It is a point worth making—well, I think so anyway—that beer lovers are less likely to come across as pretentious prats than wine snobs, even when we're rabbiting on about the grilled trout nose we're detecting in somebody's Imperial IPA. It's always worth remembering the gaffes committed by wine people over the years. Recently, we've had a book and at least one movie about the famous wine tasting of 1976, when a jury of French wine judges sampled a number of both French and Californian red and white wines, fully expecting to prefer the local varieties to the vulgar American wines. "Ah, back to France," one of them famously said on tasting a Napa Chardonnay. As we know, in a blind tasting, the French judges voted California wines the best red and the best white. To their *horreur*.

An even better story is one discovered by the superlative Calvin Trillin in 2002 (it appeared in *The New Yorker*), in which he reported that, when tasting wines from black glasses, even knowledgeable wine people sometimes couldn't tell white wines from red. That same year, a Frenchman called Frédéric Brochet gave more than fifty wine hotshots a number of red wines to judge. What they didn't know was that some of them were whites he had doctored to look red. Nobody noticed.

The practice of winemaking and drinking has all sorts of fancy names: oenology, both viniculture and viticulture, vinifaction, and so on. It is telling that most wine-related words are Latinate words, usually a sign of pretension, while the words that describe brewing tend to come from Old English or German (and sometimes Old Norse) and are more fun to say: malt, hop, sparge, wort, ullage, grist. These are good, honest words for a good, honest beverage. In recent years, beer people have adopted the pleasant word *"zymurgy"* for what they get up to, though it means, strictly speaking, the science of fermentation in general, not just for the purpose of making beer. (In looking this up, I found that the last word in my *Shorter Oxford Dictionary* is *"zythum"*: "a drink made in ancient times from fermented malt, esp. in Egypt." It's good to know that, once again, beer gets the last word.)

So, beer or wine? Ultimately, beer is good, wine is good, and sometimes there's nothing like a good gin and tonic. Let's just not be beastly to one another, and let's be flexible in our drinking choices.

Patty O'People: Drinking Outdoors

There are many human activities that just seem better when performed outdoors, and drinking beer is one. Many readers may have observed that the Canadian climate leans toward the harsh end of the scale. There are many weeks—nay, months!—when drinking beer outside would be a self-destructive act almost anywhere in this country.

All the more reason, then, that we are so quick to move outdoors at even the slightest hint of mild weather. And, once there, we are reluctant to move back inside until we begin to see ice crystals forming in our pints—which is often the same day. Just as there are Canadians who don their shorts at the first faint whiff of spring, many Canadians can't wait to sit in the great outdoors, pouring a cold fluid into themselves, regardless of the health risks.

It's the way we are: kind of nuts, in a vaguely charming way. Who is it, after all, that rides snowmobiles out on barely frozen lakes? Who goes skiing in avalanche country? Who cheerfully lives in places fraught with blackflies and mosquitoes? Canadians, my friends.

Anyone who drinks in a Canadian pub with a patio has heard it. It hasn't snowed for a couple of days, the temperature has actually risen above the freezing point, perhaps a crocus has been spotted in a protected, south-facing, sunny spot. Someone, often wearing shorts, will walk into the pub and ask, "Patio open?" Usually, the answer is no, because people who run pubs are generally smarter than their customers, though I can think of exceptions. They also run a legal risk if they allow one of their regulars to freeze to death on the premises, not to mention that it looks bad.

Some of the patio people are out there because they are no longer permitted to smoke indoors. They have been toughened by another long winter of smoking outside, and the prospect of imminent snowfall holds no terror for them. Smokers have a reason to be there.

Some non-smokers are out there, too, but only because they have been browbeaten by their smoker friends or loved ones into endangering their lives on a frozen patio. You see them out there, bundled up and shivering, wishing they were indoors with the sane people. It's too early to be drinking al fresco: the Toronto Maple Leafs are still playing, for heaven's sake. Spring has not yet arrived.

But there is always a core of Canadian drinkers who see supping outdoors as their birthright, as if it's specifically mandated by the Canadian Charter of Rights and Freedoms. Which, for all I know, it might be. And, eventually, summer does arrive, and the patio people don't look so crazy any more.

Though I bet the serious, hard core patio people get irate when they turn up at their favourite patio on a warm day and find it packed with fair-weather pations (a new word I've just made up). Where were these people in March, while I was staking out my position here? I once met a smoking drinker in Vancouver around the time of that city's smoking ban. He was resigned to drinking outside—even Vancouver gets cold sometimes—but he was already expecting to be less than civil when warm weather returned and anti-tobacco pations started complaining about his smoke.

I know pubs where people line up for a place on the patio, even though the place is all but empty inside. Give me patio or I won't drink at all (for the serious drinker, of course, this is just foolishness). Many of the patio people appear to be people who drink only in summer. I don't recognize most of them when they turn up in May. Do they spend their winters in warmer climes, so they can be patio people all year round?

For many Canadians, summer is an opportunity to sit on a dock by a clear lake, listening to a loon and sipping a frosty one. Sounds nice, doesn't it? Almost worth the four-hour drive in dire traffic to get there. Still, if you've planned your life so you don't have to battle a few hundred thousand other motorists trying to get to pretty much the same place you are, then it doesn't get much better.

For the other millions of Canadians without access to cottage country, we are left with a beer and a barbecue in the backyard, if we have one, or the pub patio. A summer long weekend in a Canadian city can be a wonderful experience, what with half the population out of town. The patio lineups mostly disappear, the bustle of city life seems to have vanished. Where is everybody, we ask, but we don't really care. Just keep 'em coming, barkeep. And, unlike our cottaging brothers and sisters, we urban drinkers aren't much worried about bugs. By Sunday afternoon, most of the air pollution caused by all the other city people driving out of town has dissipated, blown away by the prevailing winds and by now quite possibly hovering over someone's cottage miles away.

There's nothing like it. The cool condensation on your beer glass, the tang of chicken wings in the air, tempering the aroma of baking human flesh, the indolence of a summer weekend.

We all know, however, that two of the sworn enemies of beer are light and heat, and a glass of ale that has been sitting in hot sunlight will not last long. This could be part of the appeal of patio drinking: you have to do it quickly before the beer turns ugly. This is particularly true for most mainstream beers which demand to be consumed cold. Anything much above freezing brings out the flavour, and that's the last thing you want.

Drinking beer from a bottle or can would at least keep most of the light off your beer, depending on the colour of the bottle. Cans, of course, keep all the light out, and they get colder faster than bottles, though they warm up faster than bottles (I don't usually condone drinking straight from the bottle or can, as it inhibits the flavour, but as the beer threatens to warm up beyond the realms of good taste, it's not the worst thing). But pub patios offer nice, fresh, draught beer, which is a lovely thing to have, though if you're drinking by the pint you're allowing more beer to get warm. So you have to drink even more quickly, and you can see where this might lead. You might think you're getting sunstroke, but it's something else altogether. (If it's sunstroke as well, seek medical aid.)

Once again, science comes to our rescue. A website called My Science Project brings the hard nose of science to bear on the issues that confront us; that its creators have not yet won the Nobel Prize is an ongoing scandal. The rigours of their methodology can be seen in a series of experiments they conducted—and don't you wish high school science had been half this much fun?—on how to keep beer cool in hot weather.

They began their studies with a number of commercially available beer cozies, both can and bottle cozies. They then moved on to more unorthodox devices, on the assumption that you might be at a cottage, far from a store, but you might have on hand some bagels, doughnuts, or those stodgy, edible things you make out of Rice Krispies. They even provide a recipe for Rice Krispies Treats, in case you have some Rice Krispies, miniature marshmallows, and butter with you. Making a beer cozy of any of these products will help to insulate your beer, though glazed doughnuts fared less well than the others and not as well as a regular foam beer cozy. The Rice Krispies Treat actually performed very well, better than the real beer cozy, but it had a shorter shelf life and attracted ants.

Eventually, the Science Project guys tried Styrofoam, cardboard, bubble wrap, a hand-knitted beer cozy, and even one made of Lego, which looks terrific and works a bit, but not as well as you'd like (rounded Lego pieces that clung more closely to the bottle would help). The knitted cozy performed well, and looked kind of neat, though it didn't do quite as well as a normal foam cozy. It turns out that the Thermos people make a high-tech stainless-steel beer cozy that promises to keep cold drinks colder longer than anyone else's beer cozy, a claim grudgingly acknowledged by the researchers at My Science Project, who were clearly saddened by the poor performance of Lego. The Thermos product is more expensive than a foam cozy—if you shop around, you might get one for about thirteen dollars—and doesn't seem to come in your favourite hockey team colours. Whether this is a drawback is something you'll have to decide for yourself.

I don't know any pubs that offer beer cozies for their outdoor customers, though it seems a patron-friendly policy that might attract pations from far and wide. Mind you, I don't know if the standard cozy would fit a pint glass, and I'm unaware of anyone making them specifically for that purpose. There's a vast sum of cash awaiting someone here: make a pint-sized beer cozy, sell advertising space, lend them out to the patrons, retire somewhere warm.

There are many sorts of patios. There is the basic patio on a sidewalk, usually a few feet from the traffic, with all its charms. More pleasant, as a rule, is the patio out back, usually a greener, quieter place. (This was George Orwell's favourite.) I know such a patio, marred only by management's insistence on spoiling the peace and quiet by pumping pop music of the seventies and eighties into it. Just on the other side of the patio wall is a railway track, and I was pleased, one warm afternoon, that a freight train came roaring along and drowned out most of that song about the guy who's a midnight toker. One of those extremely long freight trains, it was. They talk about the Windsor-Quebec City rail corridor. Parts of this train might have been in both cities.

In many places, you might be lucky enough to find the odd rooftop patio or deck. This can be the best of all, particularly if you have a long climb to make and can justify the entire experience as a fitness program. The beer tastes even better when you've raised a sweat climbing the stairs to get to it. Sitting up on high, the city's bustle still audible but muffled, I almost pity the people swatting away the wildlife up in cottage country, the thought of the long drive home already disturbing their pastoral reveries.

Ah, summertime . . . check. Living easy? Check. Charming server approaching with offer of a fresh pint? Check. Count me in.

The Author Goes Back to School

It used to be that any shlemiel could work in a bar. I've done it myself. Turn up, pour drinks, collect money, discourage fighting. Back when I worked at the Argyll Arms in London, a very long time ago, my boss never even spoke to me about the drinking age and checking ID, or any laws at all. For that matter, when I started drinking in pubs—underage—I was seldom asked for ID, either, unless the bar staff knew the police were on their way.

The world has become a very different place. Look at the Americans (now stop looking at the Americans; they get jumpy when there's too much eye contact, and many of them are armed). There are American pubs in which absolutely everyone gets carded, which at least provides employment for the guy at the door.

Nowadays, you have to take a course to do just about any sort of job. (I can see it for airline pilots and surgeons, people like that, but most careers you learn on the job.) Don't believe me? Take a look at the want ads—if there *are* want ads any more—and you'll see what I mean: your reaction will probably be, "You need a university degree to do *that?*"

Luckily, you don't need a university degree to sling beer, but you do, increasingly, have to pass a test. This is becoming the case in a number of Canadian provinces (though a server I spoke to in a Montreal bar claimed never to have heard of such a thing) and American states. And since January 1, 2008, anyone working in a licensed establishment in Ontario—"all licence holders involved in the day-to-day operations of an establishment, as well as all managers, servers, security staff, and others where required"—must be trained and certified by an organization called Smart Serve. They don't mention it at this point on the official website, but the list even includes golf course marshals. (I used to think that "smart serve" meant that, if you gave your customers a decent measure—and maybe a beermat— you'd increase the likelihood of a tip, but it's now more complicated than that.)

As a customer involved in the day-to-day operations of a number of licensed establishments, I wondered if I could pass the test myself. Some day soon, I suspected, knowing the way these things go, we'll probably have to get a certificate just to get into a pub to drink beer. Beat the rush, I thought. Take the training, pass the test.

There are two ways of completing the Smart Serve training. You can turn up in person, watch the videos, and take the test, or you can do it online in the comfort of your own home—where you can, ahem, enjoy a pleasing beverage as you learn. So online it is.

You'll begin by parting with $36.70 ($34.95 plus $1.75 GST); if your credit card collects Air Inches, you'll be that much closer to that trip to St. John's to drink beer. If you're *in* St. John's, you're already pretty close.

Then you'll do the Online Orientation training, followed by a test they cleverly call a Scavenger Hunt, which makes it sound like more fun than it is. I got four out of five questions right, so I was already right on the money, given that you need a mark of 80 percent or higher on the final test.

And then you begin. The Course Content list is daunting, I have to say. There are six steps before you even get to Module One, but they're mostly a disclaimer that, even though you've taken the course and passed the test, you are not an actual lawyer. That, and a copyright page that says you can't reproduce any of this stuff and sell it or lend it or transmit it to anyone. Perhaps I'm not even permitted to tell you about it, so keep it under your hat. When you've finished this chapter, tear it out of the book and eat it. Wash it down with a hearty IPA.

Module One deals with the effects of alcohol on the human body, which—if you're doing this at home—you're just about now beginning to enjoy. (I'm joking, of course. I'm not taking this lightly, and neither should you. Though, if you've already opened a brew, there's no point letting it get flat.) The first step of Module One takes you to a video, which I'm still waiting to see. That's right: I said I'm still waiting to see it. What did we do with all that extra time back before we waited for things to download? My cable provider runs a series of annoying commercials that show some poor sap who can't get a signal on his cellphone and can't make contact on his laptop, always being shown up by some guy who looks like a younger Stephen Harper, which only makes it worse. Sitting here, waiting for my video to download, I feel like that poor sap, even though my cable provider is the one advertising that this sort of thing needn't happen to me. I'm lucky, anyway, that I have thirty days to complete the course and take the test. I may need that long just to download the videos. I've sent them an email; let's see what happens. I'm guessing that this might be a test of whether I have the patience to work in a bar, let alone be a golf course marshal.

Know any good stories while we wait? A fellow I know in Listowel, Ontario, sent me this story just recently. This pair of Siamese twins—

sorry, conjoined siblings—walk into a bar and grab a couple of bar stools. The bartender, although a man of the world and used to seeing the unusual, is nonetheless a little surprised. He apologizes to the two men for looking at them oddly. "Not to worry," says one of them, "we're used to it. I'm John, and this is my brother Jim. We're joined at the hip, but otherwise we're just a couple of regular guys. We work for a living—well, we work together, as you can imagine. But then, we do *everything* together. In two weeks, we're going on holiday together, off to England."

"England," says the bartender. "Nice place. You'll like it there."

"Oh, we go there every year," says John. "We go for a month, rent a car, tour around."

(Don't worry: I'm monitoring the video download. No sign of life.)

"Jeez," says the bartender, "I envy you that. Great beer over there."

"Oh, we don't like the beer," says John. "We're Molson guys, Jim and me."

"But the scenery," says the bartender, "the history, the culture."

"Frankly," says John, "we can do without all that stuff. Jim and I don't much care for it. Can't make out what the people are saying most of the time."

The bartender is bewildered. "But you go every year. How come?"

John gestures toward his brother. "It's the only time Jim gets to drive."

Well, that's the joke Bill "Army" Armstrong sent me, and I like it fine. But there's still no evidence of cooperation on the video front. I might not know much about computers, but I know how to reboot. See you later.

❧   ❧   ❧

I'm back. I went and had a look at the cat, went downstairs and watched somebody hit a golf shot on the television, then picked up a book. Still no video, no response to my email. I bet if I served a martini to someone underage or someone intoxicated, they'd respond a good deal more quickly than this. They'd be all over me.

It isn't a good start, this. I'm losing confidence. It's an hour later, and now the cat's come to look at me. And still the same message: "Transferring data from smartserve.org . . ."

❧   ❧   ❧

Day 2. I find a different e-address for Smart Serve and repeat my question of Day One. Video still not downloading. Eventually get response to second email, saying: "If you are using Mozilla Firefox as your browser, please switch to Explorer. If you are using Explorer, then check that you have the latest version of the software installed." They didn't mention that before I paid my $36.70.

Later in the day, I get one of those e-announcements that my original email has not been delivered. Even later, the author's technologically advanced wife expresses the possibility that Explorer might not be compatible with the author's Mac. The author expresses the wish that he lived in a simpler era.

❧   ❧   ❧

Day 3. Author receives another announcement that his original email to Smart Serve has not been delivered, not that it matters.

❧   ❧   ❧

Days 4 through 28. The author works on other projects. The publisher who signed the book in the first place announces that he is leaving the company, and very possibly the industry. This happens sixteen days after the author has sent the publisher The Work So Far. Not a good sign.

The author is assured by some people that Internet Explorer can be downloaded on a Mac, but they don't tell the author how. The author's Mac authority suggests he go to a library and use the computer there. The author discovers the impossibility of getting on a library computer, decides that libraries should, in any case, be buying more books rather than providing computers so that the public can access Internet porn without owning a computer. The author finds an Internet café and succeeds in locating the Smart Serve videos, so he is back on track. This adds $5.50 to the $36.70 registration charge. Still, there will be a wallet-sized certificate and a lapel pin at the end of it, if everything goes well.

❧   ❧   ❧

Day 29. The author finally does his homework on the Smart Serve program, learns how many standard drinks a 150-pound, twenty-five-year-old male can consume and still drive a car legally in the province of Ontario (three in one hour, four in two hours, five in four hours). The author becomes familiar with the Signs of Intoxication. Apparently, a bar patron who complains about the price of drinks is displaying poor judgement, a category that also includes buying rounds for strangers, ordering doubles, and making irrational statements. The author reflects on his own shortcomings in this regard.

Similarly, "becoming entertaining, animated, boisterous" is a signifier of the loss of reason, caution, or memory that also leads to lighting a cigarette when one is already lit (that is to say, the cigarette is already lit, not the customer; that goes without saying) or wanting to drive while intoxicated. To me, these activities do not occupy the same level of evil. Becoming entertaining is, I think, not a bad thing at all, certainly compared with wanting to get behind the wheel of a ton or two of machinery. People have been known to receive the Order of Canada for being entertaining. Who knew it was a sign of intoxication?

Reading the assorted Signs of Intoxication—there are five subsections—brought back all sorts of happy memories, though there are things I don't actually remember. If I've ever been drunk enough that I couldn't find my mouth with the glass, it's not surprising I wouldn't be able to recall it. And then there's "bumping into things or people and/or falling down." I can scarcely count myself blameless on that one.

The Smart Serve program seems almost designed to discourage people from entering the hospitality industry. It gives the distinct impression that the only people you're likely to meet will be repeating their stories and jokes, making sexual advances to strangers, knocking over their drinks (or someone else's drinks, which may lead to fights), or complaining about the prices. Even the fellow who appears to be holding his drink well is likely to get into a car and kill people, whose relatives will sue you and your establishment for money you don't have, no matter how expensive your drinks are.

There is, as one licensee has pointed out to me, an inherent paradox in the regulations that govern pubs. You spend good money, and lots of it, to obtain and decorate a space (a "safe and enjoyable atmosphere," as the Smart Serve people express it) and to secure difficult-to-get licences and approval from assorted levels of government, so you can do what, exactly? Sell intoxicating beverages. But the moment one of your patrons actually becomes intoxicated, which might seem the whole point of consuming said beverages, you've landed yourself in a predicament that could cost you your licence and/or land you in court. Is there another business in which selling too much of a product is an offence? I used to work in a bookstore, and at no point was I advised to watch for signs that our customers were acting oddly and buying too many books. "That guy in the Philosophy section has had enough. Get him out of here." Heck, buy enough books and you can make a sexual advance, for all I care.

Since doing my homework for the Smart Serve exam, I have begun to observe pub life in a new and different light. I walk in, and a member of the staff bids me hello in a friendly manner and, possibly, inquires as to my health. How pleasant, one might think. But no. This person, trained under the Smart Serve regulations, is practising what is called "Chat and Check." This person—let's say it's

Christine, an attractive yoga instructor, world traveller, and sporadic slinger of fine ales at Kilgour's Bar Meets Grill in Toronto—is actually trying to determine whether I've already been drinking when I arrive, whether I'm driving, what sort of mood I'm in, and whether I have a designated driver with me. Christine, I have to say, does this apparently effortlessly. You'd almost get the impression she cares.

But Christine doesn't care. She's just looking out for herself and her employers. She's deciding whether I'm a green-light customer— relaxed, comfortable, talkative, happy—or a yellow-light customer. A yellow-light guest becomes giddy, uses increasingly foul language, is "too friendly" to employees and other guests (note to self: stop asking Christine how her yoga classes are going), and threatens to become the "life of the party." Such a guest must be treated with caution. Service should at least be slowed down. Christine can slow me down in several ways: by proposing I eat something, for instance, or suggesting a non-alcoholic beverage, or simply by making herself scarce for an hour or so, neglecting to make eye contact even if I ask her about her damn yoga classes or which continent she's off to next.

Otherwise, the guest may enter the red zone. If Christine spots me buying rounds for strangers, moving in slow motion, or losing my train of thought, such as it is, I'm finished. At this point, Christine needs to take action. It's too late to suggest I order food or try a soft drink.

Luckily, she can't just beat me up at this juncture. Not yet. First, she has to demonstrate concern for my safety, after which she can ask me to leave, while remaining courteous and non-judgemental. If I persist in making unwelcome sexual advances or being quarrelsome, and show no signs of leaving, Christine can take my arm and lead me off the premises. She can use "no more force than is necessary" to remove me, unless she's acting in self-defence (and you know how I get when I've had a few). And once I'm on the sidewalk, she can't use any more force at all, which must be awfully frustrating sometimes.

This being Ontario, where we cling steadfastly to such rules as not wearing white shoes before the May 24 weekend or after Labour Day, there is much stress placed on courtesy in the Smart Serve regulations. Poor Christine has to be courteous to me even as she's popping me one in self-defence ("Take that, Nick, if you don't mind."). If Christine intervenes as I'm entering the place, either because I'm already hammered or because I am in violation of the Kilgour's dress code (and you should see what some people wear to Kilgour's), she is still encouraged to be courteous to me and conduct herself with a professional attitude, not discriminating against me on the grounds of sex, race, disabilty, or appearance.

Though, speaking of appearance, Smart Serve repeatedly stresses one thing about the sort of people who are likely to be troublemakers: they don't dress very nicely. Licensed establishments are strongly encouraged to post dress codes so they can legitimately refuse service to "undesirable persons." Obviously, shirtless, barefoot patrons are to be discouraged, as are those wearing "muscle shirts." That's fine with me: I don't own such a thing, for obvious reasons. (Equally obvious: the reason I don't wear a money belt.)

I am reminded of my old friend John Jackson, back in the early seventies. Outdoor drinking had just begun to be tolerated in this jurisdiction, and a small gathering of us went and sat at a patio on Yonge Street. The sun was beating down, and John was wisely wearing a hat as protection, being an early adopter of male pattern baldness.

A young male server appeared to take our order, and he casually mentioned that he couldn't serve us if anyone happened to be wearing a hat. He cited regulations. Presumably, there was some long-standing ban on men wearing hats in taverns, and the province hadn't got around to amending the rules to adjust for outdoor tippling. Our server courteously asked John to doff his chapeau, an offer John declined. The young man tried cajoling, but John was having none of it. The hat was there to stay, now bring us our beer. "Oh, come on, sir," pleaded the server. "It's not as if you're bald or anything." John glared and briefly removed the offending hat, before we all swanned off to drink elsewhere, probably indoors.

I recall no references to hats in the Smart Serve training modules. Perhaps the muscle shirt is the new hat. What I *did* see in Smart Serve was a reflection of Ontario values: courtesy, restraint, a discouragement of violence, and an acknowledgement that profit is a good thing. One of the methods recommended to stem excessive drinking is to encourage guests to try "premium" brands of alcohol, on the grounds that drinking better will lead to drinking slower, while still assuring good profit for the establishment. Similarly, encouraging food sales slows down alcohol absorption and makes money, while boosting higher-profit-margin non-alcoholic beverages is good for all concerned. Heck, discouraging intoxication is both fun and profitable!

I was, by now, ready to take the test. I had originally thought of taking the test blind (you get two shots at the exam), just to see if I could pass it on the basis of decades spent in licensed establishments, but they don't let you even access the test until you've taken the seven preliminary quizzes and filled in the five checklists. Having come that far, you're free to go. Then I discovered that they allow you two hours to finish the Smart Serve exam (I haven't written a two-hour exam in many decades), and I had a pub to get to. So I put the exam off for . . .

❧ ❧ ❧

Day 30. It's the last-chance saloon for the author. After today, my Smart Serve registration turns into a pumpkin. I rise early, study my blood alcohol concentration charts, run through the Signs of Intoxication again, and take one last look at the types of identification I can accept should I take employment in a tavern. Then I click on Start Quiz and prepare for a two-hour ordeal. Eleven minutes later, I punch in my answer to the twenty-fifth and final multiple-choice question. Almost instantly, I receive congratulations on having passed my test and am awarded certification number e08080100018 and a promise that I will receive my wallet-size certificate and my lapel pin by mail within three to six weeks. (It actually took a week.)

Well, that was easy, once I found a way to watch the videos. I understand more about the pressures on bar managers and staff to keep the likes of me from doing damage to ourselves and others. And I promise Christine at Kilgour's, and all the other servers who have to deal with me, that I'll try not to make inappropriate sexual advances or repeat myself or light two cigarettes or repeat myself or be entertaining. Or, most of all, repeat myself. (And what exactly are "appropriate" sexual advances?)

Now, how do I get a job as a golf course marshal?

The Biggest Damn Beer Company in the History of the Universe

Anheuser-Busch, makers of the world's most successful beer, began with a man named Eberhard Anheuser, who probably pronounced his name in an appropriately Germanic manner: Anhoyser, as opposed to Anheiser or Anhowser, as one usually hears. Eberhard is long gone, so we'll never hear it from his own lips.

In any case, in 1860, the enterprising Eberhard bought the Bavarian Brewery in St. Louis and renamed it E. Anheuser and Co. The following year, Eberhard's daughter Lily married a promising fellow named Adolphus Busch, who eventually went to work for his father-in-law and became president of the company—by now called Anheuser-Busch—when the old man went to the great mash tun in the sky.

Since then, the company has been run by a succession of Busches: August A., Adolphus III, August A. "Gussie" Junior, August A. III, and August A. IV. There was a guy called Stokes in there between 2002 and 2006, and I have no idea how he got there. All these Busches made pots of money, as did some of the people associated with them. Cindy McCain, wife of frequent presidential candidate John McCain, inherited a Budweiser distributorship in Arizona, the third-biggest in the United States, and is said to own as many as 80,000 Anheuser-Busch shares. Budweiser has made the McCains very rich indeed— rich enough to fund countless presidential campaigns.

It had been rumoured since early 2007 that InBev, the Belgian beerhemoth, was on the brink of unleashing its acquisition sharks—if you can, in fact, leash or unleash a shark; you see what I'm getting at—on Anheuser-Busch, and this came to fruition in 2008. After a bit of preliminary foreplay—or chat, as the business people say—InBev made an unsolicited bid on June 11 to buy A-B for US$65 a share, or roughly $46 billion (the share price had been $58.35 before the InBev offer, and had hovered around $47 back in February, before the takeover rumours started.)

I don't live anywhere near St. Louis, Missouri, but even I could hear the spluttering from my den. August Busch IV, the sixth generation of Busches and the big cheese of the operation, led the spluttering. A sale of the company, he insisted, would not happen "on my watch." His father, August Number III, was similarly exercised. Missouri politicians expounded on the evils of foreign ownership of a great American icon, and a protest march was quickly organized in the streets of St. Louis. Barack Obama, then running for president, did a quick check on the number of Democrats Abroad in Belgium (not enough), and announced that he was less than entirely happy with developments. John McCain, the Republican candidate, wisely declined to comment, given that his wife stood to gain large numbers of dollars from the takeover.

Websites were assembled and flags were waved. Americans who had never heard of Belgium were suddenly turning quite nasty about that little country and its thieving, rapacious capitalists. The reigning Busches got their dander up, launched a lawsuit against InBev, and announced that the acquisition would be illegal, since InBev operated in Cuba, in contravention of the Trading with the Enemy Act. The Busches also dropped dark hints that InBev would be quick to cut American jobs, because that's what they were like.

The A-B board simultaneously tried to appease shareholders by promising to cut $1 billion in costs, which sounds an awful lot like cutting American jobs, not that they'd have done anything of the sort. They also tried to buy out the 50 percent of Mexican brewery Grupo Modelo they didn't already own, in an attempt to make the company too expensive for InBev. Not content with these efforts, they also said things about InBev that weren't very nice.

InBev came back, all guns blazing, and proposed a new board for A-B, one that would include August Busch IV's uncle, Adolphus Busch IV. (Don't these Busch people have any other names? Is everybody an August or an Adolphus? They're as imaginative as their beer recipes.) This led to another surge in spluttering and public posturing. A twenty-one-year-old St. Louis man named Jordan Moore made the ultimate gesture by vowing that his plan to have the Budweiser logo tattooed on his right ribcage was now officially scrapped. According to *The Wall Street Journal,* he pledged that, if Budweiser wound up in foreign hands, he would go back to drinking Wild Turkey, the patriotic American bourbon owned by Pernod Ricard, a French company. That's the spirit that made America great.

Unfortunately for the August Busches III and IV, they owned only some 4 percent of A-B stock, less than Warren Buffett, so they had very little power, especially since Buffett and Adolphus IV were expressing an interest in cashing in.

By July 14, InBev had returned with a new offer: $70 a share, or roughly $52 billion. The tough, uncompromising response of the A-B board: Why didn't you say so? Suddenly, the lawsuits were forgotten, and nobody on the board cared whether Jordan Moore got his tattoo or not. Cries of "We're in the money!" ran through the boardroom, and joy reigned supreme (if the estimates of Cindy McCain's share holdings are accurate, the difference between the two InBev offers brought her about four hundred thousand dollars, which is better than I did on July 14, 2008.)

Those Belgians, it turned out, were decent fellows once you got to know them. One is reminded of the line attributed to Churchill when a woman said she'd sleep with him for a million pounds. He offered her ten pounds. "What do you think I am?" she protested. "We've established what you are," he allegedly replied, "we're just negotiating a price."

And the patriots out on the street? Left crying in the beer they now swore they'd drink instead: Miller (owned by the former South African Breweries, today headquartered in London, and now the second-biggest beer company in the world after Anheuser-Busch InBev).

What has any of this to do with Canada? Assuming this takeover goes through (as I write, there is talk of a lawsuit being launched by ten Budweiser drinkers), Labatt will be owned by the Biggest Damn Beer Company in the History of the Universe. As the owner of Labatt, InBev is a major player in the Canadian market. What we have seen since InBev chugalugged Labatt is that the old traditional Canadian brands, like Labatt Blue, have been neglected in favour of the big, globalized brands, brands that get all the marketing dollars. Labatt has been making Bud and Bud Light under licence for some time, and this takeover will make the Bud twins an even closer part of the family. I would expect the Labatt name to decline even further in the future. That Labatt Blue tattoo you're so proud of is likely to look a bit dated.

Sparge That Malt, Pitch That Yeast!

Like many pub-minded people, I am not at my best in the early morning—or any part of morning before opening time, for that matter. So, when the alarm went off at 5:45 one summer Monday morning, I had half a mind (and half a mind's about all I can muster at that time of day, unless I'm just coming home) to turn it off and roll over. But rolling over was not an option. No, I had a mission to fulfill that morning, a world I had to turn into a better place. I was making beer.

Brewing is a by-product of agriculture, and, like farmers the world over, brewers are inclined to be early risers. Ron Keefe is no exception. Ron begins his brewing days at something called 6:30 in the morning, a time that had been only a rumour to me for many years. Like certain degrees Celsius and percentages of alcohol by volume, 6:30 a.m. was, I assumed, a purely hypothetical figure that could possibly be created in a laboratory but was unlikely to be encountered in real life. Well, guess what: it really exists.

Since 1991, Ron Keefe has been the proprietor of the Granite

Brewery in Toronto—not to be confused with the Granite Brewery in Halifax, which is owned by Ron's brother Kevin. Kevin's success in the 1980s led Ron to think there might be something to this brew-pub game, so he learned how to brew beer, which is what he's been doing pretty steadily ever since, usually twice a week—starting very early in the morning.

I am up this early, as is my friend Bill Martin, to help Ron make a thousand litres of his Best Bitter, and there are few loftier goals than that. Ron's Best Bitter, especially in its dry-hopped, cask-conditioned version, is one of those things that makes you think warm thoughts about the human species. Human genius has given us the Goldberg Variations, the infield fly rule, Miles Davis, Stephen Sondheim, Joni Mitchell, the Austin-Healy, *Jules et Jim,* the *Pet Sounds* album, the goal scored by Jimmy Case for Brighton and Hove Albion in the 1983 FA Cup semifinal, one or two other things, and the Granite Brewery's dry-hopped Best Bitter. And what a great country to live in, where beer geeks can, in all seriousness, debate whether the Toronto Granite's Best Bitter is superior to Kevin's version in Halifax.

And what a great country to live in, where a guy with no knowl-edge of biochemistry can step into Ron Keefe's brewery early one morning and play a role in the creation of the great man's iconic ale. I'm not kidding myself here: Ron is not going to stand back and let Bill and me take any liberties with his ale. We're not going to "express ourselves" with any surprise addition of cucumber or bog myrtle. We're going to make Ron's Best Bitter the way Ron wants it made, the way his customers like it. And that's fine by me.

It's excellent beer, just as it is, made in a terrific pub. The Granite is completely wheelchair accessible, yea, even unto the bathrooms, though it's a bit cramped in the brewery, what with hoses, pumps, and things I have no names for. The pub's menu wins prizes for the inclusion of many healthy and vegetarian options, and the place has patios fore and aft for warm-weather drinking. All in all, it's a very good pub, and Ron gives every impression of being the pinnacle of human decency.

That said, I have no illusions about Ron Keefe. I have no doubt that, when he goes home at night, he is as beastly as can be to his wife, Denise, and their children. I'm sure he cusses and waves his arms about and behaves like one of those celebrity chefs. And maybe, when there aren't civilians around, like Bill and me, Ron's like that at his brewpub as well, which is why he has such staff turnover—his average employee lasting no longer than about ten years at a stretch.

All I'm saying is that I've never actually caught Ron Keefe in one of these moments, though I have high hopes this summer morning as Bill and I arrive. He can maintain that calm, cheerful exterior when he's schmoozing with the patrons, but what side will he show us when the kettles are whistling and the yeast is bubbling and a thousand litres of Best Bitter are on the line?

He begins well, letting us in with a handshake and the offer of coffee, but I'm not about to be fooled. It isn't as if you have to get up early in the morning to fool me, but we've all got up early this morning. I see it as a level playing field.

Ron takes us into the brewery. Water is already heating up around us. Ron shows us batches of his Ringwood and Peculiar ales, sitting in open fermenting tanks and topped with big, bloated, bubble-like stuff that looks like old-fashioned doughy dumplings. Yeast has been doing the Lord's work here. Soon, we are helping (or at least staying out of the way) as three kinds of malt start making their way down from a hopper into the mash tun, where they are happily cooked up in nice, warm water. The water runs gently over the malt as it tumbles in; yes, it's the sacred ritual of sparging, and it's happening mere inches away, producing one of my favourite smells. And Ron, sensing he can trust us, gives us complete liberty to add a closely measured quantity of calcium sulphate to harden the water to the right levels (remember that ale likes hard water, lager soft).

The barley in question has already been malted. Very few brewers today do their own malting; it's a cumbersome process that calls for lots of space and specialized equipment. It isn't as easy as stomping on grapes. The principle is that the barley needs to be broken down a bit if it's to work properly. The barley is left to steep in water until it softens and begins to germinate, then it is dried. What we're looking for in barley is the starch, which will be turned into sugar in the mash tun, which in turn will be turned into alcohol by the yeast. But I'm getting ahead of myself.

Meanwhile, Ron is transferring the Peculiar into another tank for its secondary fermentation. This leaves an empty fermentation tank, which requires cleaning. And this is where Bill and I are finally useful. Our Best Bitter will be going into this tank in a few hours, so we want it good and clean. Sparkling, even. The sight of Bill in a fermenting tank, only his head visible, is a life-affirming one. It is the study of a man doing good.

Eventually, by late morning, we have run hot water through our malted barley (mostly two-row Canadian barley from western Canada, along with smaller amounts of imported Carastan and black barley just for fun) three times. Ron, a good teacher who actually runs a course on brewing and beer appreciation at a local community college, shows us the fruit of each part of the process: first dark and sweet, then more amber and less sweet, finally pale and less intense altogether. By now, we have extracted all we're likely to get out of this barley. These three runnings are all finally in Ron's large kettle, and we wait for it to come to a boil.

The mash tun is now empty except for rather a lot of barley that has donated colour, flavour, and sugar to what is still not yet beer. Bill and I are both thinking that something's going to have to happen to all this grain. Like a couple of wusses, we put up no fight when Ron's assistant appears in tall rubber boots and steps into the mash tun with a shovel. To our eternal discredit, neither of us insists on doing the heavy work of shovelling the spent grains into large grain sacks, filling seven and a half of them. This stuff would be ideal to feed to farm animals, but we're in the middle of Toronto, and I can't see my carnivorous cat taking an interest. If I had brought a couple of slices of bread, I could have had what would quite literally have been a barley sandwich, but I hadn't thought of it.

Ron had advised us to bring a book, as there are some longueurs attached to the brewing process, and we are now at such a point. Bill and I read a bit, chat a bit, while Ron takes care of his weekly food specials, deals with phone calls, and gets started on the payroll. He still seems cheerful and more than pleasant. When he returns to us, it is time to add the flavouring hops to the mix. This is exciting. We have a good sniff of the Cascade hop pellets just before they make their ultimate sacrifice. In they go, bringing their own piquant brand of bitterness to the sweetness of the malt. A little later, we add some Irish moss and isinglass finings to help the beer clarify. Again, Ron puts a little murky not-yet-beer into a bottle and adds a bit of the isinglass mixture. Over the next hour, on and off, we watch the liquid turn clear, while everything else separates out.

Isinglass, as you almost certainly know, comes from the swim bladder of the sturgeon, which leads to an amusing discussion of how someone long ago figured out that the swim bladder of the sturgeon could be used to clarify beer. Never underestimate the resourceful- ness of the human brain. If life gives you lemons, make lemonade. If life gives you the swim bladder of a sturgeon, make your beer turn clear. Strict vegans wish there were no animal products in their beer; the good news is that it all drops away, so there isn't any of it in the finished product. I hope this makes you feel better.

The liquid that isn't yet beer bubbles away in the kettle, and we break for lunch (fish and chips for me, beef curry for Bill) and a pint of Ron Keefe's excellent beer. After lunch, we add some Fuggles hop pellets to contribute aroma to the beer, let it brew for another five minutes, then switch the kettle off. Ron does some interesting things with hoses, which involve cooling the fluid-that-isn't-beer and transferring it to a tall fermenting vessel, the very one that Bill and I had scrubbed to a fare-thee-well.

We are now getting close to the crucial part of the operation. Ron disappears into the walk-in cooler and returns with a white plastic pail filled with the mysterious critter known as yeast. As reported elsewhere in this book, humans didn't understand what yeast was, or how it worked, until Louis Pasteur worked it out in the nineteenth century. That's many millennia of ignorance, yet we got along fine. Eventually, we figured out that there was such a thing—monks in the Middle Ages called it "godisgoode"—and knew enough to put it in our beer. Or, strictly speaking, to put it in what was to become our beer. Without fermentation, there is no beer. Without yeast, there is no fermentation.

Everything we have done so far is prelude to the moment of truth: pitching the yeast. Ron stirs up the pail of yeast—Ringwood yeast, from the brewery of that name in England—and hands me the pail. Solemnly, I climb the ladder, trying not to spill the precious pail of tiny single-celled life forms, and, looking down into the thousand litres of what is still not beer, I empty the pail. I hear Bill, standing near the foot of the ladder, murmur, "Go, my beauties!" Millions of tiny yeast cells set to work, doing what they do best, what they were born to do. Through the almost-beer they scurry, eating sugar and turning it into alcohol. As Bill eloquently puts it (he's in advertising, so has a gift for words), the yeast cells are busily shitting and burping. They shit alcohol and burp carbon dioxide. They're making beer and carbonating it at the same time. They really are little beauties.

By now it is mid-afternoon, and there is no more we can do for our beer for now. We have handed control over to the wily and industrious yeast. Ron, still as cheerful as when we started, invites us to join him at the bar for a glass of ale. Ron's assistant is going to come in and clean out the vessels we haven't. Bill and I, taking instruction well, accompany Ron to the bar and drink beer. He even gives us nifty certificates to proclaim our usefulness in a brewery. Naturally, at the bar, we choose the dry-hopped, cask-conditioned Best Bitter. It's a bit like one of those cooking shows, where they put something into the oven and, seconds later, they're eating it. Bill looks up from his glass and announces happily that he can taste the Cascades and he can smell the Fuggles.

When we finally leave the Granite, tired and content, we're already making plans to return when "our" Best Bitter is ready to be served. Hope it's all right.

(It was just fine, thanks to Ron.)

Trains and Boats and Planes (Plus a Couple of Greyhound Buses, Not to Mention Plenty of Urban Mass Transit): Looking for Canada's Beer

The Author Gets Out of the House

I have made the point in this book that it is the nature of beer in Canada that, if you want to drink what is being brewed in this country, you have to leave your couch and your cat and hit the road. If I say to you, "Get out of town," I mean just that. Don't talk to me about beer in Canada until you've drunk beer *in Canada.* The national brands don't count.

In any case, the summer of 2008 was, by anybody's reckoning, a sorry (and soggy) disgrace in the city I inhabit. The winter that preceded it was just as unspeakable, leading local optimists to anticipate a flawless summer. Boy, were they wrong. The advantage of record summer rainfall, unlike near-record winter snowfall, is that you don't have to shovel it, but you don't have to like it, either.

So it was a blessing that I spent so much of the summer of 2008 outside Toronto. Whenever I returned home, usually to become reacquainted with my umbrella, I'd spend my time mopping out the basement or cutting the damn grass that kept growing long after it usually dies.

But inevitably it was soon time to ship out again. Having studied the Geist magazine beer map of Canada, compiled by Melissa Edwards, I thought of getting to places that seemed relevant to the beer lover, but I feared setting myself up for disappointment. Would there be anything to drink at Stubby Lake, Ontario? Might I go thirsty on Brewer Bay in Nunavut? How about on Newfoundland's Beerberry Islands, or in Beersville, New Brunswick? Is there a barley sandwich on Lac Barley, Quebec? Would there be a brew on Mount Brew, British Columbia?

In the end I decided to limit myself to an urban landscape, where there were more likely to be breweries and pubs. If I didn't get to your village, town, or city, I apologize, but it's a very big country. Goodness, it's a big country. Feel free to drop me a line and tell me what I missed. (I've already been blasted for not getting to Thunder Bay, Ontario, which I am informed is a hotbed of hard drinking. On any evening, says the fellow at the end of the bar at Kilgour's, you can see three distinct groups of drinkers: Irish drinkers, First Nations drinkers, and Finnish drinkers, all doing what they do best, or at least most often.)

You also won't find much in this section about drinking in Canada's largest city. Unless you live in Toronto, you won't want to hear about what goes on in our national capital of self-centredness. In any case, there's far too much of that sort of information in my last book, available in fine bookstores everywhere.

I calculate that I boarded twelve airplanes (two of which had just been switched because of faulty equipment, which is only slightly comforting), five trains, two Greyhound buses, and one boat, which doesn't count any number of city buses, taxis, subways, light rail systems, and the delightful urban ferries in Winnipeg and Vancouver. It makes for a bad carbon footprint, but I didn't drive anywhere, and I made every effort to drink local beer wherever I went. That was the whole point. Sometimes you have to be environmentally suspect to be environmentally sound. But don't tell David Suzuki anyway.

While everybody else in North America was lining up to see the new Batman movie, I was out there somewhere in Canada, drinking beer. Maybe somewhere near you, maybe sitting a couple of bar stools away from you. I was the guy looking around, maybe asking the bartender a question or two about local laws and customs, jotting down a few notes. Maybe we spoke briefly, you and I, before I headed out to the next place. Maybe you recommended the next place, in which case, I thank you. If you went on a brewery tour in the summer of 2008, I might have been there, too—the guy with the beard, asking the occasional question and looking skeptically at the tanks and kettles. I might have been with my wife, or with a friend or two, or maybe I was flying solo. But I was there.

The following chapters are the product of the pages of notes I kept as I crossed Canada. My notes were not always totally legible afterwards, but *you* try writing coherent notes in a dark pub after a day's battle with the taps. Just try it, and you'll see.

What I learned on my travels is that Canada is a dandy country, filled with all kinds of interesting people, a few of whom brew beer. More of them operate pubs, bars, taverns, and taprooms, a few dozen of which I investigated, from St. John's to Victoria. I mentioned already that Canada is a big country, but I'll say it again: Canada's a bloody big country. And, bless us, we grow a lot of barley. And we need to, what with all those hard-drinking Yukoners and Newfoundlanders.

There are many ways to travel across this country, and lots of reasons to do so. My reason was beer. Well, that and the places that serve beer. I didn't get to a lot of museums or art galleries or historic sites or late-summer fairs. I was on a mission. I met a lot of bartenders and barflies, and a few brewers. Those are my people, and I salute them.

Party Towns:
Drinking in Halifax
and St. John's

Halifax is a party town. I have that on the authority of Doug, our cab driver, as we journeyed into the city from the airport. If you've ever flown there, you'll recall that the Halifax airport is roughly half-way from wherever you've come from to downtown Halifax. Still, it's a pleasant, if pricey, drive through a largely rural setting, and it gives you plenty of time to get to know your cab driver.

Doug was a plain-spoken Maritimer who made it clear that he was not a big booster of Toronto, the city we had just left. He had experienced some bad times in Canada's largest city back in the early 1990s, and we could only tut-tut as he told us about them. His best story came as we arrived at our hotel. What was shaping up as another unhappy ending had a surprise twist when the Toronto police officer bearing down on him suddenly said, "Doug?" What are the odds of the copper being a transplanted Haligonian who had known Doug in high school? No charges laid.

Anne and I had flown the friendly skies of Air Canada (insert your own gags here) to test Doug's thesis about Halifax being a party town. Well, we hadn't heard Doug's thesis when we caught the plane, but it's no secret that Halifax is a lively drinking town. Doug told us that Halifax has more bars per capita than anywhere else in North America, though I've no idea where you find figures like that. (Actually, you can find all kinds of figures of that sort, each of which contradicts all the others. Try it on your favourite search engine and you'll see. There's hardly a town on this continent that doesn't claim to have more bars per capita than anywhere else, with the possible exception of Salt Lake City. Still, Halifax is a plausible choice. All those students and sailors, not to mention a committed community of pub-minded locals, add up to a lively drinking scene.)

In a very brief visit, we got to ten Halifax pubs and a brewery tour, which scratched (or, more accurately, tickled) the surface. We could have hit more than ten, but we did some duplicating (and we did enter a couple of other places and, after a cursory glance, leave without imbibing). We hit Rogue's Roost—a very good brewpub with a fine Weizen and an altogether serviceable IPA while we were there—twice, and Tom's Little Havana no fewer than three times. Tom's had been recommended to me by someone I've met exactly once, with the words "just your sort of place, I think," which was an eerily on-target appraisal. It was very much my sort of place: a bit quirky, friendly staff, nice-looking room, good beer. Since Halifax went non-smoking in late 2006, Tom's tribute to tobacco is now merely decorative, but there are lots of handsome cigar boxes on display. If you go to Tom's bathroom and then, later in the day, go to the Rogue's Roost bathroom, you may feel you've entered another dimension, but maybe it's just the IPA talking. (Try it yourself, and you'll see what I mean.)

Apart from the two principal brewpubs—Rogue's Roost and the excellent Granite Brewery (which closed its brewpub doors in 2009, but whose beers can still be found at the handsome Henry House)—

most of the quality beer to be had in the greater Halifax area comes from the Garrison and Propeller breweries. And the beer we kept returning to was Garrison's Imperial Pale Ale, named Beer of the Year at the 2007 and 2008 Canadian Brewing Awards. It's a big, hoppy beast of a beer (70 IBUs, as mentioned earlier), and at 6.9 percent alcohol it demands the drinker's respect. And it certainly got mine.

Back in 1820, which is going back a bit, a man named Alexander Keith opened a brewery in Halifax. There was a large British military garrison in town, and every soldier in it was entitled to a gallon of ale a day. Anybody who didn't open a brewery in Halifax in 1820 was a fool, and Alexander Keith was no fool. He also had the good fortune to be a trained brewer. You can see where this is going: commercial success, great wealth, social and political clout.

From the beginning, if we are to believe everything we're told in Halifax, Keith's trademark beer was his India Pale Ale, a beer he learned to make during his apprenticeship back in England. (Keith was Scottish, but, according to what I was told at the brewery, learned his brewing in England.) The India Pale Ale style, as you likely know, was devised during the period of the British Raj in India. Life in India had its charms for the Brits, but they missed their beer. By the time the beer made its way by sea to India, it had gone off. There are two ways to make beer last longer: add more hops (one of nature's great preservatives) or make the beer stronger (alcohol being another of nature's great preservatives). So, British brewers began making a beer for export that was hoppier and stronger. Now, if you've tasted Keith's IPA, you may have detected the relative shortage of a hop character. You may also have noticed that it's no stronger than, say, Molson Canadian. This is an India Pale Ale that might stand up to the trip across the harbour to Dartmouth, but not likely as far as India, even with today's transportation advances.

That said, I felt an obligation to you, the reader, to go on the Keith's brewery tour. Without asking for it, I was given the seniors' price, so I would suggest going in the morning after a fairly full day of drinking Garrison's Imperial Pale Ale. You might pass for a senior, too.

Saving two dollars was a good start. I should observe that I've been on quite a number of brewery tours in my day—big breweries, small breweries, and breweries in between. The silliest tour was the Anheuser-Busch brewery in Los Angeles, a very long time ago. I don't know what it's like now, but then, they sent you hurtling through the brewery in a sort of monorail-like contraption, then they set you loose in a large garden with several beer bars and rather a lot of exotic birds. There's nothing like drinking beer (or at least Michelob, if you could find that bar) and gawking at ostriches and emus.

There were no exotic birds at the Keith's tour, or at least I didn't notice them. Usually, brewery tours involve an employee (though once I got the brewer's mother, which takes some beating) taking you through the place, pointing out vats and kettles and, if you're really lucky, a bottling plant. At Keith's, you get actors. When I say "actors," I didn't ask to see their Equity cards. They were certainly pretending to be people they weren't, which I suppose makes them actors.

The conceit is that you're visiting Keith's brewery in 1863, which conveniently sidesteps the awkward facts that Keith's itself was bought out by the Oland family in 1928 and then sold to Labatt in 1971. The names Oland and Labatt do not crop up on the tour.

I was one of nine time travellers that particular Friday, greeted by a pleasant and comely young woman purporting to be representative of nineteenth-century Maritime womanhood. She had her hands full trying to remain historically correct while asking us to turn off our cellphones. Being fairly typical members of the human species, we were faintly embarrassed by all this pretending, but there was no turning back now. We'd paid our money, even if I'd paid two dollars less than most of the rest. (Later, during the sampling part of the tour—always the most popular part of any brewery tour—we were encouraged to say "Aye!" if we wanted a second sample. I was the only one to call out, which was a reflection either of the beer or of the diffidence of a group of strangers in a peculiar situation. Or of my drinking problem.)

Our guide abandoned us in a room, where we watched a historically accurate video about Alexander Keith and the history of his company, after which another performer took us to see the mandatory brewery tour kettles, mash tuns, and so on. Because it's 1863, he was under no obligation to inform us that the real Keith's brewery today is actually in the north end of town.

Soon, we were taken to the Stag's Head—for all we knew an accurate portrayal of a Halifax tavern of the day, where we got up to two samples of Keith's range of brews, plus some songs and an amusing story. To my surprise, I won a game of three-card brag—pure luck, I assure you—and our original guide reappeared and led us to the gift shop while singing "Farewell to Nova Scotia," even though I wasn't leaving until the next day.

To the best of my recall, this was the eighth brewery tour of my life. It was certainly the cheesiest. On at least two occasions, we were asked to recall the Keith's slogan: "Those Who Like It, Like It a Lot." Which has always struck me as an odd company slogan, appearing to acknowledge that many people don't much like the beer at all. (It's up there with Carlsberg's "Probably the best beer in the world." Well, is it or isn't it?)

The Keith's folk are selective in the sort of advertising they want us to remember. We were noticeably not asked to recall the television campaign that featured an angry Scotsman who flew off the handle at any perceived slight to his favourite beer, which he apparently liked a lot. This came at a time when half the commercials one saw on television had angry Scotsmen delivering rants about something or other. When Billy Connolly does rants, they're funny. The Keith's angry Scotsman was just annoying. The campaign was cancelled, not because viewers turned against it, but because the actor playing the role was charged with possession of child pornography. This is not mentioned on the Keith's tour—not that I was expecting it to be. (It might explain why, at the very beginning, we were informed that the people we would meet on the tour were living in 1863 and could not be expected to answer questions about what might happen after that year, any more than we can foresee what is to come.) And I'm sure that the four actors who steered us around the brewery have impeccable and wholesome morals.

I'm sure of that because the actor in the commercial actually lived in Toronto, that centre of Canadian vice and degradation. (What am I saying? The idea of vice in Toronto is having a beer at lunch, or leaving work five minutes early on Friday. Still, let's pretend that Toronto is a centre of vice and degradation.) Halifax, on the other hand, is a damn nice place filled with damn nice people. If necessary, I will remind you of the example of Jennifer Clarke, the Halifax beermonger who saved a customer's life in 2008, mentioned a few chapters ago. I'm considering starting a Jennifer Clarke Appreciation Society. Someone ought to.

Haligonians—and you have to love a place whose residents are called Haligonians—are the sort of people who immediately stop their cars when they see a Torontonian jaywalking. Not even jaywalking: they'll stop if they see you on the sidewalk, looking as if you're possibly thinking about jaywalking, perhaps later in the day, maybe after you've had a bite to eat. Haligonians seem the sort of people who, if they think you're considering having a bite to eat, will recommend where to go and then pick up your tab.

No wonder so many Torontonians move to Nova Scotia: you can walk anywhere you like and nobody will run you over. [*Editor's note:* Our legal advisors discourage readers from taking the author's advice about jaywalking in Halifax. The motorist approaching you as you blithely step out into the street may be a Torontonian driving a rented car. You will be dead meat.]

Vancouver used to be like that in the 1970s, back when only a relative handful of Torontonians lived in that city. Toronto was like that as recently as 1614, the year before Europeans arrived. I'm not sure when Toronto got its first automobile, but you can be sure a pedestrian was despatched to his or her doom shortly thereafter.

But—as I persist in pointing out—I digress. Halifax is a city Canadian drinking folk need to experience, and that means you. (If you go to Maxwell's Plum in Halifax, you'll like the array of draught beers, but be sure to ask for a room-temperature glass, not the face-numbing mugs they haul out of the freezer.) But we had to bid farewell to the Garrison Imperial Pale Ale and make our long way out to the airport again, to catch a plane for . . .

❦ ❦ ❦

St. John's. It's funny, this half-an-hour-later-in-Newfoundland business, because it's actually the other way around. Things happen half an hour *earlier* in Newfoundland, though you wouldn't necessarily notice it. The sun comes up first in Newfoundland (at least on those days when the sun comes up at all), before even the keenest Ontario workaholics are stirring. Well, the really keen workaholics with a two-hour commute are up, but that's about all, really.

If you think people in Nova Scotia are nice, wait till you get to Newfoundland. Lord-a-mercy! Though, in my experience, you're more likely to get hit by an internal combustion device in St. John's than in Halifax, not that it actually happened. We did notice that St. John's has some of those pedestrian lights that tick off the seconds remaining before the light changes. There's at least one that gives you a full minute to cross the street. Motorists wouldn't stand for that in Toronto, I can tell you.

There are few more touchy phrases in Canada than "distinct society," though I suspect "notwithstanding clause" and "*Hockey Night in Canada* theme song" come close. And I don't want to get anyone worked up, but if Newfoundland isn't a distinct society, I don't know what is.

You don't go to St. John's for the weather, unless you're an oar short of a dory. What does it tell you that the local hockey team is called the Fog Devils? (And that doesn't even take into account the snow, the rain, the wind, and the cold.) The day before we left Halifax, the weather forecast was still predicting cold, wet days for St. John's. Anne, a direct descendant of Pollyanna, said to me, as she's said so many times before, "Oh, they don't always know what they're talking about." And, as usual, she was right. Shortly after we arrived, the sun cleared out the last of the mist and the temperature jumped.

It's not a big place, St. John's, though at roughly 100,000 souls (maybe 180,000 if you include the surrounding area), it's a damn sight bigger than Deer Lake (4,827) or Dildo (3,007). Halifax, to the Torontonian, seems a wonderfully compact place, and St. John's isn't much different, though it sure is hilly. Its harbour is a busy working harbour, which keeps the city from being quaint. From just about anywhere in central St. John's, you're looking across the harbour at a bunch of Irving Oil stuff, and that's certainly not quaint, either. St. John's is a small city on a rocky island on the distant edge of a large continent, an appreciable distance from just about anywhere, which also doesn't lend itself to quaintness.

Our cab driver on the way out of town observed that there were two kinds of jobs in Newfoundland: good jobs in oil or minimum-wage jobs. Many Newfoundlanders, of course, are living and working elsewhere at any given time. A few, like Rick Mercer, are entertaining us from Toronto. Many others are in places like Fort McMurray, Alberta.

A traditionally marginal economy and geographic remoteness, to say nothing of the fog and snow, have created a people of great humour. It is no coincidence that so many Canadian comics of recent years hail from the Rock. And they're not just funny; they even talk funny. I suspect you have to leave the safety and sophistication of St. John's to hear

Newfoundland English as it is properly spoken. Certainly, I didn't hear it at the airport or at our hotel, but I heard it at a place called Kelly's Pub on George Street.

George Street is perhaps the most famous street in Newfoundland, known for housing almost nothing but pubs. I don't know if St. John's boasts of having more pubs per capita than anywhere else, but George Street claims more pubs than any street practically anywhere. You'd expect to run into nothing but tourists on George Street, but Kelly's Pub seemed full of locals. Next to us at the bar was a fellow named, apparently, Onion, a thoroughly genial barmate who bought us a drink for no apparent reason. Had this been an Ontario bar, our Smart Serve–trained bartender would have recognized "buying drinks for strangers" as evidence that Onion had reached the red zone of drunkenness, but the charming young woman behind the bar showed no signs of giving our new friend the heave-ho.

Onion and his two friends (called Sage and Garlic, for all I know) were engaged in debate about the film *An Officer and a Gentleman,* a film neither Anne nor I had seen. We were thus ill-equipped to take sides on whether it was a "gay" movie or not. One of Onion's friends argued that any film with F-18s in it was, by definition, "gay," a position I found oddly difficult to dispute. The same guy took Onion to task for not being more open-minded about the subject. "As a New-foundlander," he said, "I would hope you were less narrow-moinded."

It is said that Newfoundland English is a dialect, not an accent, another position I can't dispute. One could comprehend most of what Onion and his friends were saying, but there were invariably words one couldn't make out. It was like being back at Mondial de la Bière in Montreal: you understand much of what you're told, but there's always a key word that calls the whole sentence into doubt.

For a pub in a tourist area, Kelly's attracted a crowd of locals, certainly in the afternoon. As we left, a taxi rolled up, and we turned to see one of the bar staff helping a good-natured, elderly barfly to his cab. I'm not in need of that service yet, but I like to think that, when the time comes, I'll find a pub that takes care of me. It's in their best interest, of course, but it says something of the community nature of a pub that it looks after its people.

There are companies that offer commercial pub crawls on George Street, for tourists who don't know how to go into a pub by themselves. I am informed that these events include such traditional Newfoundland activites as kissing a cod and slamming down a measure of Screech. Sophisticated drinkers scarcely need such molly-coddling. Nor do we need to get intimate with a stuffed fish. Mind you, I don't have a certificate declaring me an honorary Newfoundlander, but I'm going to be brave about it. I'm happy that none of the barkeeps we dealt with in St. John's even suggested that we indulge in these "ancient" practices. They could tell we weren't local, but at least we didn't come across as total tourists.

One bartender advised us to stay clear of George Street, for purposes of tourist avoidance, though he acknowledged that we might want to visit O'Reilly's for the music. They're a musical lot in the Atlantic provinces. We heard some live music in Halifax, but you can scarcely get away from it in St. John's unless you go to bed early (about noon or so), which would be a mistake. We wandered into O'Reilly's our first evening, coughed up two five-dollar cover charges, and spent the next few hours in the company of Fergus O'Byrne, a Dublin-born Newfoundlander who used to be in the band Ryan's Fancy. Was he something to behold? He was indeed. He did a long solo set of mostly traditional songs, after which he was joined by three younger musicians.

The place had been somewhat busy when we arrived, but soon it was heaving with people. It seemed likely that everyone in St. John's was there. Indeed, I know exactly two people in St. John's, and

didn't they come dancing into view as the band played? We had
stumbled into the right place on the right night, though for all I know,
O'Reilly's might be the right place every night.

The following evening, acting on a hot tip from a bartender,
we went to a pub called the Ship to see a significantly folkish trio
called The Once. And no, they weren't opening for And Future
King. We had been told by another bartender that they were three
of Newfoundland's best actors and three of Newfoundland's best
musicians, which seemed to me to be hogging it all a bit. Mind you,
the bartender who told us this was himself an actor who had just
come from rehearsing a production of *The Merry Wives of Windsor*,
which he said was being done in a Southern Reconstruction–era
setting. Apparently, Falstaff comes across as something between
Foghorn Leghorn and Colonel Sanders, but Tim, the thespian barkeep, insisted that it actually worked. Tragically, we'd be leaving
town before it opened.

Back on the subject of The Once, Tim sounded unsurprised that
these three performers were multitalented. "As we like to say here in
Newfoundland," he told us, "we're maggoty with talent." I don't know
about maggoty, but The Once were very good, singing and playing a
variety of styles from contemporary to traditional, often in three-part
harmony, and sometimes in the sort of a capella arrangements that
make you glad to be human and not, oh, a garden slug.

We didn't spend all our time in pubs, you understand. We were
certainly prepared to, but the suddenly glorious weather got us out
and about and up the way to Signal Hill, which must have some
of the best vistas east of the Rockies—certainly the best vistas you
can enjoy on a short walk from the centre of a city. From there, we
walked to Quidi Vidi, a picturesque village just outside St. John's on
a postcard-worthy cove. Quidi Vidi—pronounced most commonly
Kiddy-Viddy, which almost smacks of child pornography, which I
probably wouldn't have thought of if I hadn't been reminded of

Keith's advertising campaigns a number of pages ago—is the home of the Quidi Vidi Brewery, and if there's a more scenic brewery in the country, I've yet to see it. And I've seen a few.

The building was designed as a fish-processing plant, just in time for the Cod Moratorium of 1992. Not long afterwards, aspiring brewery owner David Rees heard of the vacant building a few minutes outside St. John's and scooped it up. If you go to Quidi Vidi on a Sunday, you'll find that the only bar in the village is closed, so the only way to slake the thirst you've developed from walking all that way is to go on the brewery tour. No actors this time, just a droll local fellow named Charlie with a good line in stories.

Newfoundlanders are not an abstemious lot, heaven knows. Only Yukoners drink more than Onion and his mates, but they're both well above the national average, according to the Brewers Association of Canada, who keep good records of this sort of thing, so ought to know. (Quebec comes next, followed by Alberta; mind you, there are a lot of Newfoundlanders in Alberta these days, skewing the figures there.) And what Newfoundlanders drink is beer and rum. Look behind the bar in a St. John's pub and you'll often see one bottle of vodka, one bottle of gin, but several bottles of rum. And usually lots of beer.

If you were with me a number of chapters ago, you may recall we spoke, you and I, about the difficulties of transporting beer across provincial boundaries and of getting beers accepted by provincial liquor boards. The effect of this situation, apart from making brewing a largely provincial issue, is that smaller provinces are less likely to attract bold brewers. You need a critical mass of beer drinkers if you're going to hit the market with something that isn't mainstream.

And that's the difficulty with Newfoundland, a province with a population of just more than half a million, even if they drink half again as much beer per capita as British Columbians. There just aren't enough Newfoundlanders, at least not in Newfoundland.

They're loyal to their own brands—you don't have to explain the values of buying locally to Newfoundlanders. The problem for finicky beer drinkers from away is that the local beers aren't terribly exciting. The beer that is probably Quidi Vidi's best, 1892, named for the year of the fire that ravaged central St. John's, is described by the brewery as "generously hopped," which is true in comparison to most other local beers. Newfoundland's other microbrewery, Storm, makes a decent enough Gold and a similar Red (apart from the colour, they're not terribly different, though the Gold might have a bit more body), but again, they don't make you jump up and down with pleasure. There's pleasure in it, all right, but not jumping-up-and-down pleasure. Quidi Vidi was close to launching a new beer called Iceberg, the water for which was being harvested from icebergs. Well, it's a change from mountain streams and glaciers, but it had not been unleashed when we were there.

The enterprising beer tourist will be tempted to try some of the local brands made by the corporate giants. Recognizing the fierce independence of the local drinker, both Molson and Labatt sell beers made exclusively for the Newfoundland market that are unknown in central Canada. Labatt, in the 1990s, launched a marketing campaign for a lager called Blue Star with the following inspirational words: "Blue Star is the ultimate Newfoundland beer, for Newfoundlanders, by Newfoundlanders." Blue Star was competing with a popular Molson product called Black Horse. Labatt also has an ale called Jockey Club, while Molson counters with Dominion Ale and India Beer. I'm not saying these are life-altering beers; I'm only saying you'll be hard-pressed to find them anywhere else (and the labels don't always tell you who makes them).

Anyway, back at O'Reilly's on George Street, we're enjoying the music of Fergus O'Byrne when, as if in a dream, the only two people I know in St. John's appear before us on the dance floor. She is Janet Harron, formerly a book publicist in Toronto. He is Liam McKenna, a brewer of some renown. They're both good at what they do, and they look good on the dance floor, too. They've relocated to St. John's because Liam is opening a brewpub.

The YellowBelly Brewery and Public House is located in a wonderful old building built after the Great Fire of 1846, which is not to be confused with the Great Fire of 1892. When you're in St. John's, you'll soon be told that the buildings that survived the 1892 fire usually have gabled roofs, whereas those that came after tend to have flat ones. (You learn something on every page in a book like this, don't you?) The building is on what is known as Yellow Belly Corner, named for the yellow sashes worn by one of the Irish gangs that lived and fought in early nineteenth-century St. John's. It's three and a half storeys, plus a basement, all of which will be used to fill locals and visitors with quality ale and food.

Sadly, the complications of restoring a building of historic importance (and, let's face it, the complications of getting anything done anywhere) had delayed the opening of YellowBelly, and the pub was still not open when I was there. (There was a pub in Halifax a few years ago that had been on the brink of opening for some years, and for all I know, there may still be Haligonians who refer to it as the Opening Soon, after the sign that hung in the window for what apparently seemed a lifetime.)

YellowBelly finally did open, after a few false starts, and a welcome addition to the St. John's drinking scene it seems to be. It's owned by the guys who own O'Reilly's, so they know how to get a lot of human beings into a big space, and they had the good sense to hire Liam McKenna to make their beer. Liam is an infectiously enthusiastic young man. When you ask him if he likes Newfoundland and St. John's, you don't get a simple affirmative answer; no, you get: "Magical place. Truly inspiring: the people, the music, the landscape, the weather, the sea. We feel very fortunate to be here." That would be a yes, then.

When I talked to Liam at O'Reilly's, he was enthusiastic about Fergus O'Byrne, whom he praises as a national treasure, not that I disagree. Like many professional brewers, Liam started as a home brewer, and he originally planned to go into the wine business. Well, it's all fermentation, isn't it? While at the University of Guelph, he taught a lab course in industrial microbiology, which was about how to make beer, wine, whisky, yogurt, cheese, antibiotics, and heaven knows what else. Luckily for the beer world, he wound up in our favourite trade, working early on for the Conners brewery, which will be warmly remembered by many Ontario drinkers. One of his higher-profile gigs involved settling in Dublin for a spell with the Dublin Brewing Company. Brewing a stout in Dublin, the home of Guinness, is cheeky. To brew a stout in Dublin that's better than Guinness is to risk one's health, and he's been back in Canada for some years.

Liam acknowledges that Newfoundland, albeit a major beer-drinking province, is not an adventurous beer-drinking province, and he hopes to play a role in stretching the taste buds of his new locals. Not that he's going to do anything certifiable, you understand. He knows he's not going to fill one of the biggest locations in St. John's by brewing extreme beers. There aren't enough beer geeks in Canada, let alone Newfoundland, to fill four and a half storeys.

He started with three beers, to which he has added his St. John's stout. He calls Wexford Wheat "a crossover product," an American-style wheat beer he hopes will draw in untrained drinkers and, with any luck, get them moving on to bolder beers, like his Pale Ale and Irish Red. He hopes to expand to seasonal beers, and he's also thinking of larger facilities beyond the pub itself. Within the pub's brewery, he's using state-of-the-art Ziemann equipment made in Japan, and he has roughly the same capacity as Toronto's Granite Brewery. It sounds as if Liam's going to be in Newfoundland for some time to come. Janet's working at the dean's office at Memorial University, and they seem as happy as cods' tongues.

Speaking of which, I had always thought of cods' tongues as more a mythological dish than something you could actually order in a restaurant. Not for the first time, I was wrong. Most St. John's restaurants offer less clichéd dishes, but Velma's on Water Street promises—and delivers, at least to my untutored palate—traditional Newfoundland fare, including cods' tongues. Velma's is not what you'd call an especially hip place. It looks like someone's dining room had been transplanted from the 1950s, and it appears to attract a fairly local clientele. And the food is terrific. Velma provides a thick and wonderful pea soup that probably saves lives during a St. John's winter. And the cods' tongues, lightly battered and pan-fried with scrunchions (little bits of pork fat, but only the very healthy bits), are among the tastiest things I've ever eaten. They have been described as the truffles of Newfoundland, which to me amounts to an unnecessary glorification of truffles. After twenty-four hours of listening to me raving about them, Anne let me go back to Velma's for more.

St. John's is my new favourite Canadian city. I'll go back again for Velma's cods' tongues, for the view and the exhibits of The Rooms (the gallery, museum, and archives of Newfoundland, the view from which is so dramatic that the restaurant provides binoculars at every table), the music of O'Reilly's and The Ship, the bar at the Duke of Duckworth, the walk up Signal Hill, and Liam McKenna's ale at YellowBelly. I can't wait.

Offrez-Vous Une Autre: Drinking Beer in Montreal

The old O'Keefe brewery slogan in Quebec was "*Offrez-vous une autre*," or, translated roughly, "have another." The beer drinker in Montreal needs no such encouragement. When people ask me where the hottest place in Canada is for interesting brewing, I don't think long before volunteering the name of Quebec. Much of Canada's early beer history happened in Quebec, and the province continues to make more history every day.

I discovered Montreal in the summer of 1966, though I'm given to understand it had been there for some time already. I liked it so much I took the next two long weekends of summer to hitchhike back there. To a young man accustomed to Ontario and its dourness, Montreal was a stunning revelation. Everywhere one looked, there were people having fun. I couldn't get enough of it.

I went back the following year for Expo 67 and for more fun. There was nothing in Toronto like it—partly by law, but partly because we were insufficiently evolved. The having-fun gene was not highly developed in Toronto, mostly because we didn't need it in our environment. Where we lived, we needed the work-hard gene and the postpone-pleasure-until-heaven gene. There wasn't much evidence of either in Montrealers' DNA, and I couldn't stay away. One afternoon, when I was tired and suffering from the angst that afflicts young Ontarians, possibly to this day, a group of young locals came walking toward me. One of them, a very pretty young woman, caught my eye, smiled, and asked, *"Amusez-vous bien, monsieur?"* She didn't hang about for an answer, but a moment before, it would have been *"Non,"* and now it was *"Oui,"* thanks entirely to her. Nothing like that happens in Toronto.

For reasons I cannot imagine, let alone remember, I had stayed away from Montreal in recent years. Something to do with my Toronto genes, or maybe stupidity. Possibly a determination not to amuse myself well. When I finally got back there, in the summer of 2008 for the Mondial de la Bière festival, I no longer knew my way around. Dunn's, the famous smoked meat restaurant, had closed down, for starters, and I doubted that Chez Lou Lou les Bacchantes on Mountain Street was still there. I had the good fortune to stumble on Chez Lou Lou in 1966, and went there as often as I could, although I was nowhere near hip enough. On the Internet, you can find a photograph of Leonard Cohen at Chez Lou Lou. I am not in the background—worse luck.

My Mondial trip had left me wanting more, and I persuaded my old friend John Jackson to accompany me back to Montreal on a beer-seeking mission. Jackson's a brave lad, so we boarded a Via train and off we went. Our goal was clear. As John succinctly put it on the morning of our second day, "I didn't come here to go to a movie." Damn right, not that anyone had suggested it. We went to no movies, no museums, no galleries. We were there to drink beer, and we drank beer. Give us a job to do, and damn it, we'll do it.

Friends had given us the key to their house in Montreal, on the Plateau. Their young filmmaker son was somewhere on the Prairies doing a Fringe Festival piece, so we didn't have to worry about offending the younger generation with our sodden ways. The location was perfect. Our first day threatened rain and thunderstorms, so it seemed logical to stay within walking distance. This was no great hardship.

We started at L'Amère à Boire, a pleasing, high-ceilinged brewpub on Rue Saint-Denis. It had a nice patio out the back, but the rapidly declining weather kept us at the bar, and that was no great hardship either. L'Amère à Boire has a menu on a blackboard that promises such uncommon items as gravlax and *brandade de morue,* which appears to be some sort of Provençal way of cooking cod. They also offer a few burgers, including a lamb burger, a salmon burger, and what John described—a little insensitively, I thought—as a bunny burger, a burger of *lapin.* The *lapin* in question, it turns out, is raised by one of the brewers.

But we were there to drink, not gobble bunnies. With my cholesterol issues, who knows if rabbit might instantly kill me? Which would be appropriate revenge for the bunny. I opened with a handsome Hefe Weizen and moved to a reddish lager called Drak, praised in the menu by Stephen Beaumont for its dry, toasty character, and it was all of that. The menu insisted that it was a Czech-style beer and that *drak* was the Czech word for dragon. Huh, I said to John, there's a Belgian beer called Gulden Draak. I wonder if it's any relation. Well, it's a dissimilar beer, but it turns out that *draak* is Flemish for dragon. Fancy that. I wondered that two of the great brewing nations of the world have almost the same word for dragon. On further research, it would appear that the Germans call a dragon a *drache,* and it all appears to come from the Greek. But back to the bar.

A beer we both liked very much was something called Fin de Siècle, a tasty hybrid beer made with two kinds of English ale hops—Golding and Fuggles—and Hallertau hops, German hops used to make lagers. It also uses an ale malt with a lager malt, but for my taste, the English influences won out.

By now, the thunderstorm had subsided, so we ventured out again, looking for our next stop. It was a block, maybe two, south on Saint-Denis. Le Saint-Bock was a handsome place with twenty interesting taps (three brewed on the premises), including one cask ale. (L'Amère à Boire had a beer engine, but they were out of their signature cask beer. Timing, in comedy and beer, is everything.) My notes for Le Saint-Bock include the stunningly articulate words "really nice bar!" I have no reason to question that judgement, especially since we went back the next morning, given that they open at a civilized 11 a.m., unlike many Montreal watering holes.

Not to say that L'Amère à Boire wasn't fashionable, but Le Saint-Bock was even more so, without making us feel shabby and unwelcome. The cask ale was a bitter from a brewery called La Barberie, and a lovely hoppy thing it was. That in my belly, I was told that the Pénurie #2 from the Trou du Diable people was "the hoppiest beer we have," and it went down a treat. They were playing jazz, which confirmed my theory that people in pubs look smarter and more sophisticated against a jazz background. Even John looked reasonably intelligent, but that might have been down to the Pénurie #2.

Le Cheval Blanc is another brewpub, and I have no idea what item of Quebec legislation has, consciously or not, provoked so many brewpubs. Montreal has a lot of brewpubs, clearly more than all of Ontario, though that isn't saying much. Le Cheval Blanc was conveniently not far from where we were, and by now the threat of rain seemed much reduced. Le Cheval Blanc would appear to have once been a diner, a likelihood amplified by the looks of the bar stools and a bar John said looked like part of an Airstream trailer. He was undecided whether it was aluminum or stainless steel, but finally came down on the side of the latter. It's a long, narrow, dark room, illuminated by candles and Chinese lanterns. John, whose eloquence was rising with every sip, felt it looked "a bit New Yorky," and I didn't disagree. I enjoyed a pint of the Saison, a 5.9-percent brew described on the blackboard as an *"ale spéciale, réfermentation naturelle,"* and moved from there to an excellent India Rouge, the house IPA. It was the by-now loquacious John Jackson who pointed out that, on the large blackboard listing the prices of assorted other beverages— Jaeger, tequila, Scotch, Porto, and so on—there was toward the bottom an entry consisting solely of "Drink 5.25," suggesting that this covered anything not included in the dozen previous beverages on the roster.

Really, everything was going very well by now, so John and I made our way to Benelux, a highly regarded and very stylish brewpub on Rue Sherbrooke. I've been to a brewpub or two in my time, but never one that looked so much like a cocktail lounge. I felt that one of us should have been wearing a little black dress; John has better legs, but I didn't broach the subject. Once again we sat at the bar, and we ordered the Yakima American Pale Ale, which hit any number of spots.

The 2008 Olympics were going on, so most pubs had a television somewhere, usually behind the bar. Even a place as classy as Benelux had a large-screen set behind the bar, and we watched Simon Whitfield approaching the end of the triathlon. He appeared to have run out of gas at one point, and the barflies groaned, but then he regained consciousness and made his move. At the bar we cried out "Yes!" or *"Oui!"* according to our linquistic preferences, but some wily German had the better finishing kick and we settled cheerfully for silver, in our modest Canadian way. John's considered observation on the triathlon was, "I wouldn't be caught dead in one of those outfits." Better that than a little black dress, I thought, but again I didn't say anything.

The following day was cooler, but dry, and we broadened our horizons. Well, when I say we broadened our horizons, we had ascertained that Le Saint-Bock opened at 11 a.m., so we made our way there, stopping to admire the old Bibliothèque Nationale almost across the street from the pub. It's a splendid Beaux-Arts building with lots of lovely details and handsome stained-glass skylights we could just make out inside. They've moved the collection to a much bigger location nearby, and I have no idea what is to become of this landmark. Something good, I hope. I'm old enough to remember when cities routinely tore down beauties like this down to put up something horrible.

With which, the clock struck eleven and we crossed the street to the pub. I opted for a wheat beer from the Trois Mousquetaires brewery, which seemed a good breakfast beer. As we drank, our bartender, resplendent in a red dress, changed the beer listings on the blackboard. The cask ale was now an IPA from La Barberie, so we felt forced to offer ourselves *une autre*. Something was going on in the Olympics, and there was heated activity in the pub's brewery, centred entirely on the mash tun, as far as I could tell.

This was all very well, but eventually we had to tear ourselves away and walk downtown to Le Fourquet Fourchette du Palais, a big restaurant attached to the convention centre (or Palais des Congrès, as the French so much more grandly express it). The draw here was that it seems to be owned, or at least operated, by Unibroue, the Belgian-influenced Quebec brewery that was bought in 2004 by Sleeman, which in turn was bought by Sapporo in 2006. Miraculously, all this corporate nonsense does not seem to have had any deleterious impact on the Unibroue beers; nor, sadly, has it made Unibroue beers significantly more available in other parts of Canada.

Le Fourquet Fourchette, for a convention centre restaurant, is pretty darn good, though it lacks the more intimate charm of the less corporate places John and I had been frequenting. We had a satisfactory and good-value lunch, and my taster pack of Unibroue beers was happiness-inducing. Come to think of it, this may have been the only place we visited that served Unibroue beers on tap; I wonder what *that's* about. I'm suggesting they're now perceived as too big and corporate. We were happy at Le Fourquet Fourchette, even when the waiter dropped a fairly well-laden tray right beside us, but we were content to remove the shards of glass from our flesh and move on.

I had a plan: walk back to Boulevard Saint-Laurent and catch the Number 55 bus north. Our real goal was a pair of pubs that opened at 3 p.m., a common opening time in Montreal, but I calculated that a beer at La Taverne du Sergent-Recruteur would fill the time admirably until Dieu du Ciel opened. John pulled at the handle of the brewpub's door and encountered resistance. The place was closed, apparently for a private party. We'd been there once before and had been underwhelmed, so this wasn't a tragedy. But it did mean we had close to half an hour to kill.

Nil desperandum, as they say in ancient Rome. Just beyond Dieu du Ciel, on Avenue Laurier, is a store called Dépanneur Rahman, noted for its choice of beers. If anyone doubts that Quebec is a distinct society, take a look at the dépanneur, the small local store that sells beer and wine, among other products. The People in Charge, the guys who run most of Canada, get very antsy at the thought of beer in corner stores. "It ain't broke," said Ontario premier Dalton McGuinty when the *Toronto Star* ran a series of articles in 2008 critical of Ontario's system of beer distribution, a system carefully designed to bring comfort and succour to companies based in Belgium, Japan, and Colorado. Presumably, the definition of "broke" he had in mind was the opposite of "immensely profitable."

But in Quebec, you can buy beer in a corner store, though the choice varies significantly. If I lived at Laurier Ouest and Rue Clark, I'd be a happy man. My local pub wouldn't open till three, but in the meantime, I'd have Dépanneur Rahman, a corner store piled up with cases of beer, along with an alarming selection of individual bottles. Wow, said a couple of guys from Ontario, not inappropriately.

We made it to Dieu du Ciel just as a woman was unlocking the front door, and we quickly grabbed a table near the window. Happy as clams, we were, and we hadn't even ordered a beer yet. Dieu du Ciel is, guess what, a brewpub that also operates its own free-standing brewery outside Montreal. These people make very good beer, and the best selection of it you'll find is at their unpretentious little pub on Laurier.

They make eccentric beers at Dieu du Ciel, and they frequently give them eccentric names. We had sixteen beers on tap to choose from, from Rigor Mortis Blonde to Route des Épices. I opened with a raspberry wheat beer that looked like cream soda and was perhaps a tad sweet for my taste buds, but it found its way easily down my gullet. On cask was their Vaisseau des Songes (Ship of Dreams), and a pint of seagoing heaven it was. We finished with their Corne du Diable, a big, hoppy IPA, by which time the place was chock-a-block with people—people of all sorts, but mostly younger than us, people of most of the known sexes, people of a mostly francophone bent, as far as I could ascertain, and people partaking of pleasure. And everyone visible from our corner was drinking beer. I know beer places where, at any given time, half the punters are drinking wine or some damn thing. Not at Dieu du Ciel. It was a wonderful sight, one that made me happy—which, for an Ontarian, is an uncommon experience. Oh, and they offer accommodation upstairs; could it get any better?

About a mile north of Dieu du Ciel is a relatively new spot called Vices et Versa, a rarity in Montreal beer-drinking circles: a pub that doesn't make any beer. With so many good breweries now operating in Quebec, Vices et Versa doesn't need to. They offer twenty-nine taps, including one cask ale (though the cask was empty the day John and I got there), all from Quebec microbreweries. I started with a pint of Le Poème de la Hache, a portion of the price of which went to a group called Cyclo Nord-Sud, a Quebec organization that sends used bicycles to Africa and Latin America. As the blackboard advised, *"Buvez pour une bonne cause."* So I did. You see? Beer ennobles us. It makes us better people.

Feeling good about myself, I moved to a couple of IPAs—Hoppy, from Brasseurs et Frères, and Postcolonial from the lively Hopfenstark brewery. By now, I felt I was hitting my stride. I almost felt I could speak French, but was still just sober enough not to demonstrate it beyond the essentials of ordering beer.

We had one more stop, a place I had heard mentioned, called Réservoir, conveniently on our way home. It hadn't been designed with fellows like John and me in mind, unless we woke up one morning some considerable amount younger, but either we misunderstood them when they told us to beat it, or they were quite welcoming. We chose to read it as the latter, and they cheerfully brought us their brewed-on-premises IPA, which was much more than drinkable. In an apparent effort to save limited space, they had what appeared to be tanks of either the fermenting or bright variety stacked horizontally rather than the more conventional vertically, which roused some comment from the two oldish guys at the bar who didn't have enough French to find out the full story. If your name is Mrs. Black and you taught John and me French back in high school, I apologize for our lack of fluency. Anyway, you never taught us how to say "fermenting tank" in French.

We were now close to home—or, more accurately, someone else's home that had been placed at our convenience—and we had a train to catch back to what some call civilization (or, failing that, Toronto) in the morning. One really needs to get to Montreal more often. (*Plus souvent*. That I can remember, but how the heck do you say "fermenting tank"?)

"This Might Be the Greatest Beer I've Ever Had!": Winnipeg, Regina, Calgary, Edmonton

I'll say it yet again: Canada is a very big country. That's a thought that crops up in the human brain more than once during a Greyhound bus ride from Winnipeg to Regina.

A very big country indeed. And, although you seem to be seeing absolutely every inch of it, you're only scratching the surface. Though you'll see—and actually stop at—such places as Elkhorn, Manitoba, and Whitewood, Saskatchewan, you'll catch not a glimpse of Roblin, Wroxton, or Wadena.

Seeing all of Canada is impossible, except possibly from space, and even then you'll miss the finer points of, say, Foam Lake or Snowflake. Still, the impossibility of the task is no excuse for giving up and staying home.

If you're writing a book about beer in Canada, you need to get out to where the barley grows, out to the Prairies. Which is how I wound up on the Greyhound bus motoring along the Trans-Canada Highway.

It all started with my friend Jim Morrison. No, not *that* Jim Morrison. My friend is not buried in Paris. My Jim is a kind of historian for hire, living in Winnipeg, largely because it's right smack-dab in the middle of Canada and equidistant to archives across the country. It was also a cheap place to buy a house when Jim moved there in 2001. Passing through Toronto and hearing about my travels to the east coast, Jim suggested I visit Winnipeg to watch people drink beer in the heartland. I could stay with him, he added, reminding me that he lived in what had been, before to his arrival, a residence for an order of Catholic priests, and therefore possessed many bedrooms.

This seemed a good idea, and I thought that, since I was in the neighbourhood, I should rent a car and go elsewhere on the Prairies. Why not, I cogitated, visit the four Prairie cities that host Canadian Football League teams? So I did. Just not by car. Counting the drop fee for leaving the car a very long way from where you picked it up, driving turns out to be more costly than flying, and way more expensive than the bus.

As noted repetitively, almost obsessively, in this book, the vagaries of interprovincial beer trafficking make it imperative that the seeker of fine ales in Canada do a lot of travelling. You can't write about Manitoba beer without going to Manitoba, so I did a laundry and went, specifically to Winnipeg, the city Guy Maddin calls "the heart of the heart of the continent." (I had prepared for my visit by watching Maddin's film *My Winnipeg,* his funny "docu-fantasia" that mythologizes his native city in ways that take the line between fact and fiction to places it's seldom been.)

My non–Guy Maddin research had suggested that the most interesting brewery in Manitoba was the Half Pints Brewing Company in Winnipeg, and I had an eye on their Little Scrapper IPA. I had been in Jim's house for, oh, two minutes when he offered me a choice of beverages, which—I noticed—included beer. Beer would be nice, I said, in response to which he reached into his fridge and pulled out a pair of bottles of Half Pints' Little Scrapper IPA. Well, I thought, that was pretty easy. It hardly counts as a quest if you achieve your goals that easily. I didn't turn down the beer, though.

Through pure chance, I had never spent any time in Winnipeg. There was a short stopover on a train once, and another time I spent two hours in a doughnut shop in the middle of the night somewhere in the environs while I waited for some slight evidence of daylight so I could resume hitchhiking. Another time, I got a lift from Regina all the way to Sault Ste. Marie—a personal hitchhiking distance record if you don't count the Alaska Highway, where all the rides tend to be long ones—and we bypassed Winnipeg altogether. (The driver was a short-order cook from Florida who took a week off to drive to Las Vegas, Idaho, Banff, then home via the Soo. His idea of a week off seemed a bit bizarre to me, but I'm no psychiatrist. And I was grateful for the ride.)

So, this was my opportunity to catch up on Winnipeg, albeit belatedly. And I had company. Jim's daughter Anna was staying at the house, as were Nick Martin and Kyle Thomas, a couple of young Montreal filmmakers who were doing a show at the Winnipeg Fringe Festival. Nick had been my absentee landlord on my visit to Montreal. As observed, there was plenty of room at Jim's place, and we had been carefully billeted around the house at some distance from one another. In any case, the young filmmakers were more of a rumour than a hard fact, operating on thoroughly different schedules from the rest of us. When did they come home? When did they get up? I have no idea.

Jim lives in St. Boniface, an interesting, working-class, still largely francophone part of town. There, you'll find Gabrielle Roy's house and Louis Riel's grave, among other charms. I was about to say it's south of downtown Winnipeg, but I just looked at a map and it seems to be mostly east. It's not easy finding your way around Winnipeg; everything seems to be in a slightly different direction from your expectations. Cities built around meandering rivers are like that, and

Winnipeg has two rivers: the smaller Assiniboine, which winds its way into the Red River, which meanders a lot (and also flows from south to north, which is counterintuitive). If you don't want to get lost in Winnipeg, stick with my friend Jim.

It was not until Day Two that we got to the King's Head, which seemed to have been designated The Pub I Would Spent Most of My Time in If I Lived in Winnipeg. It's a cheerful, lively spot with a droll Irish bartender named Francis who reminded me a bit of Coach from the *Cheers* television series. One of the Half Pints seasonal beers is a lager they call Phil's Pils. A customer asked Francis for two Pils, to which Francis barked back, "You got a prescription for that?" The customer seemed merely confused, even when the bartender explained the joke, but one of his female colleagues said, "That was a good one, Francis." And I liked it, too.

Jim is a proud holder of a membership card for the King's Head. Strictly speaking, I suppose it's a club, or at least it used to be a club. Nobody asked me for any proof of my membership, though I would cheerfully have parted with the requisite five dollars to have the official card in my wallet.

The King's Head, unlike anywhere else I found in Winnipeg, had an impressive draught list that included all of the Half Pints beers— their three regular beers (an amber, a stout, and the IPA), plus the seasonal du saison. Like numerous Winnipeg bars, they had the beers from the Fort Garry Brewing Company, which I wish I had liked more than I did. For me, drinking in Winnipeg was mostly about looking for Half Pints, though it's a confusing name. If you ask for a Half Pints stout, you're not sure what you'll get or how much of it. Still, it's all part of the adventure.

My first visit to the King's Head happened with a brace of Morrisons—père et fille—and we all opened with different pints. I had the Half Pints Stir Stick Stout, a brew with a big, in-your-face coffee-packed flavour. Anna took a sip of it and declared that "it tastes like alcoholic iced coffee." She liked it enough to order one of her own, and announced dramatically, "This might be the greatest beer I've ever had!" This is strong talk, and I don't know how many of the world's great beers she's tried, but she's a young woman with a promising palate.

We also checked out a place called the Lo Pub, attached to a youth hostel in central Winnipeg. In my youth-hostelling days, I never found one with a pub attached. If I had, I might still be out there on the road. The Lo Pub, given its circumstances, is a youth-oriented place; there was a band setting up as we drank. It offers the two standard Fort Garry ales on tap, but it also stocks all the available Half Pints beers in bottles, including one of the last bottles of their seasonal Weizenbock, which I was happy to take off their hands.

On one of their brief appearances in our lives, the two young film-makers spoke keenly of their experiences at the Marion Hotel, around the corner from Jim's place. Their enthusiasm was due, at least in part, to the cheapness of the beer, but they also liked that it changed each time they went. It was a biker bar, it was a strip bar, it was a music bar—you never knew. So, Jim and I went late one night to have a look, and found the Marion Hotel in music bar mode. A house band was playing what I was told were covers, though the only song I recognized was a Beatles tune they were playing as we arrived. This was a contrast to the first place we had gone to, upstairs on the roof of a place called Pasquale's, where the canned music had featured Gene Pitney and the Everly Brothers before it went even more retro.

Apart from the punters toiling away on the numerous VLTs, the Marion was a cheerful spot. I must have too much money, because I didn't even notice if the beers were cheap. The young filmmakers would have noticed. Mind you, it had been a long day.

There are many hotels in Manitoba, because the liquor laws state that hotels are permitted to sell beer to go. How many hotels exist only to fulfill the requirements in order to be able to sell beer?

Probably quite a few. And many of these places are not just selling the odd six-pack across the bar. They have full-blown beer stores completely separate from the hotel. Certainly an eye-opener for the visitor from Ontario.

I liked Winnipeg. Mind you, I was there in July, in mostly sunny weather, which helped. The streets were busy with Fringe Festival–goers, though they were, admittedly, quieter away from the Fringe area. (On that previous visit to Toronto, Jim had been with a Hogtown first-timer, who expressed wonderment at the amount of pedestrian activity going on outside the pub we were in. In Winnipeg, he said, the sidewalks would be empty by nine o'clock.)

I liked the water bus that scoots along the rivers in summer. I liked brunch at the Fort Garry Hotel. I liked dinner at a place called In Ferno's in St. Boniface. (Anna Morrison proved to be a fan of local restaurants. As an ironic Torontonian, I assumed she was being facetious, but I was wrong. She informed me that, just around Jim's place, there were a few excellent restaurants at prices we haven't seen in Toronto for ages, if ever. In Ferno's was terrific.) I liked a lot of the old buildings in Winnipeg; although Guy Maddin says that demolition is one of Winnipeg's few growth industries, they haven't got to all of them. I liked the Half Pints beer. And I came away without a single mosquito bite, which was almost disappointing. It's like playing the Old Course at St. Andrews and never going into a bunker. I guess the mosquitoes were occupied with Anna, who was taking the brunt. And it was Anna who pointed out to me that Prairie parking lots are all wired with electricity so that drivers can plug in their block heaters. I noticed that throughout the Prairies, thanks to her.

And it was only afterwards that I discovered that Winnipeg is the sexiest city in Canada, as judged by this country's largest speed-dating service. There's a joke in there somewhere, but you'll have to dig it out yourself. Ottawa, by the way, finished last.

I could have wished that more Winnipeg bars stocked the beers of the town's best brewer, though most seemed to have the wares of the town's second-best, so they're not against buying locally. And I wish I hadn't contracted what I've come to call Louis Riel's Revenge. Late on Friday night, Jim showed Anna and me Riel's grave; by Sunday afternoon, my every waking thought was about the proximity of a bathroom. When I'm more interested in bathrooms than barrooms, you know I'm not well. I had half expected to catch encephalitis or West Nile from the mosquitoes of Winnipeg. Instead, I got the Wrath of Louis. How ignominious.

❧ ❧ ❧

Louis Riel or no Louis Riel, I was booked the next morning for a nine-hour bus ride to Regina. I sat near the back, for obvious reasons. A few decades had passed since I'd taken a Greyhound bus anywhere, but I quickly figured out the drill once more. Not that it's much of a drill. You line up, get on, go somewhere else. From time to time, you stop somewhere, and sometimes you can get off and stretch your legs or look for something to eat. Luckily for me, the Louis Riel thing had taken away my appetite.

It's funny, I think to myself sometimes, where people choose to live. Some people, through one set of circumstances or another, don't have much choice in the matter, but most of us could make a decision to live somewhere else. It's a very big world, after all, and we're mostly grown-ups. You hear about people who just change their lives and move to the south of France or a tropical island, or who get a studio apartment in Greenwich Village or buy a boat and live on it in any number of places, and you think, I could have done that. But most of us don't. I always wanted to live in Montreal, at least for a time, but I've never done it. I've lived in London and New York, but not Paris or Rome. Or Montreal, which is a lot closer.

Most people, of course, are restricted by their line of work. There's not much use living in midtown Montreal if you're a lumberjack or a barley farmer. If what you always wanted to do is grow barley on a big scale, you'll have to relocate to a place with a lot of fields. If, on the other hand, you choose to be a professor of surgery, say, you'll need to live pretty close to a medical school, which will let out Pinehouse, Saskatchewan. I believe you'd have an unwieldy commute from Pinehouse.

Some people like big cities, or medium-sized cities, or towns or villages, or the countryside. Some people even like suburbs. It would be a dull world if we were all the same, and sometimes it's a dull world anyway. But the thing is, and I think it's very interesting, that people, by and large, like where they live, whether they've lived there all their lives or just got there a year ago. That's one of the fascinating things about people.

Most people probably pretty much stay put. You get used to a place, and you feel loyal to it. I remember back in 1972, during the Canada–Soviet Union hockey series, that many Canadians were surprised how patriotic the Soviet fans were, despite their not-very-pleasant government. They weren't cheering for their government, any more than Canadian hockey fans were cheering for theirs. The White House was stunned in 2003 that the Iraqis weren't more grateful to be invaded. Mind you, Americans think everybody on the planet yearns to be American.

These are the thoughts that occur to you when you have a forty-five-minute stopover in Brandon, Manitoba. I don't know much about Brandon. Many years ago, I wrote a very small book of humour designed to be given as a get-well gift to someone sick. No, you never heard of it. Anyway, the store in this entire country that sold the most copies of this minor masterpiece was the gift shop of the Brandon General Hospital, so I've always felt warmly toward the Wheat City. Also, I once knew, very slightly, a friend of a friend from Brandon. Rodney was a judge there, and was famous for a case of indecent exposure that came before him. The male accused had been charged with flashing some poor woman outdoors in the depths of a Brandon winter, which I understand to be a cold time of year in those parts. (When I say "those parts," I mean southern Manitoba.) From his solemn place on the bench, Rodney prepared to hear the evidence, but suggested that surely the case should be heard in small claims court.

So I was ready for Brandon, where they clearly have a sense of humour. One thing you have to remember is that bus terminals are seldom in the best parts of any given town. I had a stopover once, many years ago, in Baltimore, and it was terrifying. People were afraid to get off the bus, let alone leave the terminal. They don't put bus terminals right next to major museums. The Brandon bus terminal is downtown, but I'm guessing that real life in Brandon happens somewhere else. There's not much open in downtown Brandon in the middle of the day. I walked around for a while, after I had used the bus terminal bathroom, but by the time I found the Double Decker Tavern, it was already time to hightail it back to the bus, worse luck. On the way out of town, we saw much nicer bits of Brandon, or at least the part of Brandon where the big box stores that put the downtown stores out of business gathered.

I can't avoid pointing out that, nine days after I passed through the Brandon bus terminal, a man on an eastbound bus passed through Brandon and, shortly before Portage La Prairie, brutally murdered a complete stranger. This gruesome event led to much talk of tougher security on buses, but it wasn't as if people were saying, "God, not another brutal slaying on a Greyhound bus."

Since the bus is the cheapest way to travel, if you discount hitchhiking or walking, it gets a mixed clientele. You don't see a lot of society swells on the bus—or *I* didn't—but I certainly didn't feel threatened. The bus is not just cheaper; often, it's almost the only way, given that the train doesn't go everywhere (or almost anywhere) any more. I'll admit to being shocked that the Prairies were so ill served by the railways. The Regina train station is now a casino, which shows you how crazy our priorities have become. And, because the bus stops in places you'd probably never get to otherwise—I'm thinking of Oak Lake and Virden—you see bits of Canada you wouldn't even see from the train, even if the train still existed. Anyway, the bus was fine, and nobody murdered me. Nor did I expect them to.

A little more than nine hours passed on the bus from Winnipeg to Regina, during which time I saw much evidence of agriculture. I say this apologetically, but I'm a bit of a stranger to farms and agriculture. When you come back into Canada from another country and you have to fill in that form that asks you, among other things, whether you're going to be visiting a farm in the next two weeks, I never have to think twice about my answer. Where I live in midtown Toronto, we don't have a lot of agriculture. There are a few lawns, and the woman two doors down does a very nice number in proper gardening, but you wouldn't call it agriculture. She doesn't talk much about her harvest.

So, I have no idea what I was seeing. I wanted to see barley, for obvious reasons, but it struck me on the bus that I have no idea what it looks like. Canada is one of the great barley producers of planet Earth, so statistically it's very likely I went past all sorts of barley. There were a number of fields with something yellow growing, and I have vague, distant memories of being told that yellow fields were usually mustard or canola, but I really don't know. I suspect the yellow fields weren't barley, but how would I know?

I should have asked someone on the bus, but it might have seemed odd. They didn't seem chatty, my fellow travellers, and mostly they didn't look like people who would know, either. (The fellow in the seat in front of me was from Toronto, and on one of our stops he asked me to take his photograph in front of some Prairie scene, suggesting his friends would never believe it otherwise.) There was a man who got on with his mother somewhere in rural Saskatchewan. He sat beside me, his mother across the aisle, and he seemed like he might possibly be of a rustic nature. I bet he could have told me. He could probably have told me if it was two-row or six-row barley. Heck, he could probably have told me whether it was the Selkirk or Binscarth variety of barley. Another opportunity missed. I just didn't want to seem like a total goof from Toronto who doesn't even know barley from canola. I imagined him entertaining his friends, through most of the next winter, with tales of this urban doofus he met on the bus, who claimed to know something about beer but didn't know barley when he saw it. In retrospect, would it have killed me to give him that bit of pleasure?

Apparently, it's 355 miles (572 kilometres for younger readers) from Winnipeg to Regina, and for the most part those miles all look pretty much alike. They talk, on the Prairies, about their beautiful skies, and I can see why. The sky seems to go forever. This is because there's nothing in the way, like hills. Even Toronto has a hill. It's not much of one, but you know when you've climbed it. Out there on the bus, you could feel almost a frisson when something appeared in the distance, but half an hour later, it usually turned out to be a tree or a grain elevator.

There seemed to be a hill just north of Regina, as we approached the Queen City, though I never saw it again. Perhaps it was a cardboard cutout. Anyway, soon I was in Regina itself. My hotel was two blocks away from the bus terminal, which I was glad of, though my theory of the bus terminal always being somewhere you don't much want to be was a little worrying.

Given that I was travelling solo, I had decided to give Hotwire a try. This is a website that offers you a price on a hotel room, rated with a stated number of stars and sometimes within a certain part of the city of your choice, but it doesn't tell you the name of the hotel until you've parted with your credit card information. I tried it first with my Edmonton hotel, and got a very good price on a good hotel right downtown. Regina was a bit more daunting, as the area it specified took in pretty much all of Regina and much of southern Saskatchewan. I didn't want to stay at an airport hotel or in Lumsden, but I took a chance and wound up with a Ramada Inn downtown. So far, so good.

Someday, someone's going to explain Regina to me. Someone's going to tell me about the cool part of town, where the streets are lined with bookstores and interesting shops and bistros and charming pubs filled with hepcats. Are the people of Regina keeping this quaint *quartier* all to themselves? Because I've never stumbled upon it.

Anyway, I cocooned briefly in my downtown hotel room and rested up. One thing I liked about the Prairies is that the Blue Jay games come on at five in the afternoon, which is ideal for the traveller, and particularly the alco-tourist. You can hit a few pubs in the afternoon, enjoy a little downtime with a bit of baseball in your room, then go out pubbing again in the evening.

When at last I set out, I had one destination in mind. If you say "beer" and "Regina" in the same sentence, chances are you're talking about the Bushwakker Brewpub. Such was my goal when I left the comforts (and bathroom) of the Ramada Inn. Admittedly, it was a Monday evening, but I'm used to seeing people on the streets, people walking around, going places. It was quiet in downtown Regina. Too quiet. I walked up Broad Street, seldom having to step aside to let others pass. There was slight activity at Casino Regina (formerly Union Station), but I wasn't tempted. I'm a bad loser and an infrequent winner.

You keep walking what I assume is north, under a railway underpass, until you hit Dewdney Avenue. The thought crossed my mind at some point on this journey that I had recently read that Regina was the most dangerous city in Canada, but when you're down with Louis's Revenge, you don't much care if you live or die.

Not to get ahead of myself, but a couple of days after I left Regina, there was a letter printed in *The Globe and Mail* that debunked the kind of statistics that accuse Regina of being dangerous. The writer finished by saying, "The Regina area is an awesome place to live." I bet that guy knows the charming bit of town they don't tell casual visitors about, the one with the quaint pubs and bookstores I still haven't found.

I'm going out on a limb and suggesting that Dewdney Avenue is named, not for the Toronto poet and essayist Christopher, but for Edgar Dewdney, who, as lieutenant-governor of the North West Territories, was in a position to make Regina (or Pile of Bones, as it was known at the time) the territorial capital. He nobly named it for Queen Victoria. Not so nobly, he had already bought land in the area, so he was in a position to profit from his own ruling. Well, what's the point of being a lieutenant-governor if you can't do something nice for yourself from time to time?

His avenue is a very straight, wide one with not a lot of obvious activity on it, but if you persevere you'll find the Bushwakker, and you'll be glad of it. It took me sixteen or seventeen minutes to get there from the Ramada, but I still wasn't feeling great. I would normally do it a couple of minutes faster, and my youthful wife would take another minute off my time.

There were more people inside the Bushwakker on a Monday evening than I had seen out on the streets of Regina. So *this* is where everybody was. Monday is jazz night, and jazz was being perpetrated while I was in attendance. (Wednesday is folk music night. The place is closed Sundays, unless the Roughriders are playing a home game. You get a good view of Taylor Field—or what is now called Mosaic Stadium at Taylor Field—from the front door of the Bushwakker.)

I liked the jazz, but I was there for the beer. And there was plenty of it: six lagers brewed on-site, including the 8.5-percent Procrastinator Doppelbock, and eight ales (plus, if you're so minded, fifteen single malts and eight blue agave premium tequilas). Still too delicate for a wholesale assault on the draught lists, I had a Summer Wheat and a Bombay IPA, and I regret none of it. I made my way back to the hotel, knowing that I had there a bottle of something hoppy and exotic I had bought in Winnipeg for exactly this sort of moment.

In the morning, I made a dash over to Scarth Street, which boasted an almost raffish pedestrian mall on which stands a fairly new place called Beer Brothers Bakery and Cuisine, though I had to pass possibly the worst busker in Saskatchewan to get there. If the CBC makes a reality TV show designed to choose the worst busker in Saskatchewan, this guy has the inside track. The Beer Brothers have a draught list that is fairly mainstream, though there was evidence that they sometimes serve the Half Pints Stir Stick Stout (the one that might be the greatest beer Anna Morrison has ever had), but not that day, and a selection of bottles that is a bit better. I had an Okanagan Springs Pale Ale from British Columbia, which struck me as more pale than ale, then I left to check out the Bushwakker one more time.

The Bushwakker is the brainchild of a man named Bev Robertson. Like Steve Cavan in Saskatoon, Bev is a former academic (his field was crystallography, which is something difficult) and home brewer who wound up turning professional in the beer game. Bev, who is one of the beer world's characters, used to sit in the University of Regina Faculty Club, nattering with other academics about why industrial beer in North America tasted so bad even though it was entirely possible to make good beer. In the mid-1980s, Bev was serving as chairman of the Saskatchewan Health Research Board and had the ear of the provincial cabinet, which he used to agitate for legalizing brewpubs. Legislation was eventually passed, but Bev failed to get one of the early licences. Justice finally prevailed, and the Bushwakker opened in January 1991. It was the first Saskatchewan brewpub to make decent beer, and is still the place to go in Regina.

The woman behind the bar welcomed me back as if I'd been coming to her pub for years. If I'd thought someone from the late shift would be working the early shift the next morning, I'd have changed my shirt, but it was too late to dwell on that. Have they no labour laws in Saskatchewan? I had a Regina Pale Ale, which was more ale than pale, then a modest glass of the pleasantly immodest Procrastinator. Beginning to feel like a full member of the species again, I ordered a bottle of an American beer called Fish Tale Ten Squared Anniversary Reel Ale from Olympia, Washington. The label claimed the use of ten types of hops, 10 percent alcohol by volume, and 100 IBUs, which is about as high as you can go on the bitterness scale without single-handedly cornering the entire global hop market. But what really got my attention, as an Ontarian, was the label itself: all in English, not a word in French. Not even a warning that this was a *bière forte*. In Ontario, this label would have had stickers all over it, alerting me in both official languages to the dangers of drinking a 10-percent beer. This moment was when it really hit home that I was on the Prairies.

As my unilingually head-crashing beer was slowly wearing down, I asked my friendly bartender how a fellow got a cab in this town. She kindly offered to call me one, and it arrived exactly when it should have. I couldn't have been more pleased. Now, I haven't travelled from every airport to every city in this country, but I've never been anywhere in Canada where a cab ride to the airport was fourteen dollars, counting a good big-city tip. Even the cab from downtown Whitehorse to the airport was more, and it's *no* distance.

Yes, I know, I should have taken the bus to Calgary, but it's even longer than the Winnipeg–Regina trip, and I got a fare on WestJet that was just about the same as the bus, if you don't count all the taxes and extra charges that added up to more than the fare itself. Anyway, I wouldn't have had time for a second trip to the Bushwakker. And I'd never flown WestJet before. I remember comedian Dave Broadfoot, back before Air Canada put us all on diets, joking about a flight attendant on Air Canada berating a passenger. "Eat your dinner," she said. "There are people starving on WestJet."

The aftermath of Louis Riel found me still not hungry, and I'd had a hearty bowl of soup at the Bushwakker anyway, so I had no fear of starvation on my short flight. So, soon I was in . . .

❧ ❧ ❧

Calgary. Back in Winnipeg, Jim Morrison had told me how far Calgary had spread, but even so, I was surprised to see housing developments sprawling crazily in all directions. We hear about Boomtown back in eastern-central Canada, but you have to see it first-hand to appreciate it properly. Seven years ago, I vaguely remember there being some space between the airport and Calgary. There isn't much now.

Calgary is booming so much that even Hotwire had no deals on hotels, but I stumbled upon some website I'd never heard of and got a decent price on another Ramada Inn. Unlike my Regina Ramada, this one didn't have free computer service in the lobby or a free local newspaper. (Or didn't seem to; the morning I checked out, I got the last *Calgary Herald* at ten to eight. And there was a computer in the lobby, but it cost a toonie for ten minutes.)

After an inning or two of baseball, I was out on the town. Much of downtown Calgary seemed to be closed, though it was unclear whether business was bad or half the buildings were about to be torn down for new things. The McNally-Robinson bookstore on Eighth Avenue had shut not long before I got there, but that seemed largely due to the soaring value of the building. Who can afford to sell books when the building is worth so much?

I was keeping an eye out for Brewsters, a chain of eleven Prairie brewpubs, three in Regina and four apiece in Calgary and Edmonton. Most of these pubs are in what I would consider fairly distant suburbs, but there is one in reasonably central Calgary. So off I went, and there it was. I had a pint (or what passes for a pint on the Prairies, where most of the glasses look more like about sixteen ounces) of their Hefeweizen, which, according to the menu, has been named

Best Beer at the Calgary International Beer Festival. It was okay, but to me it lacked a bit of body and oomph (to use a technical brewing term). My bartender was an amenable-seeming chap. I don't know if Alberta has its own equivalent of Ontario's Smart Serve program, but he certainly had the courtesy and professionalism I would expect. Brewsters had a kind of corporate feel to it, not surprisingly for a fair-sized chain, and I didn't anticipate anything quirky. It was darker at Brewsters than seemed strictly necessary, but fortunately, I had my reading glasses with me.

From Brewsters, I went to a spot that had been recommended, the Ship and Anchor on the bustling strip of Seventeenth Avenue Southwest. The joint was hopping, mostly with people much younger than I, and it was really dark. People younger than I don't mind darkness, even though their unwrinkled features are not necessarily enhanced by low lighting. Maybe it's because they don't read. I grabbed a pint of Wild Rose IPA and found a seat by a door, where light was coming in. I still needed my reading glasses.

There was one more spot I had in mind for my pub crawl, and that was the Hop in Brew pub. I had written down the address, which was a good thing, because the only sign of consequence outside the pub was a neon sign reading OPEN. I checked the address (213 Twelfth Avenue Southwest) and went in. I quickly detected that the Hop in Brew was The Pub I Would Spend My Time in If I Lived in Calgary. It's an old house in a largely residential neighbourhood, and it has a very pleasantly independent feel and look to it. A delightful young woman served me a pint of McNally's Reserve, and I sat down at a well-illuminated table. Given that, by this time, it was pretty much dark out, I was surprised to find a pub with a good beer selection and a winsome bartender that also allowed me to read. Still a bit off my feed, I resisted the temptation of one of the house pizzas, though the ones I saw looked good.

The next morning, I sought out and finally found breakfast, then went looking for a cab to take me to the Wild Rose Brewery, which is in a part of town I would describe as Way the Hell and Gone. I had prepared for this journey by printing out directions from Google Maps. My cabbie was unfamiliar with the Wild Rose Brewery; as a young Muslim, he was generally unfamiliar with the concept of a brewery. "They make beer," I explained helpfully. He merely frowned. He studied my Google map and directions. Calgary is a city that is divided into quadrants defined by the points of the compass. I was in Southwest, as was the Wild Rose Brewery. The driver frowned as he puzzled over the Google directions, particularly when they wanted him to go northwest on Crowchild Trail. "If I go northwest," he told me, "we will get to Edmonton before we get to where you want to go."

I told him I trusted his judgement, and we sped off in an a southwesterly direction. The Wild Rose Brewery is near the Farmer's Market, and he knew where that was, and it's pretty much within the grounds of a military base. Imagine the Americans allowing a brewery on a military base. My cabbie and I circled the area for some time, gradually getting closer, although no one we asked for directions had ever heard of the Wild Rose Brewery. We had been heartbreakingly close at one point, but turned around a moment too soon. He might have disapproved of driving to a brewery (we stayed off theology), but my cab driver got a good fare out of his marathon drive around much of southwestern Calgary.

I was keen to visit the Wild Rose Brewery because it has a taproom on the premises, and that sounded like a good thing. And it is a good thing, especially on a nice day, which this was, to be seated outdoors with a good range of ales to sample in a fairly quiet setting. It is also a smart thing to put a brewery on a military base, and three of our brave fighting persons were enjoying lunch at a nearby table. There is a long connection between the military and fermentation. Alexander Keith opened his brewery in Halifax in 1820 to satisfy the needs of a military garrison, and he never looked back. The venerable Wheat Sheaf Tavern in Toronto was cleverly located just up the street from Fort York, which is why it's still there 160 years later. If you can't make a living selling beer to the troops, you should take up another line of work.

The brewery itself is in a large Quonset hut that was once an airplane hangar. I'm sure it served our nation well as a hangar, but it's doing even better as a brewery. I ran through a number of the Wild Rose ales, and particularly enjoyed the Special Old Bitter and the IPA (tragically, I was not there on a Friday, when, at four o'clock in the afternoon, a cask-conditioned beer is tapped and served and apparently lasts no longer than that evening). Eventually, a kindly staff person called me a taxi—better to let *him* explain where in the name of God we were—and I made my way back to civilization.

I was dropped off in the busy neighbourhood of Kensington, which has a very good bookstore (Pages on Kensington), a pub (imaginatively named the Kensington Pub), a few restaurants, and a store called the Kensington Wine Market. I was interested to take a look at how alcohol was sold on a retail level in the Prairie provinces. Manitoba and Saskatchewan have government-operated liquor stores that look like government-operated liquor stores everywhere else. Manitoba also has some privately owned stores, as well as the hotel-based beer stores mentioned earlier.

Saskatchewan has a similar law governing beer sales, though when brewpubs came into existence in that province it was decided that they should also be able to sell beer for consumption elsewhere, as long as they were at least a mile from an existing hotel. I was initially confused when I sought out information about beer and pubs on the Prairies and a Regina informant told me that Saskatchewan has lots of brewpubs "due to idiotic liquor laws." Funny, I thought; Ontario has very few brewpubs, also due to idiotic liquor laws. Then I discovered this quirk of Saskatchewan law that rewards brewpubs but does not guarantee that such places are any good or make drinkable beer. It's all about off-sales. So, Bushwakker makes good beer *despite* the law, not because of it.

Alberta, as we know, privatized all alcohol sales and sold off its liquor stores in the early 1990s. Good thing or bad? The jury remains out, though there are strong opinions on both sides. Defenders of privatization point to such places as the Kensington Wine Market in Calgary, which is a handsome, well-stocked store. Its beer selection is excellent, and I overheard the store's beer guy making recommendations to a woman who wanted to stock up for a tasting. I considered fishing for an invitation to this event, but thought I might be asked to leave the store.

Not all Alberta stores are like the Kensington Wine Market. As I walked back to my hotel, I wandered into another liquor store at Sixth Avenue and Eighth Street Southwest and noticed a sign just inside the door: "We ask that you keep your shopping under *15 minutes.*" I hadn't felt as unwelcome in a liquor store since the bad old days in Ontario, back when drinking was an official sin. Maybe in Alberta it's a privatized sin. I kept my shopping well under fifteen minutes. More like about fifteen seconds, and I left empty-handed.

Proponents of liquor privatization invariably express confidence that prices will drop once government inefficiency and unionized staff are replaced by entrepreneurial know-how and minimum-wage employees. That makes immediate sense, but I didn't see a lot of bargains in Alberta stores. When I compared prices of products I knew, they were more expensive than in Ontario, which may be simply a factor of the Liquor Control Board of Ontario's abnormal buying power. Or are Albertans so oil-rich that price is no object?

After freshening up in my hotel room and watching yet another inning or two of baseball, I headed back out onto the mean streets of Calgary. Seven years before I had visited the James Joyce, a handsome mock-Irish pub downtown, and decided to see how things were going there. Its stretch of Eighth Avenue is also called Stephen

Avenue Walk, which I had read somewhere was the place to discover what's trendy in Calgary. I saw nothing that looked particularly trendy to me, unless a lot of young people hanging about, apparently waiting for something to happen, is trendy. The James Joyce was busy on an early Wednesday evening, but I found a seat at the bar. The beer list was so dispiritingly conventional that I ordered a gin and tonic, which did me a world of good. Bert Grant, one of the great American craft beer pioneers, used to carry a vial of hop juice with him to add a little flavour to the bland beers that were ubiquitous at the time, an idea that still strikes me as clear evidence of genius.

Another bar I had spent some time in back then was a place called Bottlescrew Bill's. I remembered it as being funkier than it is today, but my memory is suspect. I was blessed with a very friendly bartender at a well-lit end of the bar, and I decided to try some Yukon beers. The only time I had previously made it to that territory of enthusiastic drinkers (remember that they're far and away Canada's leading per capita consumers of practically any sort of alcohol you can name), there were no local beers beyond homebrew to be found up there. That changed in 1997 with the birth of what is now the Yukon Brewing Company.

Bottlescrew Bill's didn't have Yukon's beers on draught, but they offered a couple of bottles. I had a Yukon Gold, billed as an "English style pale ale," and was pleased enough to follow it with a seasonal brew called Lead Dog Ale. At 7 percent, this is clearly a beer designed to do battle with the Yukon winter, and I'd give it more than half a chance.

Bottlescrew Bill's doesn't mention this on its website, but it has very possibly the nicest bathroom in Calgary, not that I've tried them all. I bade my cheery bartender good night and headed back to the Hop in Brew. If a pub's that good, it's worth going back. My bartender was a different comely young woman from the previous evening—the fortunate regulars are spoiled for choice, if you ask me—but every bit as welcoming. I settled on an Alley Kat Full Moon Pale Ale from Edmonton and got comfortable. I learned that the pub had been created by a Dutchman and his Canadian wife, Dick and Carmen Hoppener, and that all the things I liked about it—the beer, the quiet, the absence of television—were the result of deliberate policy choices. If Dick and Carmen have not been awarded the Order of Canada, a terrible mistake has been made.

The music, which on both my visits was not terribly loud, seemed to be what I tend to call "indie," just because I'd never heard any of it before. If I had been staying a third night in Calgary, I'd have gone there again, but early the next morning I set out for . . .

❧ ❧ ❧

Edmonton. Back on the Greyhound bus, but for only three and a half hours this time. And, again, no murderer that I could see. The Calgary bus terminal is discreetly tucked away on the fringes of downtown, just far enough away to provide business for a cab driver. It was an uneventful trip to Edmonton, stopping briefly in Red Deer. And the Edmonton bus terminal was quite handy to my hotel—my bargain room at the Westin.

Unlike anywhere else I had been on this trip to the Prairies, Edmonton seemed to have a vibrant downtown area. (I learned later that Calgary had long banned people from living downtown, which seems insane if true. They're making up for it now with condo towers.) This perception may have been helped along by the presence of the Taste of Edmonton festival, which was going great guns about a block from my temporary residence. I had bought plenty of food for the bus ride, so I wasn't terribly hungry, but I spotted the beer tent and got stuck in with a bottle of Alley Kat Full Moon and had vague sensations of happiness.

Each of my four Prairie CFL cities seemed to have exactly one very good brewery, and Edmonton's is Alley Kat. Started in 1994 by Neil Herbst, a home brewer who had been laid off from a provincial government job, Alley Kat is making some more than decent beers. The difficulty lies in finding them in Edmonton. As I write these words, the Alley Kat website is recovering from a makeover, but what it needs is a list of pubs in which its beers can be found.

Trying to be of service to you, dear reader, I make an effort to perform some research before I land in a new city. My research on Edmonton was proving more difficult. Where was the great pub of Edmonton? Where was its King's Head, its Bushwakker Brewpub, its Hop in Brew? I'm still looking. I had begged the users of the Toronto website The Bar Towel for information about the west, and I had learned plenty from them. A beer drinker named Mark from Regina was particularly helpful, but his view of Edmonton was summed up in two words: horrible pubs. Those are strong words, and I hoped they were false.

I went for a long walk in Edmonton. I went and checked out the Chateau Louis liquor store, which boasted a not-unimpressive array of beers, then headed south again. Near the Alberta Legislature, you'll find a bridge called the High Level Bridge. If you walk across it, you'll discover how it got its name. It's a *very* high-level bridge, with wonderful vistas of the North Saskatchewan River a very long way below. If you're uncomfortable with heights, this is perhaps not the bridge for you. There is another one, called—and you're not going to believe this—the Low Level Bridge. They're plain-spoken people in Alberta. They call things the way they see 'em.

I was aiming for 82 Avenue, known to all as Whyte Avenue, which is where much of Edmonton's nightlife seems to assemble. Like Calgary, most of Edmonton's streets are numbered, but, rather than emulating Calgary's quadrants, Edmonton went with a system whereby the centre of town is generally to be found near where 101 Avenue meets 101 Street, from which point the avenues climb in number as you go north and the streets climb in number as you go west. Clear? It actually works, assuming I've got it right. If you're at, say, 10135

100 Street, you know you're between 101 and 102 Avenues, as long as you can remember which ones are streets and which are avenues. Carrying a compass might help.

Whyte Avenue is a long stretch of street with moments of interest along the way. I found a place I had heard about called the Black Dog, but the beer choice was disappointing and the room dark and noisy. I looked in at a couple of other places and finally settled down at the Wunder Bar. I was just in time to get in at the end of happy hour, during which Amber's Pale Ale could be had for a generous three dollars. Count me in, I said.

The Wunder Bar has a lot of Germanic decoration, including numerous German national football jerseys, but Germany was represented by only a few bottled beers. I had hoped for draught Weihenstephaner Hefeweizen (a man needs a dream), but I got Amber's Pale Ale. Still, at a mere three spendolas, I wasn't complaining. What I didn't see, at Wunder Bar or anywhere else I went, was Alley Kat beers on tap. It made me glad I had drunk some in Calgary.

I don't want to rouse the already keen feelings of rivalry between Alberta's two major cities, but it seemed odd that, to drink Edmonton's best beer on tap, you should have to travel to Calgary. The late writer Pete McCarthy had a set of travel rules to live by, and Rule Number One ran along the lines of: when you get there, buy a local paper and go for a drink. While I was reading the *Edmonton Journal* at the Taste of Edmonton beer tent, I came upon the line, "Edmonton will only become the Toronto of the West over Calgary's dead body." This struck me as odd, because I had assumed that neither Edmonton nor Calgary even *wanted* to be the Toronto of the West. I thought that Albertans would rather be the Moncton of the West or the Yellowknife of the South, or even the São Paulo of the North, than be associated in any way with the heathen Toronto. To be fair, over the entire western trip, I had never volunteered that I live about three miles from the Toronto Stock Exchange, but when asked—as I often was—where I was from, I never prevaricated. I admitted to Toronto, but never once was I abused or insulted. Given that the West is so much richer than Ontario these days, it would be a bit gratuitous to abuse me. At this time, they had all the money, and what I still think of as the Reform Party was in power in Ottawa, so there wasn't much for them to complain about. Consequently, everyone was very friendly to me.

I didn't stay out late, partly because I couldn't find a really good pub, but also because I had an early flight back to godless, jobless Toronto the next morning. And, as I discovered in the morning, Edmonton's airport is a hell of a long way out of town. I seemed to have been in the back of a taxi for an hour or two when I saw a road sign promising the airport in only another nineteen kilometres. I began to form a theory that Calgary and Edmonton actually share an airport. If you approach it from the south, you see signs reading "Welcome to Calgary Airport." From the north, the signs say "Welcome to Edmonton Airport." If you can measure a city's claim to being world-class (a Toronto obsession) by the cost of a taxi to the airport, Edmonton is right up there: four dollars more than Toronto, thirteen dollars more than Calgary (eat your heart out), and more than four times the price of getting out of Regina. I've got my receipts.

❧ ❧ ❧

So, can a boy from Toronto have a good time on the Prairies? You bet he can, though the chances improve if he doesn't come down with the Curse of Louis Riel. Also, I would think, if he goes in summer (though, of course, there isn't much of this country that's a gift in January, despite the annoying phone calls we all get from friends in Victoria when the flowers start blooming). I liked the enthusiasm everyone had for their local CFL team, and that team news was always the biggest story in the sports pages. I wish Toronto were more like that. (When I got home, I read about my city's buildup to an exhibition game the Buffalo Bills were playing in Toronto, including a very amusing story about the official tailgate party—no freelance tailgating was to be permitted. Welcome to Toronto. And what's with this NFL envy, anyway? These guys need four downs just to take a football ten yards; you must be joking.)

Other than that, I hope someone reads this book and sets up a perfect pub in Edmonton, if only to prove me wrong. I hope more Winnipeg pubs start serving Half Pints beer, and that the Fort Garry Brewing Company sees Half Pints—and not Molson and Labatt—as its competition and lifts its game accordingly. I hope that Francis, the bartender at the King's Head in Winnipeg, lives a long and happy life; ditto both the bartenders who served me at the Hop in Brew in Calgary. I hope to hear from someone in Regina who will let me in on the secret places they never tell visitors about, and I'll be curious to see Calgary when they finally get it finished. I should live so long.

West by Northwest: Vancouver, Whitehorse, Victoria

When you've spent much of your summer underneath an umbrella, and when the discussion around town is about whether we'll break the all-time rain record, you might feel a certain reluctance to go to Vancouver. I've been there before, and I know that it rains from time to time, which is putting it charitably.

Then there's my past history in Vancouver, which has a lot to do with trying to find somewhere to drink. The very first day I spent in Vancouver, a Sunday back in 1971, I wasted a lot of time and energy walking to a beer store that was, of course, closed, (I had been living in California and had forgotten Canadian ways). Subsequent visits have been more successful, but only a bit.

In the late 1970s, when we visited my brother in Vancouver, he sang the praises of the new "neighbourhood pubs" that had been introduced. The problem was that there wasn't one in his neighbourhood. We had to drive rather a long way to a neighbourhood pub, which seemed to defeat the purpose. I have since read that the provincial legislation that permitted neighbourhood pubs dictated that such pubs could not be opened within a mile of each other, or of another licensed establishment, and required the consent of a sizable majority of residents within some absurd radius. Small wonder there were hardly any of them.

This time, I did more research. I found the CAMRA Vancouver website and contacted Rick Green, president thereof. Within moments, I received a return email (who says these BC people are laid-back?) proposing a meeting and suggesting some watering holes I might find appealing. Bingo!

Shortly after arriving, my wife, Anne, and I set out for a pub called the Irish Heather. To get there, we had to walk through the heart of the Downtown Eastside, which was as dispiriting as the newspapers suggest. It was, however, mere steps from the only Vancouver pub that serves cask-conditioned ale every day of the week. I was told this several times by different people, so I believe it to be true. There are other Vancouver pubs that have cask nights, but as of August 2008, the Irish Heather was the only full-time cask provider.

Not that our bartender knew a lot about it, though perhaps he was new. The room itself was new, the pub having just moved across the street from its former venue, dislocated by Vancouver development. The cask ale in question was described tentatively by the bartender as a red ale, but it was in fact R&B Red Devil Pale Ale, and very fine it was, too. "This beer's darn good, first rate," exclaimed Anne, taking the words from my mouth. We stayed on for another, despite our eagerness to get to our next stop.

Which was the Alibi Room, a restaurant/bar Rick Green had billed as having the best selection of draught British Columbia craft beer in the province. This got my attention, because previous visits to Vancouver had revealed a slowly growing number of brewpubs but almost nowhere to drink other local beers. I was aware of a developing craft beer presence in BC, but couldn't find anywhere to drink the damn stuff.

The place to drink it is the Alibi Room, though not on Mondays, when they close. All those other days of the week, however, are fair game, though they don't open until late on weekdays. When we turned up, the place was almost empty, but we were advised to find ourselves a table pronto because they expected to be busy. We sat by a window with a view across an expanse of railway tracks over to North Vancouver and the mountains. It wasn't raining now, and the vista was a good one. Our charming server delivered one of the country's best draught beer lists: eighteen British Columbia craft beers from sixteen different breweries, plus a rotating guest tap, occupied that evening by Rogue Dead Guy Ale from Oregon.

It's a big room in an old building, and the place—as predicted—filled up quickly. Between us, we had beers from Old Yale, Nelson, and Spinnakers (two different ales), and finished with Swan's Extra IPA. My halibut cakes were a trifle precious for my plebeian tastes, but Anne's Canadian cheese plate was excellent. To describe us as happy at the Alibi Room would be to understate the case.

Sunday was one of those Vancouver days with a variety of weather that ranged from bad to worse. Not to be daunted, we made our way to the Yaletown Brewing Company, then took that very cute little ferry thing to Granville Island. It's almost worth living in Vancouver just for the cute ferry thing, though it's been raining whenever I've used it.

(It's no use complaining about the rain in Vancouver. It's like complaining that people aren't friendly in Toronto or that the alpine skiing is a bit underwhelming on Prince Edward Island. It's just the way things are, and they're not going to change for you. Years ago, I was in Jasper, Alberta, with a woman of my acquaintance. We fell into conversation with a couple from the American northeast. And how were they liking Jasper? Well, just fine, for the most part, except that they found the mountains a little high for their taste. You see what I mean?)

Granville Island was bustling, as Granville Island tends to be on a Sunday, rain or shine. It is the home of two more brewpubs, one attached to Granville Island Brewing, Canada's first post-Prohibition microbrewery. I can recall, back in 1984, the excitement of the news that Canada was getting a microbrewery, even if it was more than two thousand miles from where I lived. It may have been that very year that Anne and I went out west. I toured the brewery, tasted the product (which at the time was a single lager), and brought home a two-four. Try bringing a two-four on an airplane as carry-on luggage today—or, better yet, don't.

The other brewpub is Dockside Brewing at the Granville Island Hotel. The place has a lovely view of False Creek, and—having stayed there for the Vancouver Writers Festival in 2001, I can testify—the hotel is very nice. Let's just say that I am less enthusiastic about the beer.

Still, we were due at a restaurant/bar called The Whip, and you don't want to turn up late for a place called The Whip. Or perhaps you do; it's a matter of taste and predilections. At four o'clock on Sunday afternoons, The Whip serves up a cask-conditioned ale—you will like it, or else—and it was there that we met up with Rick Green and some of his CAMRA Vancouver mates. We were drinking Heroica Oatmeal Stout from the Steamworks Brewpub, and enjoying it—to the point that it was only as we were leaving that I noticed that The Whip also had a couple of Storm Brewing's beers on tap. It turned out to be the only place I saw that offered Storm brews, and they weren't at the Great Canadian Beer Festival in Victoria two weeks later, so I cannot enlighten you as to the quality of their apparently quirky beers.

Rick and the others were jolly company, with lots of useful information about the state of brewing in the area. Between these brave souls struggling to advance the world of beer and the cask-conditioned Heroica Oatmeal Stout, it was worth the journey. On Rick's advice, we walked a few blocks afterwards to Brewery Creek, the sort of beer store I never expect to see in Ontario. As one who lives in Toronto, I always assume the world's best beer stores are in Buffalo, New York, so it was a pleasure to see a Canadian store that could give Buffalo a run for its money. They really had some remarkable beers.

We wound up at the Dix BBQ and Brewery for their IPA and dinner. Dix is part of the same pub group that owns Yaletown and four other places, but it felt a little less corporate than Yaletown. The room was brighter, and the piped-in music was earlier classic rock than Yaletown's: Janis Joplin and David Clayton-Thomas rather than Phil Collins and Sade, if that matters to you.

Monday was the sort of day you hope to see in Vancouver: warm and sunny. Anne went shopping in the morning, I had a quick gander at the Vancouver Public Library, which is one of my favourite buildings anywhere, and we met up at the Railway Club. Now, I'd heard of the Railway Club, but for reasons that are mostly to do with out-and-out foolishness, I'd never been there before. People had even recommended it to me. No wonder I'd never taken a total shine to Vancouver: I'd never been to the Railway Club.

The Railway used to be a club, and you can still become a member and get discounts on evening music events. We were told—by the owner, who seemed trustworthy—that the Railway's was one of the first three liquor licences granted by British Columbia at the end of Prohibition, and the only one still extant. I was directed to a framed poster in the back room, a relic from the late Prohibition days when voters were about to decide the fate of the noble experiment:

RESULTS OF PROHIBITION
THE BAR-ROOM Has Gone
DRUNKENNESS Has Been Reduced 92 Percent

Four of the Five Provincial Jails Closed
PENITENTIARY COMMITMENTS Have Been
Reduced 50 Percent
PREMIER OLIVER SAYS
"The Act has Proved of Great
Benefit to the Province"
WHY TURN BACK THE CLOCK?

It was an eloquent plea, but I was too happy in the Railway Club, and this was no time to take the pledge. The main area is a lovely room, long and narrow, with a lot of wood and plenty of windows, so it's nice and bright during the day. It's a place that feels like home, if home had a number of draught beer taps. The beer choices were not all adventurous, and the Tree Pale Ale I wanted to try was out of stock. But they had Phillips IPA, which was exactly the kind of beer that had drawn me out to BC in the first place. If I ever get so jaded that I complain that the only beer I can drink in a given bar is Phillips IPA, shoot me. All right, this is Canada; no one I know owns a gun. So hit me repeatedly with a rolled-up *Vancouver Sun* until I succumb to my wounds.

If I lived in Vancouver, I'd spend a lot of time at the Railway Club, at least during the afternoon, before the Alibi Room opens and before the bands start. All I know about the bands at the Railway Club is that some of them have amusing names, but I've learned that you can't always judge anything by its name.

I had already decided that I liked the Railway Club, but by the time I'd returned from admiring the Prohibition poster, it had become even better. Anne had asked about the apparatus suspended just below the ceiling and running around the room, whereupon a switch was flipped and an electric train started up. The icing was well and truly on the cake now. Some of the boxcars bore ads, one of them for the brewery whose beer I was gratefully drinking, and the owner told us that the advertising paid for the train. I'm as unhappy as you are about the invasive nature of modern advertising, but I can happily endure ads on an electric train in a pub.

I would have been content to remain at the Railway Club all afternoon, but I was on a mission. Rick Green had urged us to visit a brewpub called Central City out in Surrey, conveniently located near the SkyTrain, an entrance to which was just as conveniently located near the Railway Club. It's worth going to Central City Brewing just for the half-hour ride: rapid transit with vistas. Get a day pass for the Vancouver system. It's a dollar (in 2008 dollars) cheaper than the normal fare going to Surrey and back, and you can use it anywhere for the whole day. And there's a brewpub in it for you at the end.

When you come down the stairs from the Surrey Central Station, keep heading more or less straight and walk through a parking lot. Attached to a tall, modern building (that seems to be in part related to the Surrey campus of Simon Fraser University) is the pub you're looking for. Why it's called Central City when it's clearly out in what I would brutally call the sticks, I don't know, but don't let that stop you.

Central City Brewing is a big, modern place with lots of windows and a patio. The brewer, Gary Lohin, a tall, enthusiastic fellow, makes a variety of beers, and we tried the Red Racer Pale Ale, Boomers Red Ale (a tasty ESB), and the Empire IPA, named the 2008 best beer of BC by the CAMRA folk—and I can see why. It's a big, unapologetic IPA clocking in at 6.5 percent. This being BC, of course, and not Ontario, Central City has its own canning line and liquor store. Order a pizza and a six-pack, and they'll deliver it free. (I apologize to Ontarians for making them feel inadequate).

The SkyTrain ride back downtown was just as impressive as the trip to Surrey, and we decided to use our transit pass to take the SeaBus over to North Vancouver to have a look at Sailor Hagar's, a pleasant enough place (with a very decent view) that used to be a brewpub but which brews no longer. We downed a pint or two of Howe Sound Bengal IPA and headed back across the water for another quick one at the Irish Heather, after which Anne produced an impressive noise in the direction of a cab driver and got us a lift to Yaletown, where we were to meet Colin Jack, one of the principals of an operation called Just Here for the Beer. It's a corporate name with some charm, let's face it. It's sexier than Royal Bank of Canada or a few others I could think of. Colin and his business partner conduct educational sessions about beer, and they run an annual beerfest in Vancouver called the Canada Cup of Beer, held at UBC's Thunderbird Stadium on Canada Day. All in all, I began to feel I was getting a handle on beer drinking in Vancouver, and I was liking it more and more.

But Colin had a day job to get to the next morning, and we had a flight to catch. A sunny, beer-filled day in Vancouver was all well and good (actually, it was *very* well and good), but Whitehorse beckoned. If Yukon drinkers consume more beer per capita (and more everything else per capita) than Canadians anywhere else, I needed to check this out. Were they really drinking all this beer, or were they pouring it down the drains just to keep the numbers up?

❧ ❧ ❧

I had been to Whitehorse once before. It was 1971—I got to a lot of places in 1971, including Pocatello and Gila Bend—and I hitchhiked to Whitehorse and Dawson City. Even though I started that particular trip in Vancouver, Whitehorse was a very long way away. First of all, you hitchhiked to Dawson Creek, up in northern BC. That's only 736 miles. Over paved roads, through places like Williams Lake and Prince George.

Once you get to Dawson Creek, you're approaching halfway there. Nowadays, driving on straight, paved roads—or, actually, one very long, fairly straight, paved road—it's only 894 miles from Dawson Creek to Whitehorse. Back in 1971, when you, dear reader, were probably just mewling and puking in your bassinet, the road from Dawson Creek to Whitehorse was still unpaved. It was the Alaska Highway, a gravel road built during World War II to get supplies up to Alaska. Just in case the enemy tried to strafe the road and make it even more impassable than it was, they built the highway—and I use the word "highway" loosely—in a constantly curving shape. Imagine the drunkest you've ever been but still able to sort of walk. Now, picture the trajectory of your walk, weaving a little left, then a little right. Now, imagine you're seeing that from above, weaving about from left to right amidst a landscape of trees, rocks, and lakes. That, my friend, was the Alaska Highway in 1971.

To add insult to all that, they had posts beside the road marking the number of miles you had come, and those miles ticked by very slowly—you can drive only so fast over a gravel road that keeps changing direction. Whitehorse, as I recall, was at Mile 918, which is about 1,477 kilometres. I got a lift outside Dawson Creek from a guy from California driving a Jeep-like thing. He already had another passenger, a fellow from Vancouver who didn't have much money but did have an interesting variety of illegal substances, which he peddled to the young guys working the gas stations along the way.

After what seemed like a few weeks, we arrived in Whitehorse. The guy from California was headed for Alaska and didn't want to linger, but I can't tell you how thirsty you get after nine hundred miles of gravel road. We stopped at the first bar we saw and ordered up some beer. A young native man came in, looked around in a shifty manner, then headed for our table. "You guys want some acid?" he asked. "No," replied my friend from Vancouver, "but do *you* want some grass or mescaline?"

Our new business contact raised his eyebrows. "You guys staying long?" Alas, we were just drinking our beer, then heading for the Chamber of Commerce for some maps. Our friend nodded and told us he needed to go to the pool hall to talk to his friends. We drank up and went to the Chamber of Commerce. On our way out, we saw a long but orderly queue of young native guys standing outside. An RCMP cruiser passed by as business was transacted on the sidewalk, after which we got back in the Jeep-like thing and headed back out on to the gravel highway toward Alaska.

It turns out that you can get to Whitehorse much more easily nowadays, though with today's luggage restrictions you probably can't take that much dope on the plane. With my contractual deadline, there was no time to hitchhike, so, reluctantly, my wife agreed to fly.

The weather wasn't nearly as nice in Whitehorse as it had been the day before in Vancouver, but at least it wasn't snowing. It's a small airport, though they seemed to be rebuilding it. One of our co-passengers seemed to think it a boondoggle, but I couldn't comment. He was a Newfoundlander who bristled slightly at the news that we were here because Yukoners drink more beer than people anywhere else in Canada. "More than Newfoundlanders?" he asked incredulously.

We arrived at our hotel just in time to see a Mountie—an honest-to-god Mountie, I tell you—deliver a snappy salute to a lady getting into a vehicle. That got my attention. I'd been to a passel of Canadian cities this summer and not seen a single Mountie. Was he a prop? Not at all. It turned out that we were sharing a hotel in Whitehorse with the lieutenant-governor of Prince Edward Island. And that's the kind of country this is, friends. I heard her being interviewed later in the lobby, and she seemed very jolly. And no, cheeky monkeys, the Mountie did not taser her.

There are tourist sites in Whitehorse, as you'd expect, but I was still on a mission. A beer mission. Checked in, we went downstairs (it wasn't a very high hotel) to the bar, happy to see four taps devoted to the local brews from the Yukon Brewing Company. Our bartender, a delightful woman named Jan (originally from Acton, Ontario), gave us a good rundown of what goes down in Whitehorse. She informed us that only hotels are permitted to operate bars, though there was talk that the law might change. Perhaps, by the time you read this, it has.

I liked Jan. She saw nothing unusual or blameworthy about my beer mission, when it was explained. She told us that a bright young spark in town was setting up a brewpub at the Capital Hotel, but typically, it was nowhere near completion yet. She pointed out some of the other bars in town and explained how I would get to the local brewery. It was, she said, just past the four-way stop, of which there's just the one in Whitehorse, though once this book appears they'll probably put in another one, just to appear more cosmopolitan. Don't do it on my account. If all you need is one four-way stop, why mess with it? It isn't as if there weren't traffic lights in town.

According to something I read, the Whitehorse airport services flights from Vancouver, Fairbanks, Calgary, Edmonton, Toronto, and—the one you might not have expected—Frankfurt, though only in summer. One of the first tourist handouts I picked up was in two languages: English and German. The Germans, it comes to pass, are keen visitors to the Yukon, and we heard numerous speakers of that language during our stay. Funny people, the Germans. They love the Wild West, and Germany is one of the hotbeds of American Civil War re-enactors. I was beginning to see why beer consumption is as high as it is in the Yukon. I half-expected to see a busload of Czechs turn up. We did meet a very nice Dutch family, and they weren't afraid of a drink.

Whitehorse boasts a population of only about twenty-five thousand, roughly a quarter of the population of St. John's, so it's not a big place. That said, there are plenty of places to drink. The bar at our hotel, the Westmark, was more than pleasant, but one needed to get out. There's a vaguely chalet-style place at the Edgewater Hotel and a sports bar at the Best Western. The High Country Hotel bills itself as the best hotel in town, which raises the question of why the lieutentant-governor of PEI would stay at the second-best. It did have a nice-looking patio, though I'll bet it looks nicer if it's several degrees warmer and not raining. Coasters Bar and Grill is a big place with an upside-down airplane—it might have been a Spitfire—suspended from the ceiling. Clearly the happening place in Whitehorse, Coasters hosts a lot of live music. And if you find its Facebook page, you'll see that it lists its specialties as: Drinks. My kind of place. The missus and I were on the Yukon Red Ale, a very decent drop of beer.

The missus, however, balked at the 98 Hotel. Jan, the Westmark bartender, described it as not that bad a place, and said that she herself occasionally went there. It did, she admitted, smell a bit. Well, some days we all smell a bit, and the 98 Hotel claims to have the second-oldest liquor licence in Canada, so I had to go. I hope you would, too. It might smell a bit, but the 98 was very busy in midafternoon. It had probably been busy for a number of hours, given that it opens at nine in the morning. You can join the 98 Breakfast Club—I would have done, but I'm not a morning person.

It's a fair-sized room with animal hides on the walls and quite a number of guns suspended from the ceiling behind and above the bar. I don't imagine there were many members of the board of the Whitehorse Opera Society at the 98, but the place certainly wasn't wanting for business while I was there, drinking my Yukon Gold (it used to be called Arctic Gold, but Molson had a product that used the word Arctic somewhere in the title and brought their lawyers to bear on the Yukon Brewing Company, which then had to change the name).

I liked Whitehorse and its spirit, and we had an excellent dinner at a surprisingly upmarket restaurant. Many of the people we met were from somewhere else originally but had been drawn to the Yukon and never wanted to leave. (Whitehorse, thanks to a unique geographical situation, is in fact the driest city in Canada, not that there was much evidence of that on our rather soggy visit. Still, there's no getting around the long, cold, dark winters; the locals claim it's not too bad.) Our other bartender at the Westmark, a Québécois named Francis, didn't want to be anywhere else. There's a little tourist train that goes along the Yukon River, which is good fun, and our conductor was a young man from Colombia whose family had moved up there. He certainly seemed happy enough.

The service we received in Whitehorse was almost unfailingly friendly, despite a labour shortage that becomes more pronounced as students return to school. A sign in the window of one coffee shop warned that they'd be closing early because they had no one to work. We had one fairly bellicose server in a hotel bar; one of her colleagues explained that there was nothing they could do about her because there was no one to replace her. I wouldn't want to replace Loretta, who served us breakfast at the Westmark; I'd never have breakfast anywhere else if I lived in Whitehorse.

When you're in a town that has the only Canadian brewery north of 60 degrees latitude, you feel an obligation to pay a visit. Or at least *I* do. Having toured Canada's easternmost brewery at Quidi Vidi in Newfoundland, I was drawn to Canada's northernmost. Given Yukon drinkers' taste for beer, opening a brewery in the north made sense. Alan Dawson, like many craft brewers, moved from home brewing to attempting to make a living at it, and he seems to have done well. The brewery recently expanded and is considering going into distilling spirits. (Yukoners drink more spirits than anywhere else in Canada as well.)

I was one of a dozen visitors on the free daily brewery tour, led by a former Ontarian named Ken, who is also a high school teacher. Ken showed us around, answered our questions, made a few jokes, introduced us to the guys operating the canning machine, talked up the company, then led us back out to the front room for tasting time. The lager was clearly an attempt to hit the market of people who don't much like the taste of beer, and the Gold was something similar in an ale. It is worth noting that, in the Yukon itself, the company now outsells Molson Canadian, the brand that has owned the territory for years. And good for them. Things started to get interesting with the Chocolate Brown, and got even better with the Yukon Red and the Big Fluke IPA. The Lead Dog Ale, which I had enjoyed at Bottlescrew Bill's in Calgary, is something you'd want plenty of during those long winters, and the Midnight Sun Espresso Stout, made in collaboration with a local roaster, was really good, and I don't even drink coffee.

Not everyone is as enamoured of the Yukon brews as I was. A server in a restaurant we stopped in told us that the place had been broken into twice in recent months, and that the kids who did it had stolen all the alcohol except the Yukon beers. Kids today.

❧ ❧ ❧

The days are long in Whitehorse, even at the end of August, but it was dark the next morning when we got up to catch our flight out of town. I'm a big-city guy—Toronto's too small for my taste—but I could see what all these people liked about Whitehorse. It's in a beautiful setting, the people are friendly, and, according to Ken at Yukon Brewing, there are fifty-two places to drink, fifty-one of which sell his beer. And, to Anne's pleasure and surprise, there are two Starbucks locations. There's a very decent bookstore on the main street, and an excellent second-hand bookstore as well. Plus, you don't have to hitchhike there any more.

But we were on the big silver bird once again, this time to Portland and Seattle. Well, if you're a beer lover who lives in Toronto and you get to Vancouver, you feel it would be a waste not to go to two great beer towns. This, however, is a book about beer in Canada, and the best Yukon dog team couldn't drag out of me what we got up to in the American northwest. The Horse Brass in Portland, Brouwer's in Seattle—it's all a closed book. I won't even tell you what wonderful beers were on tap at the ballpark in Portland, where we watched the Beavers beat the Salt Lake Bees. I will, however, report that Anne's judgement on America, expressed in a Portland saloon, was, and I quote, "It's a great country to get drunk in." And it is, but you can get drunk in Canada, too. Trust me.

From Seattle, you can take a boat to Victoria, which was our next, and last, stop on the 2008 See Canada and Drink It Dry Tour. Victoria seems a very long way from St. John's, and it is—3,167 miles, apparently, but who's counting? (An even more impressive 5,097 kilometres, if you're that way inclined.) There's salt water, and a lot of it, at both ends. And there's beer, and a lot of *it*, too, at both ends.

The first time I went to Victoria, many moons ago, a small group of us was almost barred from entering a mock-English pub because one of our number was wearing blue jeans. Victoria was overbearingly proper in those days. There is still tea at the Empress Hotel—four afternoon sittings, I understand—but the brewing I had in mind had a lot more to do with barley and hops than Assam or Darjeeling.

According to my calculations, there are seven breweries in the city, or one for about every forty-seven thousand residents of Greater Victoria, which is impressive. To put this in context, however, we have to consider that Victoria has an unnaturally large number of retired people. These are people who can drink all afternoon, seven days a week. Victoria also gets a lot of tourists, surely not all of whom do nothing but swill tea at the Empress. Certainly in summer, between the year-round residents and the cruise ship arrivals, daytime Victoria resembles a City of the Very Old. By early- to mid-evening, however, a transformation takes place. Either the old folks have suddenly discovered a fountain of youth, or they're all tucked up and snoozing, yielding the city to young people. Within about an hour, the average age of people on the streets of Victoria drops by thirty or forty years. It's interesting to behold. Between the old 'uns and the young 'uns, Victoria supports two terrific bookstores, Munro's downtown and Bolen Books in the hinterlands, so there's a lot of reading going on along with all the drinking. I like a town like that.

Like Vancouver, Victoria is a city of brewpubs. Four of its seven breweries are brewpubs, two of them quite venerable. Swans Hotel, on the Inner Harbour, is located in a 1913 building and looks, from the outside, like a small English hotel. It's a busy place inside, offering a variety of beers, two or three on cask. The Buckerfield's Bitter is served in a cask-conditioned form, and I wish their Extra IPA, at a meaty 6.8 percent, were as well. They also boast a 7-percent Raspberry Ale and an 8-percent Scotch Ale, so there's no need to leave sober. Swans has been brewing its mostly English-style beers since 1989. They offer live music in the evening, which you can take as an attraction or a warning. You can tell it's a happening place; we were minding our own business at the bar when who hove into sight but Toronto beer writer Robert Hughey and his wife, Caroline. Sit at a bar long enough, and most of the people you know will turn up.

From Swans, a pleasant walk (once you know where you're going) across the bridge and along the water brings you to Spinnakers, a "gastro" brewpub that occupies a place in Canadian beer history. Back in 1982, a beer enthusiast named John Mitchell did battle with the BC government for the right to brew beer that wasn't made by a company called Molson, Labatt, or Carling O'Keefe. He wanted a brewpub, but the authorities insisted that his beer must not be made on the premises. So he put the brewery just down the street and started the Troller Pub in Horseshoe Bay, near Vancouver. It was Canada's first brewpub (at least in the modern era). Two years later, he sold out his interest and joined with Paul Hadfield to open Spinnakers, Canada's first in-house brewpub. Mitchell and Hadfield were allowed to open a brewpub, but not in a residential district, hence the distance to the pub. It is now, of course, surrounded by condominium developments. Mitchell, a decade or more later, went on to be the first brewmaster at Howe Sound Brewing Company. He is a giant in Canadian brewing.

Spinnakers might have been forced to open slightly out of town, but they got the last laugh. I've never been to a brewpub (or practically anywhere) with a better view. To sit on the patio of the upstairs taproom, drinking very good beer and looking out over the entrance to Victoria Harbour and the Strait of Juan de Fuca to the mountains of Washington State in the distance is one of the beer drinker's great pleasures. I hate to admit it, but there's nothing quite like it in Toronto. Watching boats come and go, watching seaplanes landing and taking off, Anne and I kept saying inane things like "gosh" and "holy cow." And we meant it. Sorry, am I rabbiting on a bit? Did I mention that the beer is good, some of it cask-conditioned? Spinnakers is apparently the first place in Canada (and very possibly North America) to make cask-conditioned beer commercially. Like Swans, Spinnakers offers accommodation, so you never have to go anywhere else.

Unless you're on a beer mission. We were required to get to the Canoe Brewpub, not far from Swans and even closer to the water. It's a modern place in a large warehouse space, and it was bustling while we were there. There was speculation that many of the brewers from the nearby beer festival were gathering, but I don't know if that's true. We enjoyed their River Rock Bitter, and noticed that Canoe must be one of the very few British Columbia breweries that doesn't make an IPA.

After drinking and eating at Canoe, we walked over to Hugo's Brewing, the final brewpub, but we had clearly arrived late. I could tell that Anne wasn't comfortable with the noise level, because her ears were bleeding. It seems you need to see Hugo's by day unless you're a devotee of pounding, music-like aural sensations. It was really very loud. We fled to the nearby Strathcona Hotel, recommended by Central City brewer Gary Lohin as a place to drink BC beers. Built as an office building in 1913, the Strathcona has been a hotel since 1918, and claims to have the world's only rooftop beach volleyball courts.

Who knows? It might even be true. I don't remember seeing any any-where else, but I don't get to as many rooftops as I'd like.

The Strathcona says it has seven different rooms in which to drink, including a "hillbilly" bar, but after two solid weeks of alco-tourism our livers pleaded for just one, and we settled on the pub-like Sticky Wicket. Sitting at the bar with our Phillips IPA, which we liked better than the same company's Blue Back Pale Ale, we talked to our fine bartender about Victoria, beer, and life in general. We were curious to know what we had missed at Hugo's, and he allowed as how their Super G, a beer made with ginger and ginseng, was a good thing. I resolved that next time I'd find out, but I'm told that Hugo lost his lease and is no more.

By now, it was September. The nights were drawing in and my publisher wanted his manuscript, so we bade farewell to the fleshpots of Victoria, got tucked in like the geezers and geezerettes we'd seen in daylight, and readied ourselves for one more early getaway, this time homeward.

It had been a very good trip. We'd seen weather of many sorts, met some very good people of many sorts, and consumed countless beers, similarly of many sorts. We Canadians really need to get out more and take a look at more other Canadians. We're everywhere, it turns out. We're in St. John's and we're in Whitehorse and we're in Victoria, and we're pretty much everywhere else as well. Here's to Frère Ambroise, and the Keefe Brothers in Halifax and Toronto, and Steve Cavan in Saskatoon, and the Montreal beerslinger who wouldn't take my beer coupons at Mondial de la Bière, and John Mitchell, who got all this craft beer business going in this country, and Jan the bartender in Whitehorse, and Liam McKenna in St. John's, and Bev Robertson in Regina, and Dick and Carmen Hoppener in Calgary, and—hell—everybody who makes good beer, everyone who sells it, and everyone who enjoys it. Here's to us.

Bibliography

Kingsley Amis. *The Everyday Drinker: The Distilled Kingsley Amis,* Bloomsbury, 2008. There's a fellow in the UK who turns up at beer festivals, hawking T-shirts and other stuff commemorating the drinking fame of the late Oliver Reed. The serious drinker is more likely to respect Kingsley Amis, a prodigious drinker and writer about drink. This volume is a complilation of three books Amis wrote on the subject, and should be seen as compulsory (and often very funny) reading.

Charles Bamforth. *Grape vs. Grain,* Cambridge University Press, 2008. Bamforth is a beer guy from the University of California, Davis, and there's room at his table for both beer and wine, but he does a good line in comparing the two and decrying the notion that wine is somehow inherently superior. As a beer scientist, he has great respect for the consistency and quality control of the big corporate brewers, which doesn't mean that some of us much want to drink them.

Stephen Beaumont. *The Great Canadian Beer Guide,* 2nd edition, McArthur & Company, 2001. The great Canadian beer expert travelled far and wide to taste as many Canadian beers as he could. The book reads a bit like ancient history today—a lot of the beers have bitten the dust, and lots of others have appeared in the meantime—but Beaumont's overview of Canadian brewing remains valuable. I spoke to him in 2008 (at a gin party, of all things), and he suggested we were unlikely to see a third edition of this book. It's a lot of work, and it's instantly out of date. That's what the Internet is for.

Paul Brent. *Lager Heads: Labatt and Molson Face Off for Canada's Beer Money,* HarperCollins Canada, 2004. Brent is a business writer, and this is a first-rate study of the business of beer in this country, particularly of the often hilarious battles between Molson and Labatt.

Robert A. Campbell. *Demon Rum or Easy Money: Government Control of Liquor in British Columbia from Prohibition to Privatization,* Carleton University Press, 1991.

Robert A. Campbell. *Sit Down and Drink Your Beer: Regulating Vancouver's Beer Parlours, 1925–1954,* University of Toronto Press, 2001. British Columbia's adventures with alcohol have been documented better than those of most other provinces, largely because of Robert Campbell.

Martyn Cornell. *Beer: The Story of the Pint,* Headline, 2003. Apart from E.P. Taylor, there's not much Canadian content in this thorough history of British beer, but don't let that put you off.

Michael Dunn. *The Penguin Guide to Real Draught Beer,* Penguin, 1979. The world of beer has changed a time or two since 1979, but this remains an interesting and worthwhile look at the British beer scene during the early years of the real ale revival.

Susan Goldenberg. *Snatched!: The Peculiar Kidnapping of Beer Tycoon John Labatt,* Dundurn Press, 2004. To my knowledge, the only book-length study of the kidnapping of any major Canadian brewer.

T.R. Gourvish and R.G. Wilson. *The British Brewing Industry, 1830–1980,* Cambridge University Press, 1994. This is a hefty, very serious book about exactly what its title suggests.

Craig Heron. *Booze: A Distilled History,* Between the Lines, 2003. So, this academic goes into a bar and comes out with an excellent examination of Canada's drinking history. It's a very good book.

Albert John Hiebert. *Prohibition in British Columbia,* 1969. This very informative master's thesis, available online, seems to have sparked interest in BC's brief but lively Prohibition history.

C.W. Hunt. *Booze, Boats and Billions: Smuggling Liquid Gold,* McClelland & Stewart, 1988.

C.W. Hunt. *Whisky and Ice: The Saga of Ben Kerr, Canada's Most Daring Rumrunner,* Dundurn Press, 1995. Mr. Hunt clearly takes an interesting in alcohol smuggling. His 1988 book is a general look at the subject; the 1995 book deals more specifically with one smuggler.

Michael Jackson. *Michael Jackson's Beer Companion*, 2nd edition, Elan Press, 1997. The late Jackson produced books that were gorgeous to look at and were full of information. This is both.

Margaret McBurney and Mary Byers. *Tavern in the Town: Early Inns and Taverns of Ontario*, University of Toronto Press, 1987. I am a better person for owning this book, a study of early life— particularly early drinking life—in Ontario, with lots of photographs by Hugh Robertson. It's sadly out of print, but can be found.

Christopher Mark O'Brien. *Fermenting Revolution: How to Drink Beer and Save the World*, New Society Press, 2006. O'Brien is an often earnest beer activist who is very convincing on the subject of how beer can save the planet. Honest.

Maureen Ogle. *Ambitious Brew: The History of American Beer*, Harcourt, 2006. I enjoyed this book, which takes us from 1844, when Phillip Best arrived in Milwaukee, to the present. I had never made the connection between income tax and Prohibition until I read Maureen Ogle.

Nicholas Pashley. *Notes on a Beermat: Drinking and Why It's Necessary*, Polar Bear Press, 2001; Collins Canada, 2008. Most of what I know about drinking beer and hanging out in pubs is either in the book you're holding or in this earlier volume.

Simon Rae, editor. *The Faber Book of Drink, Drinkers and Drinking*, Faber, 1991. Lost in the process of a major home renovation, this book came back into my life after more than two years, and I remembered how much I enjoyed it. Rae assembles writings ancient and modern, from Homer to Garrison Keillor. I'll be in no hurry to lose it again.

C. Gordon Richardson. *Alcohol, a Defence of Its Temperate Use,* National Liberal Temperance Union, 1888. Nineteenth-century prohibitionists were given to stretching the truth when it came to promoting their cause, particularly when it came to presenting scientific evidence against alcohol, and the author of this book, a chemist, goes through the teetotallers' arguments and demolishes them. The Liberal Temperance Union promoted moderation in the use of alcohol, but deplored attempts to control drinkers through legislation.

Richard Rohmer. *E.P. Taylor: The Biography of Edward Plunket Taylor,* McClelland & Stewart, 1978. Rohmer wrote this book while Taylor was still alive, and his admiration for his subject is pronounced. Taylor was a very interesting man, but many of us still can't forgive him for closing down dozens of breweries.

Christine Sismondo, Heather Siemens, and Amanda McFillen, eds. *Bottoms Up!: Spirited Reflections on Drinking in Canada,* University of Toronto Museum Studies Program, 2007. This thin, yet lively volume was published to accompany a fine exhibition of the same name, mounted at the Steam Whistle Brewery in 2007. It comprises eleven pieces about drinking in Canada, some by students in the program, others by people who haven't been students in many years, including the author of this book. This is where I found Bridget Ker's fine piece about the medicinal use of alcohol.

Allen Winn Sneath. *Brewed in Canada: The Untold Story of Canada's 350-Year-Old Brewing Industry,* Dundurn Press, 2001. Sneath, who has toiled in the beer trade, has written a very good history of Canadian brewing. As a serious history, it really should have an index, but there we are. I consult it frequently enough that, by now, I should have compiled my own index for it.

Ruth Spence. *Prohibition in Canada: A Memorial to Francis Stephens Spence,* Ontario Branch of the Dominion Alliance, 1919. Published when the temperance forces had attained their zenith. Canada was dry, except for beer and wine in Quebec, and the United States was on the brink. The daughter of one of the great campaigners wrote this in-depth study of how it all happened. She claims to be objective and unbiased, but there is a triumphant tone to it nonetheless. She offers more detail than most of us really need, but it's an indispensable history.

Tom Standage. *A History of the World in 6 Glasses,* Doubleday Canada, 2005. Standage is usually a technology writer, and his study of six beverages that have changed human culture—three of them alcoholic, three alcohol-free—makes the argument that each is a kind of technology. It's a very enjoyable read.

Gord Steinke. *Mobsters and Rumrunners of Canada: Crossing the Line,* Folklore Publishing, 2003. More about Canadian entrepreneurial know-how during Prohibition.

Shirley E. Woods, Jr. *The Molson Saga, 1763–1983,* Doubleday, 1983. When Shirley Woods wrote this book, Molson was still a proud Canadian-owned corporation, and the book is an inspirational study of a great brewing family. I was mostly interested in the early years, and Woods does a good job of bringing late-eighteenth-century Montreal to life.

Acknowledgements

This book happened because I accepted a lunch invitation from a tall gentleman named Lloyd Kelly. If Lloyd offers to buy you lunch, you should take him up on it, as long as you don't mind doing months of work as a result. Neither of us was thinking "book deal" at the time, but a good lunch nicely washed down can make odd ideas come into fellows' heads. This book is just such an odd idea. (Lloyd also introduced me to the word "cenosillicaphobia," the fear of an empty glass.)

Lloyd left me pretty much alone for some time, then gently suggested he should get a look at what I was up to, given that he was my publisher and all. I sent him what I'd done to that point, and, sixteen days later, Lloyd announced that he was leaving the publishing industry, which I did not take as a vote of confidence. It also seemed an overreaction; I mean, it was only an early draft. Lloyd had the good grace to suggest that the two events were unrelated, but an author is bound to draw his own conclusions. The work in progress was handed on to Brad Wilson, who, despite having known me for some years, accepted this new responsibility with surprisingly good grace, and even—dare I say it—with apparent enthusiasm.

I have been made to feel very welcome by everyone at HarperCollins Canada, which includes (but is not limited to) Nita Pronovost, Noelle Zitzer, Rob Firing, Sharon Kish, Allegra Robinson, Lloyd Davis, Norma Cody, Jeremy Rawlings, Terry Toews, and two of the finest sales reps in the book trade: Kathryn Wardropper and Jennifer Flanagan. And I'd better mention David Kent as well.

It was Diane and Peter Waldock who brought me back to the world of writing books as well as selling them, and I owe a refreshing glass or two to them, as well as to Pat Cairns, Fortunato Agliaoro, Kevin Harper, and all at North 49 Books.

Thanks are required as well for beer-swilling friends, particularly Bill and Carol Martin, John Jackson and Mary McMillan, Jim Morrison and his daughter Anna, Glen Sutherland (who actually made notes on a placemat), Christine Sismondo, Patrick Kennedy, John Gilbert, and my friend and technical advisor, Patrick Lee. Cass Enright, who created BarTowel.com, and Greg Clow, who has done much to enhance it, have made beer drinking in Ontario much more tolerable by helping drinkers find good beer and good pubs and allowing us to communicate with one another. Bar Towel is exactly what the Internet was meant to be, only crankier. Why doesn't every city have a Bar Towel? Thanks also to Bar Towellers who have shared their knowledge and enthusiasm.

I have been helped along the way by, in no particular order, Stephen Beaumont, Craig Pinhey, Liam McKenna, Ron Keefe, Steve Cavan, Gary Lohin, Rick Green, Bev Robertson, Colin Jack, Todd Bailey, Gord Holder, Robert and Caroline Hughey, and Mirella Amato.

We all owe gratitude to the people who make good beer across Canada and the people who create quirky, pleasurable establishments in which to drink that good beer, particularly the publicans who go out of their way to support excellent local breweries.

ACKNOWLEDGEMENTS

I write in this book about beer festivals, an activity that requires bloody hard work and administrative nightmares without much hope of profit. Worst of all, festival organizers have to stay reasonably sober so they can deal with the inevitable dramas that crop up. And afterwards, everyone complains because it was too expensive or the beer wasn't hoppy enough or the weather wasn't good. I've never met Jeannine Marois of Mondial de la Bière in Montreal, but my hat is well and truly off to her. Praise goes also to Gerry Hieter and John Rowling and their team (especially Claudia) at the Great Canadian Beer Festival in Victoria. In Toronto, where I live, the best beer festivals are put on in pubs. Since 2005, Ralph Morana has been holding a Cask Days festival at his Bar Volo. Every year he says he'll never do it again, and every year it gets better. Ralph and Aina and their family deserve more praise than I can give them here. George Milbrandt at C'est What treats us to his regular Festival of Small Breweries, and has been doing so, amazingly, since 1989. In the summer of 2008, the Victory Café held its first cask ale festival, and followed it up with a winter festival. Many hands went into these fests, but special praise is owed to Blake Smith and Maz and Neil Brereton.

No one can write a book of non-fiction without access to a good library, and I am blessed with the Toronto Public Library system, whose collections and staff are hard to beat. I got much use from the *Toronto Star* Newspaper Centre in the basement of the Toronto Reference Library, a wonderful source of newspapers of the past.

I don't know what single fellows do when they write a book, but I've been married half my life and practically all my writing has happened since I made the trek down to City Hall. Coincidence? Ask my wife. Thanks for, well, the whole package, Anne—still the Evergreen Bride.

Index

Aberdeen, Lady, 24
Aberdeen, Lord, 24
Adams, Michael, 67
Adnams Brewery, 95
advertisements, beer, 59, 116,
        126–34, 138
    audience, 127–28
    compared with hockey
        commercials, 132
    the "liquid" and the "package,"
        128
    regulations on, 116, 131–32, 136
    sexuality and, 128, 131–32
    on YouTube, 133–34
Advertising Standards Canada
        (ASC), 131
aftertaste, 140
airplanes, charter, 60
Alberta, 35, 50, 57, 117, 241, 274
alcohol abuse, 26–28
*Alcohol: A Defense of Its Moderate
        Use* (Richardson), 42–43

alcohol content of beer, 45, 55, 66,
        71, 138
alcoholic beverages. *See also specific
        topics*
    number of enterprises selling,
        30–31
    purchasing, 51
ale, 97, 105, 160–61. *See also under*
        lager
    beer and, 99, 100
    cask-conditioned, 163–64
    "real," 162, 163 (*see also*
        Campaign for Real Ale)
Alimony Ale, 186
Alley Kat, 276–77
Ambroise, Frère, 12
American beer, 71–72, 75, 76. *See
        also specific brands*
American National Minimum
        Drinking Age Act of 1984, 69,
        70
ANBL stores, 118, 119

Anchor Steam Beer, 149–50
Anheuser, Eberhard, 214
Anheuser-Busch (A-B), 71, 75
    history, 214–17
Anheuser-Busch brewery, tour of,
    233
Austria, 3–4

Bamforth, Charles, 191, 194
barley shortages, 156–57
"barrooms," 55
bars, 55
    employees at, 203
Basques, 10
Bass, 15
Bass Charrington, 106–7
Beaumont, Stephen, 12, 248
beer. *See also specific topics*
    attitudes toward, 1
    authorization of sale by the glass,
    55
    future of, 155–59
    ingredients, 89–90, 98 (*see
    also* beer production; *specific
    ingredients*)
    shipping/transporting, 14–15, 18, 44
    temperature, 128, 130 (*see also*
    coldness of beer)
    terminology, 196
beer bottles, 76
    characteristics of, 73–76
beer consumption, 2
    in various countries, 2–5
beer cozies, 200–201
beer geeks, 152–53
"beer goggles," 91–92
beer industry, acquisitions and
    mergers in, 104
Beer of the Year, 232

"beer parlours," 58
beer prices, 156, 158–59, 190–91
    at beer festivals, 171–72
beer production, 104, 194
    environmental effects, 95–96
    ingredients needed for, 155–58
    innovations in, 136–43, 150, 162–63
        (*see also specific innovations*)
beers
    extreme, 187
    names of, 182–88
        animal-related, 187
        naming beers after their styles,
        183
        old-fashioned, 183
        provocative, 184–88
    strong/"stronger," 66, 186, 187
        (*see also* alcohol content of
        beer)
    taste, 128, 140, 183 (*see also*
        bitterness of beer)
Beer Stores, 117
Belgium, 101
Bell's, 70–71
Best Bitter, 219
"beverage rooms," 58
bitterness of beer, 153, 183, 186. *See
    also* craft beer revolution
Blackened Voodoo Lager, 184
Black Horse, 242
Black Label, 77
Black Oak Brewery, 183
Blue Ribbon, 133
Blue Star, 242
boats used for transport, 37
Bohemia, 100–101
bootlegging, 37–41, 51–52
Booze: a Distilled History (Heron), 29
Boston Beer Company, 71

Bottlescrew Bill's, 275
Brading Breweries, 104
Brandon, Manitoba, 262–63
Brannon, Janet, 116
breast enhancement, beer and hops
    for, 91
Brendan the Navigator, St., 10–11
Brent, Paul, 141
Brewed in Canada (Sneath), 12
Brewers Retail, 51
brewery tours, 96, 229, 241, 293
   of Anheuser-Busch, 233
   of Granville Island Brewing, 284
   of Keith Alexander's brewery,
     231–35
   of Uley Brewery, 94
brewing. *See also* Granite Brewery;
   specific topics
   as by-product of agriculture, 218
   words that describe, 196
Brewing Corporation of Ontario, 104
brewpub/microbrewery revolution,
   98–99
brewpubs, 219, 231, 248–49, 270
   first modern Canadian, 150,
     296–97
   in Ontario, 272
   Prohibition and, 150
   in Quebec, 249
   in Saskatchewan, 268, 272–73
   in the United Kingdom, 107
   in Vancouver, 282–83
   in Victoria, 296–97
Brewsters, 270
Brickman, Jim, 76
Britain, 13, 79, 88, 106–7
British Columbia (BC)
   craft beer revolution in, 150
   regulations in, 55–59, 114

Prohibition in, 36, 44–45, 55,
   285–86
   women and drinking in, 57–58
Bud Light, 138, 139
Budweiser, 72, 75, 81, 152
Budweiser American Ale, 154
Buffett, Warren, 216
Busch, Adolphus, 214–15
Busch, Adolphus, III, 214, 215
Busch, Adolphus, IV, 216
Busch, Lily Anheuser, 214
Bush, George H.W., 69
Bushwakker Brewpub, 266–68, 274
Byers, Mary, 21, 22

Cabot, John, 10
Caledonian Friendship Society, 60
Calgary, 270–80
Calgary International Beer Festival,
   271
Campaign for Real Ale (CAMRA),
   107, 162, 166, 175, 282
Canada. *See also specific topics*
   breweries in, 104–6
   who first brewed beer in, 9, 10
Canadian Breweries, 106
Canadian Brewing Awards, 232
Canadians, reputation for drinking
   beer, 2
Canoe Brewpub, 297
cans, 200
Capone, Al, 37, 39, 46
carbon-neutral beer, 95–96
Carbon Trust Innovation Award, 95
Carling Black Label, 106, 107
Carling Breweries, 104
Carling O'Keefe, 75–76, 106, 132,
   246
cask ale, 163–64

Cavan, Steve, 179–81
Central City Brewing, 287
certification to work at licensed
    establishment, 204. *See also*
    Smart Serve
C'est What, 80
Charles, Prince, 88
charter flights, 60
cheese and beer, 193–94
Chinese restaurants, 115
Chiniquy, Charles, 29–30
Clarke, Jennifer, 94, 235
climate change and crop shortages,
    156–57
coaching routes, 21–22
coldness of beer, 128, 130, 199–200
Colt 45, 137
Coors Light, 72, 81, 138
Coors of Canada. *See* Molson
Coors of Colorado, 129
Cornell, Martyn, 99, 100
Corona, 81
craft beer, 151–53
    in British Columbia, 282–83
craft beer revolution, 149–51
craft brewers, American, 187
Crannóg Ales, 96
Cuba, 37
Cummings, Mr., 23
Curaçao, 96
Czech Republic, 3–5. *See also*
    Bohemia

Dawson, Alan, 293
deaths related to beer, 121–25. *See
    also under* Vancouver
Delerium Tremens, 115, 183
Dépanneur Rahman, 252
Detroit, 17

Dieu du Ciel, 252–53
distillers and distillation, 41–42
Dix BBQ and Brewery, 285
Dockside Brewing, 284
doctors prescribing alcoholic
    beverages, 43, 90–91
Dog and Temperance Bill, 23–24
domestic beer. *See* imported vs.
    domestic/local beer
Dominion Ale, 242
Dominion Brewers Association, 74–75
Dow Ale, 124, 125
draught beer, 57, 79, 130, 282
Drewry, Edward, 18
drinking age, 67–70, 113, 203
drinking hours, 113, 114
driving, drunk, 113
drunkenness, 53
dry areas, 30–31. *See also*
    Prohibition
dry beer, 139, 140
Dunkin Act of 1864, 30
Dunlop, Dr., 23

East Green, 95–96
Eckhardt, Fred, 136, 137
Edmonton, 276–79
Eisbock, 141, 142
Elders IXL, 106
election days, 114–15
English beer, 79. *See also* Britain
environmental effects of beer
    production, 95–96
Expo 67, 59–60, 246

families, brewing, 108
feminism, 57
Ferguson, Howard, 45, 46, 49
Ferguson Beer, 45

fermentation, 254
longer, 137, 140, 161, 221
Fermentation Revolution (O'Brien), 102
Festival of Beer at Fort York, 171–77
festivals, beer, 165, 166, 179–81
differences between various, 167
premise of, 165
rules regarding, 168–69, 178
Fin de Siècle, 248
Findlay, W.C., 38
food and alcohol sales, 113, 114, 116. *See also* restaurants
Formosa Springs brewery, 13
Fort Garry Brewing Company, 258, 259
Fraser, Shaun, 118
freezing beer. *See* ice beer
French, 11

Gablinger's Diet Beer, 136
Garrison brewery, 232
gender segregation in taverns, 58. *See also* women
George Street in Newfoundland, 238, 239. *See also* O'Reilly's
Germany, 165–66, 291
global warming and crop shortages, 156–57
Globe, The, 33, 36, 45, 47
Godunov, Alexander, 142
Gooderham and Worts company, 42
grains. *See also* beer, ingredients; *specific grains*
shortages of, 156–57
Granite Brewery, 218–24, 231
Grant, Bert, 275
Granville Island, 284
Granville Island Brewing, 284

Great American Beer Festival (GABF), 166–67, 175–76
Great British Beer Festival (GBBF), 166
Great Canadian Beer Festival (GCBF), 177–79
Great Canadian Stubby, 74
Great Depression, 104
Great Good Place, The (Oldenburg), 88
Great Lakes Brewery, 95
Greeks, ancient, 195
Green, Rick, 282, 284–85, 287
Groll, Josef, 100
Guinness, 15, 75, 79–80
Gulick, Charlton R., 90

Hadfield, Paul, 296
Half Pints Brewing Company, 256–58, 280
Half Pints Stir Stick Stout, 258–59
Halifax, 230–36
Haligonians, 235
Head, Francis Bond, 22, 23
health, beer and, 89–94, 121, 191–92. *See also* medical uses of alcohol
Hébert, Louis, 12
He'brew beers, 187
Heineken, Alfred, 96
Heineken, Gerard Adriaan, 15
Heineken WOBO (World Bottle), 96
Herbst, Neil, 276–77
Heron, Craig, 29
Hieter, Gerry, 177
holidays, 114–15
home, drinking at vs. away from, 20, 83–88. *See also* public drinking
homogenization, 106

Hop Bomb "S.T.F.U." Pale Ale, 184
hopheads, 153–154
Hop in Brew pub, 271, 275–76
hoppiness, 153–154
hoppy beers, 184, 186, 242
hops, 99–100, 135
    growing, 156
Hopslam Ale, 71
hop syndrome, 155–56
hotels, 55, 59
    licensed to sell beer, 45
Hughey, Robert, 296
Hugo's Brewing, 297
Hunter, Patrick J., 74
Hurshman, Lewis, 94

ice beer, 141–43
Iceberg, 242
I'm Alone (ship), 39–40
immigration, 99
Imperial Pale Ale, 232, 233
imported vs. domestic/local beer, 14,
    15, 78–82, 195
InBev, 81, 128–29, 139, 216
India Beer, 242
India Pale Ale, 232
indigenous cultures, 9–10
inns, 21, 23
    temperance, 23–24
international bitterness units (IBUs),
    153
Inuit, 9–10

Jack, Colin, 288
Jackson, John, 247–52
Jefferson, Thomas, 24
Jewish beers, 188
Jockey Club, 242
Jordan's Hotel, 22

Keates, Nancy, 158
Keefe, Kevin, 219
Keefe, Ron, 218–24
kegs, 116
Keith, Alexander, 109, 110, 232–35,
    272
Keith's, 129
Kelly's Pub, 238–39
Kensington Wine Market, 274
King's Head, 258
Kirin, 139
Klein, Ralph, 117
Koch, Jim, 156
kosher beers, 188
Kuntz Brewery, 104

Labatt, 81, 104, 106. *See also*
    Guinness
    Anheuser-Busch, Budweiser, and,
        75
    InBev to be owner of, 217
    Molson and, 105, 141, 142, 149,
        242
    Olands and, 110
Labatt, Henry, 17
Labatt, John Sackville, 17–18
Labatt 50, 97, 133
Labatt Blue, 19, 81, 217
Labatt Dry, 140
Labatt Dry Light, 140
Labatt Genuine Draft, 141
Labatts family, 16–17
Ladies and Escorts rooms, 58, 61
Lafontaine, John, 32
lager, 136, 139, 248
    vs. ale, 74, 97–100
        East vs. West and, 97–101
Lager Heads (Brent), 141
Lassandra, Florence, 40

Laurier, Wilfrid, 31
"lawn mower beer," 148
Lawson, Stephen, 40
Le Cheval Blanc, 249
legislation, 19, 30, 111–20. *See also*
    liquor boards; Prohibition;
    specific topics
  post-Prohibition, 51–52, 112
  in United States, 67
Le Saint-Bock, 249
licensed premises
  distribution of, 31–32
  qualifications and training to work
    at, 203–5
  types of, 20–23
light beer, 80, 136–39
Lincoln, Abraham, 29
liquor, 41–42
liquor boards, provincial, 15, 51,
    119–20
Liquor Control Board of Ontario
    (LCBO), 51, 52, 61, 115, 119,
    274
liquor permits, 51, 54–55
liquor sales, privatization of, 119–20,
    274
liquor stores, 61
  government-run, 38, 45, 50–52,
    104, 117, 118, 273
liquor traffic, 33
"lite" beer. *See* light beer
Little Scrapper IPA, 256–57
local beer. *See* imported vs.
    domestic/local beer
Lohin, Gary, 287
Lo Pub, 259
low-carb beer, 143

Macdonald, John A., 23
Mackenzie, William Lyon, 22, 23
Maddin, Guy, 256
malt liquor, 136–37
Manitoba, 35, 256
marijuana, 13
marketing. *See* advertising
Marois, Jeannine, 171
Massei, Joe, 17
Maximum Ice, 142
Maytag, Fritz, 149
McBurney, Margaret, 21, 22
McCain, Cindy, 215
McCain, John, 215
McCoy, Bill, 39
McKenna, Liam, 243–45
McMillan, Mary, 169
medical uses of alcohol, 42, 43,
    90–91. *See also* health
Meister Brau Lite, 136
Michelob Ultra, 143
Michigan, 68, 70
microbreweries, 70, 77, 150,
    162, 175, 242, 253, 284. *See
    also* brewpub/microbrewery
    revolution
Miller, 76
Miller Genuine Draft (MGD), 141
Miller High Life, 76
Miller Lite, 136, 137
Mitchell, John, 296, 298
moderation. *See* temperance
Moderation League, 105
Molson, 104, 106
  advertising, 128
  E.P. Taylor and, 105
  history, 15–16, 29, 76
  Labatt and, 105, 141, 142, 149, 242
  mergers and, 106

(Molson , *continued*)
  partnerships, 81
  in Quebec, 29
Molson, John, 15–16, 18, 19
Molson Canadian, 19, 81, 97, 129
Molson Canadian Ice Draft, 142
Molson Export, 97, 105
Molson Golden, 105
Molson Special Dry, 140
Molson Stock, 128
Molson XXX, 143
Mondial de la Bière festival, 168–73,
  247
Montgomery, John, 22
Montreal, 16, 246–54. *See also* Expo
  67
  brewpubs, 248–53
Montreal Anti-Alcoholic League, 32
Moosehead Breweries, 109, 110, 118
Morrison, Jim, 256–58
Mullen, Denton A., 53

National Breweries, 104
national brewing, 105
National Liberal Temperance
  Union, 43
"near bear," 55
neighborhood pubs, 281–82
New Belgium Brewing, 95
New Brunswick, 36, 54, 118–19
Newfoundland, 2, 236–39, 241–42,
  244
  beer consumption in, 2
  history, 10–11
  Prohibition in, 36
newspapers, 46
Notes on a Beermat (Pashley), 160
Nova Scotia, 35, 54, 235
  bars in, 114

nudists, beers for, 187–88
nudity in bars, 116

Obama, Barack, 215
O'Brien, Christopher Mark, 95, 102
Ogle, Maureen, 32, 33
O'Keefe, Carling, 132. *See also*
  Carling O'Keefe
Oktoberfest, 165–67
Oland, Derek, 110
Oland, Sid, 110
Oland, Susannah, 109, 110
Olands, 108–10
Oldenburg, Ray, 88
Ontario, 54–55, 104–5. *See also*
  Liquor Control Board of
  Ontario
  beer stores and sales, 117
  brewpubs in, 272
  hops vs. tobacco farming in, 156
  Prohibition in, 35, 36, 47, 51, 104
  public drinking in, 54
  pubs in, 114
O'Reilly's, 239–40, 242–45
organic beer, 96
Orkney Brewery, 186
outdoors, drinking, 197–202
Owades, Joseph L., 136

Pabst Blue Ribbon (PBR), 133
Paddock Wood, 180–81
pasteurization, 106
  and unpasteurized beer, 141, 161
patio people, 198–99. *See also* pub
  patios
Perdue, Sunny, 156–57
Perri, Rocco, 40–41
Peterborough, 52
Peterson, David, 117–18

Phillips IPA, 286

Picariello, Emilio, 40

Pilsner Lager, 18–19

Pinhey, Craig, 119

Prince, Colonel, 23

Prince Edward Island (PEI), 30, 32, 40, 54

privately owned stores, 117, 118, 273

privatization of liquor sales, 119–20, 274

Prohibition, 9, 18, 20, 36–44, 112

  American defenders of, 46

  beer during, 44

  crime and, 37–38, 45, 46 (*see also* bootlegging; Capone, Al)

  as disaster, 46–47

  economics and, 38, 41, 46–47

  ending of, 44–45, 50–52

  feminism and, 57

  imposition of, 35, 37

  lingering effects of, 50–52, 84, 87, 113, 150

  movement toward, 27–34 (*see also* temperance movement)

  hypocrisy in, 29–30

  popular support for, 47, 50

  in the United States, 67

  ways around, 36–37, 43–45

  years of, 35–36

Prud'homme, Louis, 12

Pub Is the Hub, 88

public drinking, 53–54, 56, 57, 59, 86–87. *See also* home

pub patios, 198–99, 201–2

pubs, 83–86

Quebec, 13, 241, 246

  forbade women from entering taverns, 57

liquor stores, 117

  Prohibition and, 29, 31, 36, 104

  stores selling beer in, 252

Quebec breweries, beer names of, 185

Quebec City, 124

Quidi Vidi, 240–42

Railway Club, 285–87

railways, 22

RateBeer.com, 143

Reagan, Ronald, 67

Red Cap Ale, 76

"refreshing," beer as, 98, 116, 136, 148

Regina, 261–69

religion, 31

restaurants, 114, 115, 192–93

Richardson, C. Gordon, 43

Rimstead, Paul, 132

Robertson, Bev, 268

Roblin, Mr., 24

Rogue's Roost, 231

Rothman tobacco company, 106

Royal York Hotel, 55

saloons, 45, 55. *See also* inns; taverns

Sam Adams, 71

Sam Adams Utopias, 71, 190

Saskatchewan, 15, 36, 45, 112, 273

Schirf, Greg, 184

Scott Act of 1878, 30

seated, drinking while, 56–57

Séguin, Napoléon, 31

sexuality, 115, 128, 131–32. *See also* nudity in bars

Shea, Patrick, 18

Sheppard, Thomas, 21

Sixpack, Joe, 90

Skullsplitter, 186–87
Sleeman, 108, 117
Sleeman, John, 108
Smart Serve, 204–13
smoking bans, 112, 198
Sneath, Allen Winn, 12, 15, 29
Spence, Ben, 53
Spence, Ruth, 28, 30–32, 53
Spinnakers, 296–97
Standage, Tom, 194
standing up while holding alcoholic
    beverage, law against, 56
stand-up bars, 45
Stella Artois, 81
Stella Artois Légère, 139
St. John's, 236, 237, 239–45
St. Lawrence River, beer dumped
    into, 125
Storm, 242
"stubby," 75–76
sunlight, 199–200
Swans Hotel, 296

Talon, Jean, 12–13
Tavern in the Town (McBurney and
    Byers), 21
taverns, 22, 53, 55–58
    politics and, 22
    temperance, 23–24
taxes, 23–24
Taylor, Edward Plunket, 18, 19, 74,
    103–6
television. *See also* advertisements
    Canadians and beer on, 2
temperance, 45
    defined, 26, 27
temperance houses, 23–24
temperance movement, 25–26
    original goal of, 27

temperance unions, 28
Tories, 118
Toronto, 21–23, 228, 235–36
    Festival of Beer at Fort York,
        171–77
    Prohibition in, 36
Toronto Telegram, 52, 53
training to work at licensed
    establishment, 204. *See also*
    Smart Serve
transporting/shipping alcohol, 14–
    15, 18, 37
travel, 21, 61
Troller Pub, 296

Uley Brewery, 94
unions, 119
United States and Canada, alcohol
    and drinking in, 65–72. *See also*
    American beer; *specific topics*
Utopias, 71

Vancouver, 97, 281–88
    alcohol-related deaths in, 38
    laws regarding women and
        alcohol in, 57
    prescriptions for alcohol in, 43
    Prohibition and, 38, 47
Vices et Versa, 253
Victoria, 98–99, 163, 295–98
Vikings, 10
violence in taverns, 56
Volstead Act, 39, 52

Walkerville, 70
War Measures Act, 31
Wasatch Brewery, 184
Wellington Brewery, 163
Wexford Wheat, 244

Wheat Sheaf Tavern, 273
Whip, The, 284
Whitehorse, 288–94
Whyte Avenue, 277–78
Wild Rose Brewery, 272–73
Windsor, 69, 70
wine, vs. beer, 189–96
Winking Judge, 150
Winnipeg, 256–61
women
  in advertisements, 128
  at beer festivals, 169
  legislation regarding, 57–58
  vs. men in beer industry, 102–3
  in taverns, 56, 57, 84

Women's Christian Temperance
  Union (WCTU), 27
wood alcohol, 37–38
World War I, 31, 32
Wright, Chas, 94
Wunder Bar, 278

YellowBelly Brewery and Public
  House, 243
Youngman, Henny, 159
Yukon, 2, 36, 241, 290–94
Yukon Brewing Company, 275, 292
Yukon Gold, 292

Zulach, Rudolf, 45

Anyway, here comes Mr. Smith himself with a huge basket of provender that would feed a factory. There must be sandwiches in that. I think I can here them clinking.

—Stephen Leacock,
The Marine Excursions of the Knights of Pythias